Introducing the New Testament

A M Hunter

INTRODUCING
THE NEW TESTAMENT

Third Revised Edition

SCM PRESS LTD

334 00696 1

First published 1945
reprinted six times
Second edition 1957
reprinted five times
Third edition 1972

© SCM Press Ltd 1945, 1957, 1972

Printed in Great Britain by
Northumberland Press Ltd, Gateshead

Contents

Contents

PART FOUR

THE WRITINGS OF THE OTHER
APOSTOLIC MEN

EPILOGUE

Preface

When I wrote this Introduction in 1945, I sought to mediate the findings of New Testament scholars in a simple and untechnical style. Many, I am grateful to say, found it useful. But since the first edition treated only the major books, when the SCM Press invited me to revise it in 1957, I included all twenty-seven.

In the years since the book first appeared, a lot has been happening in New Testament studies, e.g. new translations like the Revised Standard Version, the New English Bible and the Jerusalem Bible, and the discovery of documents like the Dead Sea Scrolls which illuminate, at this point and that, the background of the New Testament. In Gospel research form criticism, which succeeded source criticism, has itself been followed by 'redaction criticism' (or the history of editing). A 'new look' has been coming over John's Gospel. We have discovered that 'dear doctor Luke', besides being a historian, is also a theologian with a viewpoint of his own. New light has been shed on such riddling documents as Hebrews and Revelation. And so on.

In this latest edition I have sought to take account of these things. It has meant a complete revision of the whole book, and in many cases a radical re-writing, in order to exhibit the progress of New Testament studies. But I have not altered the general format and lay-out of the book.

This is not merely a historical Introduction to the New Testament. In each discussion of a New Testament document I have deliberately tried to show its continuing relevance for the world in which we live. If anyone should protest that it is no business of the New Testament scholar to aim at 'edification', I make no apology. Unless I have wholly misunderstood it, the New Testament is an 'edifying' book – not in any narrowly pietistic sense but in the true sense of the New Testament word for 'edification', *oikodomē*, namely, the upbuilding of the life of the church in faith and hope and love.

The Rev. David G. Gray, my friend and neighbour (recently retired from St Peter's, Dundee), deserves my warmest thanks for his careful reading of the proofs.

Ayr   A. M. HUNTER

PART ONE

Introductory

PART ONE

Introductory

1

Why We Study the New Testament

If an unbeliever, or some seeker after God, were to ask us, 'Why should I study the New Testament? What is there in this book which I find in no other?' how should we answer him?

People talk much nowadays about the English Bible as literature. T. H. Huxley called it our 'national epic'; Quiller-Couch 'the most majestic thing in our literature'; and Macneile Dixon, 'the chief ornament of our language'. Is it for its splendours of expression that we should read it? The story is told of an eminent English poet that one morning his wife invaded his study and set him to read 'a portion of God's Word'. He obeyed, and a little later when his son came in and saw what he was reading, the poet looked up and said, 'My boy, you should always read your Bible. There's nothing like it for your style.' Does this story contain the reason why we should read the New Testament? Is it for its literary interest that we should study it, especially as it comes to us in the stately cadences of the forty-seven men who made the Authorized Version?

No; as a matter of fact, from a purely literary viewpoint, the New Testament is inferior to that other volume which is usually, and rightly, bound up with it, the Old Testament. (Examine any anthology of English prose, and you will see that the literary man finds far more to praise in the Old Testament than in the New.) To be sure, there are not a few passages in the New Testament which hold an unchallengeable place in the world's literature. So fastidious a critic as Robert Bridges pronounced the parable of the Prodigal Son 'a perfectly flawless piece of work'. To praise Paul's 'Song of Songs' in I Cor. 13 is to 'varnish sunlight'. Where will you find a finer piece of pure eloquence than the roll-call of the heroes of

faith in Hebrews 11? And what can excel in splendour the description of the 'new Jerusalem' in the last chapter of Revelation? Nevertheless, it is not for this reason that we bid men study the New
Testament. It is true that a man may begin studying the New
Testament with a purely literary concern and end up by valuing
it for a quite different reason. A case in point was E. V. Rieu to
whom we owe the Penguin Classics. When his son (a lay-reader)
heard that his father had begun to translate the Gospels, he said,
'It will be interesting to see what father makes of the Gospels. It
will be still more interesting to see what the Gospels make of him.'
And it was. When E. V. Rieu had finished, he confessed that his
work had changed him. The Gospels, he wrote, 'bear the seal of
the Son of Man and God; they are the Magna Carta of the human
spirit. Were we to devote to their comprehension a little of the
selfless enthusiasm that is now expended on the riddle of our
physical surroundings, we should cease to say that Christianity
is coming to an end – we might even feel that it had only just
begun.'[1]

Nonetheless, it is not as literature, not for its style primarily,
that we ask men to reckon with the New Testament.

Is it, then, for its pure and lofty moral teaching? Christianity
being admittedly a method of goodness – God's way of making bad
men good – is it because we have in the New Testament a match-
less guidebook to the good life that men ought to study it? Is it as
the world's supreme text-book on ethics that the New Testament
merits the attention of all interested in the problem of right living?

This is the answer of some. But if the peculiar virtue of the New
Testament lies in its ethics, clearly three-fourths of it must be regarded as irrelevant. For, since most of the New Testament's finest
moral teaching is to be found in the Sermon on the Mount, three
or four chapters of St Paul, the Epistle of James, and a few other
passages, we must, on this view, conclude that the bulk of the New
Testament is, for all practical purposes, so much literary dross
which we may safely throw away. Some people think that this is
what ought to be done. They lavish their praise on the Sermon on
the Mount and the thirteenth chapter of I Corinthians; but they
can only regret that these treasures come to us embedded in a
fantastic framework of myth and supernaturalism. What we ought
to do, they say, is to preserve this precious ethical residuum, 'de-

[1] E. V. Rieu, *The Four Gospels*, Penguin Books 1952, pp. xxxiif.

mythologize' the New Testament generally, and consign most of the miracles to the limbo of forgotten things. Thus the eminent Jewish scholar, Joseph Klausner, would like to preserve what he calls 'the book of the ethics of Jesus'[2] (presumably the Sermon on the Mount) after ridding it of its 'wrappings of miracle and mysticism'. And doubtless many of our modern humanists hold much the same view.

Of course no Christian could ever countenance such a proposal. To jettison the miracle and mysticism would be to jettison much of what makes the New Testament precious to him – the reality of the Resurrection and the miracle of the abiding and indwelling Christ – and while he may feel uneasy about this or that 'mighty work' attributed to Christ, he realizes that a New Testament comprising only a few selected ethical passages would be something very like *Hamlet* with the Prince of Denmark left out. Besides, a very casual knowledge of the New Testament tells him that this proposed purge of the New Testament is quite impracticable; for, whether we like it or not, the religion of the New Testament, which includes miracle and mysticism, and its ethic belong together as root and fruit. In short, the notion that we can wander through the Gospels and Epistles, as through a garden, plucking here and there an ethical flower for the adornment of our philosophy of life, is a quite arbitrary procedure.

No; the peculiar virtue of the New Testament does not lie in its ethical glories; not for these primarily do we read it.

Others there are who, finding the essence of Christianity in 'Christ's views about God and the Sermon on the Mount', think that it is in these that the value of the New Testament lies. This is roughly the standpoint of (theological) liberalism. It values the New Testament because we find in it the highest and purest 'message about God and the good'.[3] Behind this view lies the assumption that Christianity is the last and loftiest construction that man has put on the Infinite.

The Christian idea of God, for example, is the sublime discovery of that religious genius, Jesus of Nazareth, the Columbus of the spiritual world who 'by searching has found out God'. Moreover, in the teaching of this genius meet all our highest ideas of human

[2] Joseph Klausner, *Jesus of Nazareth*, Allen and Unwin 1943, p. 414.
[3] This was the phrase of Adolf Harnack (1851-1930), perhaps the greatest of the liberal theologians.

conduct. Morality, as we see it in the Sermon on the Mount, has come forth from his hands a new creation, and in it we are to find the noblest expression of man's duty on this earth. Because the New Testament is the repository of this lofty teaching about God and man's duty, we ought to study and prize it above all the religious classics of mankind.

This is an advance on the previous view. Let us not speak scornfully of men who find in the New Testament no more than this. Yet let us also be clear that, if it is in 'Christ's views about God and the Sermon on the Mount' that the peculiar virtue of the New Testament lies, then once again most of it ought to go into the waste-paper basket, or be preserved only for its antiquarian interest. For the logical consequence of this view is that the New Testament theologians – Paul, John, the Writer to the Hebrews and the rest – who found in Christ not the spiritual Columbus of our race but in a real sense the very God himself stooping low for our redemption – ought to be dismissed as misguided enthusiasts who turned 'the beautiful idyll of Galilee' into a cosmic drama of redemption. This view runs counter to the whole tenor of the New Testament. The New Testament writers never lead us to suppose that the precious thing they have to give us is men's thoughts about God, however sublime; what they claim to give us is God's Word – his final Word – to men about himself and his purpose. And now, as the children say, we are really getting hot ...

For what then (to come to the crux of the matter) are we to study the New Testament?

It is a cardinal canon of criticism that in dealing with any great work our prime endeavour should be to understand (as Aristotle would say) 'the thing it was to be'. If, applying this canon to the New Testament, we ask what its writers aim to give us, the answer is neither belles-lettres nor superfine ethics, nor even lofty views about God, but Good News *from* God – authentic tidings of God's good will to redeem and deliver sinful men. And to this day, when simple men and women go to the New Testament, this is what they seek. They do not seek fine literature: they can get that elsewhere, in Shakespeare and many another. They do not seek merely moral light and leading: they can get that in the writings of many a good and wise man of this world. They do not even seek views about God: they can get these in any handbook of comparative religion. No, beset behind and before with sin and guilt, perplexed and bewildered by the burden and mystery of life, they seek 'a Word from the Beyond for our human predicament'. And it is just because the New Testament is, from the Gospels to the Apocalypse, one triumphant testimony that God has spoken this Word that it occupies a unique place in the literature of the world. That is to say, the importance of the New Testament is that it claims to be the record of a unique self-revelation of God on the stage of human history. a revelation which gives the key to all history's inner meaning.

That revelation may be summed up in various ways:

'In Christ God was reconciling the world to himself' (Paul).
'The Word became flesh and dwelt among us' (John).
'God has spoken to us by a Son' (Hebrews).

But, however varied be the expression, it is always the record of the inconceivable condescension of God to us men in the person of Jesus Christ his Son.

No other set of religious books in the world makes this astonishing claim. As an American scholar has finely phrased it, 'If there be any true myth, if the Divine Nature has at any time and in any wise revealed itself to men, if any voice shall ever reach us out of the infinite circle of silence, where else shall we look for it but to the words of the Gospel?' In so saying he but echoes one of the greatest of the Apostolic Fathers, Ignatius of Antioch: 'Jesus Christ is the Word of God which came forth out of silence.'

There are three things to be said about this revelation and its record:

First, it is a revelation that comes by *action* rather than by words, by deeds rather than by doctrines. This is just to say that it is the revelation of 'the living God', the God who is known by what he does, the God whose character is to be discerned in the stuff of history. 'The highest cannot be spoken,' said Goethe, 'it can only be acted.' It is the claim of the New Testament that the All Highest has once for all acted in a special series of events in history – the coming of Christ – in such a way as to show men for ever his innermost heart. As Browning put it:

> What lacks then of perfection fit for God
> But just the instance which this tale supplies
> Of love without a limit? So is strength,
> So is intelligence; let love be so,

Unlimited in its self-sacrifice,
Then is the tale true and God shows complete.

Second, to claim that the New Testament records a unique self-revelation of God is not to say that God may not reveal himself generally in other ways. Indeed, you will find in the New Testament several passages which declare that God has not left men 'without some clue to his nature' (Acts 14.17 NEB) in creation, providence and history, apart altogether from the revelation in Christ (cf. Rom. 1.19f.; 2.14f.). But the New Testament writers do insist that in the record of God's dealings with a special people, the Jews, given us in the Bible and culminating in the coming of Christ, and the creation of a new people of God which is the Christian church, we have history as a process of divine self-revelation.

Third, it is because the Bible, with the New Testament as its climax and crown, is the record of that revelation that we say it contains the Word of God. The matter has never been better expressed than it was by William Robertson Smith of Aberdeen when he stood arraigned for heresy: 'If I am asked why I receive Scripture as the Word of God, I answer with all the Fathers of the Protestant Church: Because the Bible is the only record of the redeeming love of God, because in the Bible alone I find God drawing near to man in Christ Jesus and declaring to us, in him, his will for our salvation. And this record I know to be true by the witness of his Spirit in my heart whereby I am assured that none other than God himself is able to speak such words to my soul.'

2

Language, Text and Canon

Before we 'clap into it roundly', there are three preliminary questions to be answered:

In what language was the New Testament originally written?

Can we be sure we have the New Testament books substantially as they left their writers' hands?

How came the twenty-seven books of the New Testament to be gathered together and made authoritative Christian scripture?

1. All the New Testament books were originally written in Greek. On the face of it this may surprise us. Aramaic, a language akin to Hebrew, was the mother-tongue of Jesus; and though he was probably able to speak Greek, it was in Aramaic, not Greek, that he preached and taught. Further, the masters of the civilized world in those days were the Romans, and we might have expected that Latin would have been the language in which the New Testament books, addressed as they were subjects of Rome, would have been written. Why then did Paul, for example, use Greek and not Latin when he wrote to the Christians in Rome? And if the language of the New Testament was Greek, what sort of Greek was it? Four or five centuries before Christ Plato had philosophized in Greek, Sophocles had written tragedies in Greek, Demosthenes had delivered orations in Greek. Did Paul, Luke, John and the rest of them use the same Greek?

The answer is Yes and No. The language they used was Greek, but it was by no means the same Greek as men had spoken in the days of 'the glory that was Greece'. Their Greek is called 'Classical Greek'; the Greek of the New Testament writers is called 'Common Greek' (or, 'the *Koinē*', which is Greek for 'the common [language]').

This *Koinē*, or Common Greek, was in Christ's time the international language of the day, very much as English is today. Alexander the Great, of Macedon in Northern Greece, had played a main part in making it so. In the fourth century BC not only did Alexander conquer a great part of the known world, but he took with him his language wherever he marched. Thus, what had been once the tongue of a small country became the international language of the world from the gates of India in the East to the Pillars of Hercules in the West, and all round the Mediterranean.

It was in this international language, Common Greek, that the New Testament writers composed their Gospels and Epistles.

In the last eighty to a hundred years a flood of light has been shed on this Greek by the discovery in the sands of Egypt of what are called the papyri. These are business documents, tax receipts, private letters, etc., written in Common Greek during the centuries before and after Christ. A study of them helps us to fix more precisely the meaning of many New Testament words. Thus we now know that the prodigal son did not vaguely 'gather all together', as the AV has it (Luke 15.13). The Greek verb *synagein* here means 'turned it into cash', viz. his share of his father's property. So, in II Thess. 3.11, where, according to the AV, Paul reproaches some Christians in Thessalonica for 'walking disorderly', the papyri show that Paul's Greek word means 'playing truant' from their work on the excuse that Christ might be coming back at any time. Or, again, when St Peter bids his readers 'desire the sincere milk of the Word' (I Peter 2.2 AV), the Greek adjective *adolos* means 'unadulterated' – milk without admixture of water.

Yet it would be wrong to say that New Testament Greek is simply the Common Greek of the Roman world in the first century AD. If it were, how are we to account for the puzzlement of classical scholars when they come to read New Testament Greek? The strange and alien element which they find in it is Semitic. It is the Hebraic background of the writers glimmering through their Greek, intruding itself into their grammar, affecting the meaning of the words they use.

An analogy may help to make the point. Readers of *The Pilgrim's Progress* know that John Bunyan is a master of Saxon prose. Yet his prose is not simply Saxon prose, it is Saxon prose with a biblical accent, because Bunyan had steeped himself in the English Bible. Just so New Testament Greek is Common Greek with a

Semitic accent. This is what we might have expected; for all the New Testament writers, save Luke, were Jews. Some of this Semitic element in their Greek is due to the influence of the Hebrew scriptures and to the Aramaic spoken by Jesus and his first followers. More often the Semitic cast of New Testament Greek springs from the fact that the Bible which most early Christians used was the Septuagint – a slavishly literal translation of the Hebrew Old Testament made at Alexandria two or three centuries before Christ. Inevitably the style of the Septuagint coloured the Greek which evangelists and apostles wrote, and many of the New Testament's key-words can only be understood against the background of the Hebrew Old Testament and its Greek translation.

Two examples must suffice here, to show how New Testament Greek words are stained with Hebrew meaning. A good one is 'the church'. For an Athenian the Greek word *ekklēsia* signified the *assembly* of his fellow-citizens for political purposes. (The word is so used in Acts 19.32,39,41.) But when the early Christians called themselves 'the *ekklēsia*' or (more fully) 'the *ekklēsia* of God', they were claiming to be God's own people. The key to this un-Greek use of the word is to be found in the Septuagint. There, as a rule, *ekklēsia* translates the Hebrew *qāhāl*, which is the usual Old Testament word for Israel as the people of God. To an Athenian of the first century AD 'the *ekklēsia* of God' would have been a verbal nonsense, but to a Jew it would have been luminous with meaning.

Or take the word 'repentance'. The Greek is *metanoia*, and for a Greek like Plato it meant 'change of mind'. But the word on the lips of John the Baptist or of Jesus means something more drastic and existential – not simply 'grieve' but 'turn'. So when Jesus called for 'repentance', he called for a complete 'change of direction', a right-about-turn. This is because the New Testament's idea of 'repentance' reflects that of the Old Testament prophets and means a radical returning to God. (Other good examples of Greek words stained with Hebrew meanings are 'parable', 'law', 'covenant', 'righteousness' and 'glory'.)

To sum up. If New Testament Greek is Common Greek as spoken in the first century AD over most of the known world, it is Greek shot through with the Semitic idioms of the Bible, as was Bunyan's prose with those of the English Bible.

2. Eighteen centuries have passed since the New Testament was

written, and inevitably the question arises, do we now have its books in anything like their original form?

We do not, of course, possess the 'originals' or 'autographs', as they are called. These have perished. But we know what they looked like. All were *papyrus rolls*. The papyrus (from which comes our word 'paper') is a plant of the sedge family which grows abundantly in marshy spots like the Nile Delta. When the old paper-makers set to work, their first task was to extract the pith from the papyrus reeds and cut it into fine strips. These strips they laid side by side vertically before crossing them with others horizontally, to form a page, generally about ten inches long and five broad. The rough sheets were then soaked in water and treated with gum, and after drying in the sun and polishing with an ivory roller were ready for use. All you needed now was a reed pen (*kalamos*) cut with a pen-knife into proper shape and some ink made from soot, gum and water. (In II John 12 and III John 13 you will find mention of such pen and ink.) If you had skill at it, you would do your own writing; but if you were a busy man, you might dictate to a scribe (cf. Rom. 16.22: 'I Tertius, who took this letter down, add my Christian greetings' NEB).

A single papyrus sheet would suffice for a short letter like Paul's to Philemon. For longer works like Luke's Gospel you had to join many sheets together to form a roll, perhaps thirty feet long. If the roll was meant to be read often, it would be equipped with a stick at each end, for winding and unwinding.

Such was the format of the New Testament autographs. But if these have perished, can we be confident that we know what was originally written on them? After all, for about 1400 years (roughly from AD 100 to 1450, the years between the writing of the books and the invention of printing) the New Testament was copied by hand. To err is human, and copying by hand perforce produces a crop of errors. No scribe, however expert, can avoid occasional mistakes. No later copyist finding such mistakes is likely to resist the temptation to correct his predecessors' slips. Thus errors arise and are perpetuated. Since the New Testament ran these risks for so many centuries, can we be sure that the best text we have today is close to what the original writers wrote?

The answer is: We can – thanks to the discovery of thousands of New Testament manuscripts and the study done on them by experts called 'textual critics'.

When King James's famous forty-seven men made the Authorized Version in 1611, the MSS available were few and late and contained many errors. When the Revised Version was made in 1881, the position had greatly improved. At the Revisers' disposal were famous MSS like Codex[1] Vaticanus (now in the Vatican) and Codex Sinaiticus (now in the British Museum), both going back to, roughly, AD 350. Today we have some 4,500 Greek MSS of the whole or parts of the New Testament. The Chester Beatty papyri, found in 1931 and including most of the New Testament, belong to the third century and the Bodmer papyri go back to about AD 200.[2] Earliest of all is a papyrus fragment of some verses in John's Gospel which is to be dated about AD 130.

Besides these Greek MSS we have also at our disposal for recovering the true text (*a*) the Versions i.e. early translations of the Greek New Testament into other languages like Latin and Syriac, and (*b*) the many quotations from the New Testament found in the writings of early Church Fathers like Tatian and Irenaeus.

Such are our materials. When we remember how meagre are those for the texts of classical writers – we have only one MS of the Roman poet Catullus – clearly the men who work on the text of the New Testament (and they are still at it) suffer from an embarrassment of riches. How they detect and eliminate errors and evaluate the worth of MSS, we cannot discuss here. But we may quote the verdict of one of the greatest, F. J. A. Hort (who, along with Bishop Westcott, produced in 1881 the most famous modern edition of the Greek New Testament): 'The words in our opinion still subject to doubt can hardly amount to more than a thousandth part of the New Testament.' Hort probably underestimated the element of uncertainty. There still remain quite a few places where the experts disagree about the true reading. For example, in Rom. 5.1, did Paul write 'We have (*echŏmen*) peace with God' or 'Let us have (*echōmen*) peace with God'? Nevertheless, anybody today who uses the Revised Standard Version or the New English Bible may rest assured that his English translation is based on a Greek text which comes as near the 'autographs' as makes no material difference.

[1] A codex is a MS in *book* form as distinct from a roll, which it began to replace in the second century.

[2] Chester Beatty, an American, and Bodmer, a Swiss, are two modern Maecenases (patrons of letters) who purchased the MSS from Egyptian dealers.

3. Our third preliminary question is about the canon. Derived from the Hebrew *kanna*, the word originally meant a 'reed' or 'cane', later a 'measuring rod', and so a 'standard' or 'rule'. (Paul so uses the word in Gal. 6.16: 'Peace and mercy be on all who walk by this *rule*.') So it came to signify 'the rule of faith' – the list of sacred books accepted by the church as authoritative in matters of faith and life. Our question is: How came the twenty-seven books now in our New Testament to achieve that authority?

Jesus wrote nothing; and when the little people of God started on its great career, the only scripture Christians had was the Old Testament which, in the light of the coming of Christ, had become a new book for them. But alongside the Old Testament stood 'the words of the Lord Jesus' now being authoritatively quoted in the church (see Acts 20.35 or I Cor. 7.10), and the story of his earthly ministry written by Peter's friend, Mark, about AD 65, to be followed in the next thirty years by the other three Gospels. At first these Gospels circulated locally; later they gained wider currency. But fifteen years before Mark's Gospel appeared, Paul had begun to write letters to the churches he had founded. These were read at what we would call 'congregational meetings', and afterwards lent to sister churches where they were copied. Moreover, in the second half of the first century there appeared other letters associated with the names of apostles – like I Peter and I John – which were similarly prized and copied. So, book by book, the New Testament began to grow. Not that our New Testament books were the only ones. Others there were like the *First Epistle of Clement* to the Corinthians, and a sort of early *Pilgrim's Progress* named *The Shepherd of Hermas*, books known nowadays as 'The Apostolic Fathers'. Further, in the second century came some highly fanciful Gospels and Acts designed to fill in gaps in the early Christian's knowledge of the Lord and his apostles. These latter make up what we now call 'The Apocryphal New Testament'.[3] How were our twenty-seven books separated from these and raised to canonical rank?

The first point to seize is that the process was largely informal and unofficial. We err if we imagine a committee of venerable churchmen sitting round a table with several piles of books on it (Gospels, Epistles etc.) and gravely weighing the merits of each

[3] See M. R. James, *The Apocryphal New Testament*, Oxford University Press 1924.

book until finally they had a small pile of twenty-seven ready for publication. In the initial stages councils and committees played a very small part.

The next point is that the process of inclusion and exclusion was very gradual. The New Testament did not suddenly spring into being like Athene from the head of Zeus in the Greek fable. Something like three centuries elapsed before the scattered writings were collected into the New Testament as we know it today.

The story of how the New Testament canon was formed is long and (to be candid) very dull.[4] It will be enough to mention two important dates in it. By the year 200 the main contents of the New Testament had been decided. Only seven of our twenty-seven books – Hebrews, James, Jude, II Peter, II and III John, and Revelation – still had a question mark over them. (We know this from a document called 'the Muratorian Fragment' which lists the books deemed canonical in the church of Rome about that time.) The other date is 367, the year in which Athanasius (better known as the champion of orthodoxy against Arius) in a famous Easter letter defined a canon of twenty-seven books which corresponds exactly with the New Testament as we have it today. After that, it only remained for various councils to ratify decisions already reached by the good sense of the church at large.

What causes compelled the church to form a canon? One was the emergence of a host of Christian writings of dubious value and authority – the apocryphal Gospels and Acts. The church had to decide which books preserved true Christian tradition and teaching. Another was the infiltration into the church of heresies like Gnosticism. Derived from the Greek word for knowledge' (*gnōsis*), this many-sided religious movement was at its peak in the second century. It promised escape for man's spirit imprisoned in this evil world of matter through a so-called divine 'knowledge' brought from the spirit world by a redeemer-revealer who, his work accomplished, returned whence he came. (*The Gospel of Thomas*, recently found in Egypt, is a Gnostic book.) If the church was to guard her members against this false teaching, necessity was laid on her to say where true doctrine was to be found.

What criteria did the church employ? Two, commonly known as 'apostolicity' and 'public lection'. That is to say, the two criteria

---

[4] See J. N. Sanders' essay on the NT canon in M. Black and H. H. Rowley (eds.), *Peake's Commentary on the Bible*, Nelson 1962, pp. 679ff.

were (*a*) the belief that the book came from apostolic circles; and (*b*) the fact that it was regularly read with profit in the church These two tests ensured that a book had something 'salutary' to say to Christians and that what it said originated in the circle to whom God's saving revelation in Christ was given.

Comparing the books now in the canon with those which were excluded, we cannot doubt that the early church showed sanctified common sense in their choice. As their Lord had bidden his disciples (I Thess. 5.21, which is an uncanonical saying of Jesus),[5] they 'tested all things and held fast what was good'.

[5] For proof of this see my *Exploring the New Testament*, Saint Andrew Press 1971, pp. 123-5.

3

The Contents of the New Testament

The New Testament is really Volume Two in the story of salvation which is the theme of the whole Bible. If Volume One begins with the Creation and the Fall of Adam (which is Hebrew for 'man'), Volume Two records how

> A second Adam to the fight
> And to the rescue came.

It tells how, 'when the time had fully come', God fulfilled the promises made through his prophets to Israel by sending his Son Jesus to be his people's Messiah or Deliverer; and how, when they rejected him, the new people of God went forth to proclaim the salvation he had brought to the wider world.

The New Testament comprises twenty-seven books; but some are very short; and, altogether, the New Testament is only about a third of the length of the Old Testament. These twenty-seven books we may classify as follows:

First, we have four documents called 'Gospels' which, at first, look like biographies of Jesus but which, on closer study, hardly answer to our modern ideas of biographical writing. Next comes a volume of history, the Acts of the Apostles, which, as its preface shows (Acts 1.1), is really a sequel to the Third Gospel. Then follow twenty-one documents which we know as Epistles (the New English Bible calls them 'Letters'). The term is very elastic, because it covers many literary types, from a massive theological treatise (Romans) to a charming little private letter (Philemon), and includes a highly rhetorical homily (Hebrews) and an ethical scrap-book (James); and the whole is rounded off with a book of apocalyptic visions known as the Revelation of St John.

To this collection of twenty-seven books Paul, who has fourteen
Epistles ascribed to him[1] in the Authorized Version, and Luke,
who wrote both the Gospel bearing his name and Acts, are the
chief contributors; but modern scholars count some dozen different authors in the whole New Testament.

In our New Testament the books are not arranged chronologically. In point of time Paul's Epistles ought to stand first, with
either I Thessalonians or Galatians at their head. Among the
Gospels, Mark should come first and John possibly last. Moreover, not Revelation (which was written about AD 95) but II Peter
should, in strict chronology, stand last. However, we are going to
consult the reader's convenience by taking the books in the
general order in which they appear in the Bible: Gospels, Acts,
Epistles, Apocalypse – an order which, in spiritual logic, can be
justified; for Matthew, the first Gospel, with its emphasis on Jesus
as the fulfiller of Old Testament prophecy, helps to bind the two
Testaments together, and Revelation, coming at the end, supplies a
perfect climax to the story of salvation with its message of the
judgment and victory of God.

Our first section will deal with the four Gospels. After con-
sidering how the Gospels came to be written, we shall study the
literary connection between them ('the Synoptic problem') and
conclude with a chapter on each of the four.

The subject of our second section will be 'The Early Church
and St Paul'. We need to remember that the Gospels, which end
with the Resurrection, tell us only what 'Jesus *began* to do and to
teach' (Acts 1.1). The acts of Christ did not cease there; they were
continued in the acts of his 'special messengers' or apostles. Our
first study will therefore be the book which forms the bridge
between the Gospels and the rest of the New Testament – the Acts
of the Apostles. Of the apostles we know most about St Paul, and
to his life we shall devote a chapter, not only because it is intrinsically important – did he not claim, with justice, to have 'worked
harder' for the gospel than any of them?[2] – but because it supplies a framework into which we can dovetail his letters. They fall
into three classes: (1) Six Travel Epistles: Galatians, I and II
Thessalonians, I and II Corinthians and Romans; (2) Four Prison
Epistles: Ephesians, Colossians, Philemon and Philippians; and

[1] One of them, Hebrews, erroneously, as we shall see.
[2] I Cor. 15.10.

(3) the Pastoral Epistles: I and II Timothy and Titus.

Our third section will deal with the writings of the other apostolic men, often called the 'Catholic (or General) Epistles' because they were not addressed to specified churches or individuals. Finally, we shall have to say a word about the most enigmatic book of all which ends the New Testament – the Revelation made to John the Seer of Patmos, often called 'The Apocalypse'.

Reading this survey of the New Testament, the reader may well exclaim, 'What a literary hotch-potch or farrago the New Testament is! Can there be any common theme running through all this diversity of documents?' So, we have added an epilogue called 'The Unity of the New Testament', to show that there is, and that it can be summed up as 'One Lord, One Church, One Salvation'.

PART TWO

The Four Gospels

4

How the Gospels Came to be Written

'Gospel', a fine old English word from 'god spel', good news, translates the Greek word *euangelion*.

Originally, this meant the reward given to a man bringing good news. Then it came to denote the good news itself. Then – and this is its New Testament sense – it came to signify God's good news proclaimed by Jesus and embodied in him. (For Jesus came not merely to preach the gospel, but that there might be a gospel to preach.)

Life always precedes literature, and we do well to remember that the good news was being proclaimed before a scrap of Christian literature existed. But in the first Christian generation (roughly AD 30-60), if there were no written Gospels, there was a *kērygma*. This rugged Greek noun (derived from the verb *kēryssein*, which means to do a herald's work) means a 'proclamation', or preached message, and thanks to modern scholarship[1] we can roughly reconstruct its content.

A comparison of the apostles' speeches in Acts 2-10[2] with some passages in Paul's letters where he is quoting early Christian 'tradition' (e.g. Rom. 1.3f.; I Cor. 15.3ff.) yields an outline of the 'proclamation' which formed the first good news. A reporter's summary of it would have read something like this:

The prophecies are fulfilled and God's new order has dawned,
The Messiah, born of David's line, has come.

[1] See C. H. Dodd, *The Apostolic Preaching and its Developments*, Hodder and Stoughton 1936.
[2] These speeches are not verbatim reports of what Peter and the others said; but they probably represent generally the original preaching of the apostles, and in Peter's to Cornelius (Acts 10.36-43), so Semitic-sounding is the Greek that it looks as if it were based on an Aramaic source.

He is Jesus of Nazareth, the Servant of the Lord, who
  Went about doing good and healing by God's power,
  Was crucified according to God's purpose,
  Was raised from the dead on the third day,
  Is now exalted to God's right hand,
  And will come in glory for judgment.
Therefore repent, believe this good news, and be baptized for the forgiveness of your sins and the gift of the Holy Spirit.

In the beginning, then, was the *kērygma*, and this 'proclamation' was the earliest gospel with which Christ's apostles went forth to evangelize the wider world. Of course there would be different emphases in this early preaching according as it was addressed to Jews or to Gentiles. But its core or kernel remained constant. Thus in I Cor. 15.1-11, after quoting a summary of it which must go back to within a decade of the Resurrection, Paul comments: 'Whether then it is I or they (Peter, James, John and the rest), this is what we all proclaim.' The earliest gospel, therefore, as we need sometimes to remind ourselves, was not the Sermon on the Mount but a proclamation about a cross on a hill and an empty grave and God's saving action disclosed therein.

Two things must be said about this earliest preaching of the good news. First, the apostles did not simply recite their *kērygma* to their hearers in a 'take it or leave it' fashion. Otherwise, on the day of Pentecost, Peter's hearers would not have been 'cut to the heart' (Acts 2.27), as they are said to have been. The apostles preached 'existentially', as we would say nowadays, made their message a matter of life or death. Holding their preaching to be a part of the gospel itself – an act prolonging and declaring God's saving work in Christ – they were at pains to *contemporize* it, to confront sinful men and women urgently with God's saving deed in Christ and to challenge them to respond to it by the decision of faith (which meant taking God at his word in Christ). This is why Paul could say: 'The gospel is the saving power of God for everyone who has faith.... It is as if God were appealing to you through us. In Christ's name we implore you, Be reconciled to God' (Rom. 1.16; II Cor. 5.20).

Second: the *kērygma* we have outlined gives only the bare bones of what the apostles said. We may take it as certain that they filled the outline in. And if we ask with what they did so, the answer is: with stories about Jesus and his ministry among men and how he came to the cross at last.[3] There was no lack of such stories, for many still lived who had seen and heard Jesus 'in the days of his flesh', or knew people who had companied with him in Galilee or Judaea, and could recall his gracious consorting with tax-gatherers and sinners or his 'mighty acts': how he had healed the sick, or blessed little children, or stilled a storm, or fed a great multitude, or made life new for a fallen woman or a despised inspector of taxes; or, on the last evening, in an upper room with his disciples, used broken bread and outpoured wine to symbolize his approaching death and the inauguration of God's new covenant with men. Indeed, in every great centre of early Christianity – Jerusalem, Caesarea, Antioch, Rome – there grew up cycles of stories about Jesus which the Christians passed from one to another when they met for worship or held common meals, and which the apostolic preachers wove into the fabric of their sermons. At this stage memories were still fresh and vivid, and no need was yet felt for written records of the story of Jesus.

But what about the *teaching* of Jesus? The outline of the *kērygma* we have given says nothing about this. Yet we must not suppose that the early Christians forgot, or ignored, all the memorable sayings of him 'who spoke as never man spoke'. The preservation of some sixty of his parables and the 106 verses of the Sermon on the Mount (Matt. 5-7) – to take two examples – is proof positive that they did not. Indeed, there is ample evidence that they treasured up the sayings of Jesus for the light and leading they afforded on the problems of Christian life and practice. St Paul, for example, was not ignorant of what Jesus had said. In Rom. 12-14 his exposition of the 'Christian Ethic' contains ten echoes of the words of Jesus, and from time to time he was wont to refer to 'Words of the Lord' (see I Cor. 7.10; 9.14; 11.23ff.; Acts 20.35) to settle hard questions in his churches. (This is what he meant by 'the law of Christ', Gal. 6.2.)

So we may be sure that from the very beginning men remembered the sayings of Jesus, prizing them no doubt for their own sake – because they were the words of their exalted Lord, now 'King' and 'Head of the Church' – but also, as we have just seen, for their practical value – as a design for Christian living. And somewhere about the year AD 50 a collection of the sayings of

[3] See note at end of chapter.

Jesus was made to serve as a guide to Christian behaviour for those who had been converted by the Gospel preaching.[4]

Thus the materials later to be woven into our written Gospels took shape during the generation that followed the Crucifixion and Resurrection. This is the period of *the oral tradition* – the period when men still preferred 'the living and abiding voice' of eye-witnesses to any written record of Jesus. It was a time when memorable stories about Jesus or sovereign sayings of his were prized for their immediate usefulness and interest. Christian hands were full of precious things, but as yet there was no urgent desire to weave them into a crown.

That time was to come. A generation had gone past since Jesus had died and risen; a generation in which 'the hallowed fire of the gospel' flew from Jerusalem to Rome. Many of the eye-witnesses had now 'fallen asleep': James, son of Zebedee, and James the Lord's brother had been killed, and the two leading apostles Peter and Paul had been martyred in Rome. Now it became increasingly important that the story of Jesus should be set down in writing before the time should come when there would be none left able to say, 'I remember Jesus in his earthly life.' Besides, converts were flocking into the young churches; converts who needed instruction in the Christian faith. In short, the need for a written record of the Lord Jesus began to be urgently felt, and with the need came the man.

That man was John Mark, the friend and (according to tradition) 'the interpreter' of Peter. He it was who wrote in Rome the earliest Gospel. What materials for it lay ready to his hand? To begin with, he had a general knowledge of the course of Jesus' ministry result-ing from his association with Peter – an outline that could be filled in with stories about Jesus. Some of those he included were in fact reminiscences of Peter; but also at his disposal were many other stories circulating orally in the Christian circles in which he moved. With these Mark wove his crown. This was somewhere about AD 65, just after the Emperor Nero's savage attack on the Chris-tians in Rome. In the next thirty years three other men whom we know as Matthew, Luke and John were to follow his example.

[4] See the next chapter on 'The Synoptic Problem'.

NOTE

The story of the Passion was probably the first part of Jesus' story to be woven into a connected narrative – probably well before AD 50, if we may judge from the piece of tradition about the Lord's Supper (I Cor. 11.23ff.) which is set in the context of 'the night of his arrest' (NEB).

Very early the Christians found themselves confronted with the 'stumbling-block' of the Cross, as Paul called it. How could a crucified Messiah be the mediator of God's salvation? To answer this objection, they found they had to tell the story of the Cross and tell it as a whole. That in fact they did so is proved by two things: (1) a stronger thread of continuity runs through the record of Christ's Passion than through any other part of the Gospel tradition; and (2) the sequence of events in all four Gospels is roughly the same. Moreover, all is set down with a sobriety which suggests early and faithful reporting.

But it was not enough simply to proclaim the Cross and the Resurrection. Inevitably their hearers wanted to know more about the earthly career of the Lord who had died to redeem them, and had risen again. So the Passion narrative had to be prefixed with stories of how the good news all began.

5

The Synoptic Problem:
A Literary Puzzle

The first three Gospels – Matthew, Mark and Luke – are commonly called 'the Synoptic Gospels' because they give a 'synopsis', or common outline, of the story of Jesus. Place the contents of these Gospels side by side in columns, and you soon become aware of 'the Synoptic problem'. It is posed by the remarkable parallelism existing among the first three Gospels. In three different biographies of some great person (e.g. Martin Luther) you might not be surprised to find the same incidents recorded. What is strange in the first three Gospels is to find the same incidents in the story of Jesus described in practically the same words.

These similarities are just those which if they occurred today in three different newspapers, you would attribute to their having one or more special correspondents in common, whose dispatches had been freely edited. We therefore infer that each of these Gospels, though independently written, must have drawn much of its materials from a source, or sources, available to one or both of the others.

The discovery of these sources is the Synoptic problem. The first attempt at a solution was the *oral tradition* theory. Behind the three Gospels, it was suggested, lay a common oral tradition about Jesus, more or less fixed as far as the core was concerned. This solution was abandoned because it failed to explain the minute linguistic resemblances among the Synoptic Gospels. (Compare Matt. 9.6; Mark 2.10; Luke 5.24, where an insignificant parenthesis – 'He said to the paralysed man' – is common to all three.) Only a *documentary* theory will fit facts like these. In other words, if very similar matter occurs in one or more evangelists, we must attribute it to their common use of one or more written sources.

An explanation of this kind is now generally accepted. It is called 'the two document theory', and it holds that two basic documents underlie the Synoptic Gospels. They are: our Gospel according to Mark and a sayings-source generally referred to as 'Q' (from the German *Quelle*, 'source').

The first principle of this theory is:

The priority of Mark

By this is meant that the earliest account of Jesus' ministry is found in Mark, and that Mark was used as one of their main sources by Matthew and Luke. In support of this various arguments can be marshalled:

(*a*) *Common subject-matter*

Matthew contains nearly all Mark (606 of Mark's 661 verses reappear in Matthew), and Luke about a half of Mark (the actual figure is 350).

(*b*) *Common wording*

Matthew and Luke often repeat the exact words of Mark – in fact, Matthew reproduces 51% and Luke 53% of Mark's language.

(*c*) *Common order*

Matthew and Luke follow Mark's order of events; and when one of them departs from it, the other keeps to it.

These are not the only arguments. A fourth can be founded on the alterations of Mark to be found in Matthew and Luke (e.g. Matthew alters Mark 10.18, 'Why do you call me good?', to 'Why do you ask me about the good?'). And a fifth can be based on Mark's preservation of Jesus' Aramaic words like *Abba* or *talitha cum*, which Matthew and Luke omitted, doubtless because they meant little to their readers.

All this evidence builds up to one conclusion, that the first of the sources used by Matthew and Luke was Mark.

The second principle of the 'two document theory' is:

The probability of Q

Both Matthew and Luke contain many verses not in Mark. More

than two hundred of these they have in common, often in almost identical words, and these mostly sayings of Jesus. Take, for instance, the parable of the Mote and the Beam (or, as the RSV has it the Speck and the Log):

Matt. 7.3-5	Luke 6.41f.
Why do you see the speck that is in your brother's eye, but do not notice the log that is in your own eye? Or how can you say to your brother, 'Let me take the speck out of your eye,' when there is a log in your own eye? You hypocrite, first take the log out of your own eye, and then you will see clearly to take the speck out of your brother's eye.	Why do you see the speck that is in your brother's eye, but do not notice the log that is in your own eye? Or how can you say to your brother, 'Brother, let me take out the speck that is in your eye,' when you yourself do not see the log that is in your own eye? You hypocrite, first take the log out of your own eye, and then you will see clearly to take out the speck that is in your brother's eye.

Another good example is Matt. 11.25-27: Luke 10.21f. (part of what is called 'The Great Thanksgiving'). Passages like these indicate the use by Matthew and Luke of a second *written* source, nowadays commonly called 'Q'.

Three arguments point to its existence:

The first is the high percentage of *verbal agreement* between Matthew and Luke (just illustrated) in sections where they do not depend on Mark. The second is the striking agreement in the *order* in which these sayings of Jesus appear in Matthew and Luke. And a third is the presence of *doublets* in Matthew and Luke: that is, they report sayings of Jesus *twice* – generally in a slightly different form but in substance identical – once in the part taken over from Mark and once in the parts which only Matthew and Luke have. An example is the saying about 'taking up the cross'. Matt. 16.24 and Luke 9.23 are from Mark 8.34; Matt 10.38 = Luke 14.27 from Q.

Q has not survived, but by comparing these very similar verses in Matthew and Luke we can reconstruct a large part of it. When this is done, we find that Q consisted almost entirely of sayings of Jesus. Much of it can be recovered from the great sermon in Matthew and Luke (Matt. 5-7 and Luke 6.20-49) and from Jesus' charge to his disciples when he sent them out on their mission to preach and heal.

Why was this collection of Jesus' sayings made? The answer would seem to be that it was meant as a guide to Christian behaviour for new converts to the faith. To the first disciples who had entered the Kingdom of God Jesus had sought to show how God meant the men of the Kingdom to live. What more natural than that a Christian leader should make a collection of his sayings to show converts the kind of life and conduct to which their living Lord was calling them?

But who made this collection of Jesus' sayings?[1] About AD 100 Papias, Bishop of Hierapolis, said: 'Matthew compiled the oracles (*logia*) in the Hebrew (i.e. Aramaic) language, but everyone translated them as he was able.' Now that statement does not fit Matthew's Gospel, which is *not* a translation from Aramaic into Greek. But it may well refer to Q which (*a*) is a collection of dominical 'oracles'; (*b*) existed originally in Aramaic; and (*c*) was translated by various persons. If we cannot prove beyond all doubt that Matthew (who must have been an educated man) was the compiler, the tradition favours him, and he is much the likeliest candidate in the field. The strong interest Q shows in Gentiles suggests that it was put together in Antioch, the cradle of Gentile Christianity, probably about AD 50.[2]

Matter peculiar to Matthew and Luke

When we have detached from Matthew and Luke what they derive from Mark and Q, we find that each evangelist has much matter peculiar to himself.

Thus, 'Special Matthew', or 'M', amounts to more than 300 verses. Some of these are quotations from the Old Testament, showing how Jesus fulfilled prophecy. Apart from these, M comprises numerous sayings and parables – many woven into the five great discourses which are a feature of this Gospel – plus some dozen narratives, from the birth story at the beginning to tales about Judas and Pilate and some strange happenings in Jerusalem during the last week. For this special matter the evangelist relies on his own sources of information; but how far they are oral reports or written sources, nobody can say for certain.

[1] For a full exposition of the argument see T. W. Manson, *The Sayings of Jesus*, SCM Press 1949, pp. 15-20. Manson proceeds to give us a reconstruction of Q and a brilliant commentary on it.

[2] One or two modern scholars have questioned 'the Q hypothesis'. For a convincing defence of it see Vincent Taylor's article 'The Order of Q', *The Journal of Theological Studies*, April 1953, pp. 27ff.

What is clear is that much of M has a strong Jewish colouring, which suggests it originated in Jerusalem.

What of 'Special Luke', i.e. the matter peculiar to Luke in chapters 3-24, which we may call 'L'? (The birth stories in Luke 1-2 Luke probably got from the Jewish-Christian churches of Judaea.) Mark and Q account for roughly one half of Luke's Gospel. The other half consists of material peculiar to Luke. It comprises stories and teaching – narratives like the Sermon in the Nazareth Synagogue, the Woman who was a Sinner, the encounter with Zacchaeus and the Walk to Emmaus, plus a wealth of parables, among them some of the greatest, like the Good Samaritan and the Prodigal Son. How did 'the beloved physician' come by this precious material? The preface to his Gospel (Luke 1.1-4) implies that, besides written sources, like Mark and Q, Luke had *oral* ones. We therefore infer that the L material, which shows signs of Luke's own interests and style, is oral tradition about Jesus which Luke had himself collected and written down. If we ask where and when, the likely answer is: in Christian circles in Caesarea, in AD 57-59, while Luke stayed near Paul during his two years' imprisonment (Acts 21.8).

Mark, Q, Special Matthew (M) and Special Luke (L) – these are the four strata of tradition about Jesus to be found in the Synoptic Gospels.[3] The first, Mark, is to be connected with Rome; the second, Q, with Antioch; the third, M, with Jerusalem; and the fourth, L, with Caesarea.

Let us set forth our conclusions in verse:

> The problem solved is stated here:
> Our Mark did first of all appear;
> For Luke and Matthew used him, both.
> But Luke and Matthew, nothing loth
> To add some more, used Q (for 'Quelle')
> And each a special source as well.[4]

If, after this study of the Synoptic Problem, anyone should feel

---

[3] The student will find English texts of Q, M and L in my *Work and Words of Jesus*, SCM Press 1950 (appendices at the end of the book).

[4] The last line might also be expressed thus:

'And special sources M and L'.

Quelle, note, is pronounced Kvelle; but the poetic licence may be pardoned for the sake of a mnemonic!

shocked at the literary ethic – or lack of it – which allowed Matthew and Luke to 'crib' from Mark, let him remember that the law of copyright, a consequence of the invention of printing, did not then exist. In antiquity, when books were copied by hand, commercial copyright had no value; and ancient historians felt themselves free to use portions of their predecessors' work, without the courtesy of quotation marks.

Form criticism and redaction criticism

'Source criticism', which we have been discussing, takes us back behind our Gospels to their written sources. But about fifty years ago three German scholars – K. L. Schmidt, M. Dibelius and R. Bultmann – began a fresh approach to the Gospels now generally known as 'form criticism'. Let us, they said in effect, try to get back behind all documents to the time of the *oral* tradition, when accounts of what Jesus did and said were passing freely from mouth to mouth in the Christian communities, and discover by whom, in what community and for what purpose each piece of the gospel tradition was used before any gospel-maker wrote it down. It was the belief of these form critics that, with the exception of the Passion narrative, the stories now in our Gospels originally circulated as independent units – 'pericopēs' is the technical term. And it was their hope that by a new kind of study of these pericopēs they could get even nearer to Jesus as he really was.

The Gospels, they argued, are folk literature, and by applying tests of form and style derived from other folk literature, we ought to be able to classify the various materials in the Gospels. Having classified them, we may then remove the editorial framework provided by the evangelists, recover the original form of the pericopēs, and decide for what practical purposes – preaching, or teaching, or worship – the early Christians preserved them.

Accordingly, with Teutonic thoroughness, they arranged the Gospel pericopēs, like moths in a museum, into various classes and sub-classes. Among the narratives they found 'pronouncement stories' like Mark 2.15-17, which culminates in Jesus' saying 'I came not to call the righteous but sinners'; or 'miracle stories', like the tale of the healing of the Leper (Mark 1.40-45); or 'legends', like the story of the boy Jesus in the Temple (Luke 2.41-52); or 'myths', like the story of Christ's baptism (Mark 1.9-11). (These last two titles are unfortunate, for to the ordinary reader they

suggest the stories are untrue. The form critics did not necessarily mean this.) Similarly, they categorized the words of Jesus as
parables, prophetic sayings, apocalyptic sayings, etc. It all sounded
scientific, though, as we now see, such classification did not
notably advance our understanding of the Gospels. Worse, the
new science soon got a bad name because in Bultmann it took an
unnecessarily sceptical turn; and we were left wondering how
many of the Gospel stories were true, and how many were inven-
ted by the early Christian communities.

Half a century later, we can detect the errors and failings of the
first form critics. Let us mention four. (1) They seemed to assume
that all the eye-witnesses either died or disappeared just after the
Resurrection – an assumption to which Paul gives the lie in I Cor.
15.6. (2) They assumed that all the early tradition about Jesus was
quite unfixed and relatively unreliable, though the first Christians,
who were Jews, had a serious care for the faithful and controlled
transmission of their Lord's words and deeds. (3) They drew
dubious parallels between oral tradition in other cultures, where
the time of transmission runs into centuries, and oral tradition in
the Gospels, where it is a matter of two or three decades. (4) They
were prone to assume that the *form* of a Gospel story or saying
was a reliable criterion of its authenticity, which of course it is not.

What has been the upshot of it all? In this country, largely
because of Bultmann's 'disseminated scepticism', form criticism
has had a cool reception; and even in Germany, the leading
scholars now take a much less radical approach to the historical
value of the Gospels. Thus, whereas Bultmann once affirmed that
the Gospels yield little, if any, reliable information about Jesus,
his pupil Bornkamm[5] declares that they are 'brimful of history'.

But, if we rightly condemn the excesses of the early form
critics, let us also acknowledge that, when the new method is
judiciously used, as, for example, by C. H. Dodd in this country
or by J. Jeremias in Germany, it can illuminate 'the tunnel period'
of the early church (say, AD 30-50). It does help us to understand
how Christ was preached in the growing communities of the faithful, first by the eye-witnesses and then by 'the servants of the
Word' (as Luke calls them), until the stories became stereotyped
and were finally committed to writing by the evangelists who

[5] Günther Bornkamm, *Jesus of Nazareth*, Hodder and Stoughton 1960,
p. 26.

strung them together and edited them. Form criticism, then, in moderate doses, has its value; but 'too large a dose [of it] might well reduce one to the condition of a man who stands before a Raphael and keeps on asking where the artist got his paints'.[6]

Criticism of the Gospels never stands still. First, as we have seen, came *literary* criticism which sought to lay bare the documentary sources underlying the Gospels. It was followed by *form* criticism which interested itself in the pre-literary tradition of the Gospels. The latest critical technique to emerge from Germany is known as 'redaction criticism', or 'the history of editing'. This starts where form criticism left off, for the interest is now switched from the oral tradition itself to the actual people, Matthew, Mark and Luke, who gave the Gospels their final shape. These evangelists (the new critics tell us) were no mere compilers of traditional material: they were men with their own individual theological viewpoints which can be seen from the way they edited the materials at their disposal. So far from being simply collectors of tradition, they were, each of them, theologians in their own right. Study, for example, the way in which Matthew has edited Mark's story of the Rich Young Ruler and you will find that, by making five changes in it, he has made the story serve his own didactic purpose and so revealed himself as a 'church' theologian. Or study Luke's Gospel, and you will discover that he has his own particular angle on history and eschatology. He sees time as divided into three eras – the Old Testament era ending with John the Baptist, the middle era which is the time of Jesus, and the third era which is the time of the church, and lasts from the Resurrection to the End. Thus the new critics aim to lay bare the theology of the various evangelists.

Unfortunately, so far, their findings are often mutually contradictory, and it is clear that much of their work belongs to the realms of hypothesis and speculation. Inevitably so, for how can we decide for certain what in any Gospel is the work of the final editor and what may have been introduced by an early reviser or

---

[6] E. V. Rieu, *The Four Gospels*, Penguin Books 1952, p. xix. The reader will find good accounts of form criticism in Vincent Taylor, *The Formation of the Gospel Tradition*, Macmillan 1933; A. T. Hanson (ed.), *Vindications*, SCM Press 1966; Stephen Neill, *The Interpretation of the New Testament 1861-1961*, Oxford University Press 1964, pp. 232-62. In *The Birth of the New Testament*, A. and C. Black 1962, C. F. D. Moule brilliantly shows how a constructive use can be made of it.

even found in the material as it came to him?

Perhaps when the dust raised by the new critics has settled a little, we may see more clearly. Meantime we may summarize the result of their labours by saying that they have called in question the earlier view that the evangelists were primarily historians, not theologians. They have shown us (though we had an inkling of this long before) that Matthew had a strong 'church' interest and that Luke was both historian and theologian, i.e. he used his history in the service of his theology. These are emphases which we will discuss when we consider the individual Gospels and Acts. If the student is interested in the new criticism, he will find it summarized in J. Rohde's *Rediscovering the Teaching of the Evangelists*, SCM Press 1969. But one cannot help wondering whether it will take us much further than the older 'Introductions' to the New Testament which pointed out the characteristic interests of the four evangelists.

6

The Earliest Gospel

In 1933 the Reichstag in Berlin was set on fire; and the Nazis, looking round for a suitable scapegoat, fixed the blame on the Communists, many of whom they executed. About 1900 years earlier a similar thing happened in Rome. In the winter of AD 64-65 a great fire devastated two-thirds of the city. The mad emperor Nero, who is said to have been the incendiary, found his scapegoat in the new sect of the Christians who were popularly suspected of all sorts of nameless crimes. A 'killing time' ensued, and among its victims were two Christian leaders named Peter and Paul.

According to reliable tradition it was shortly after this that a little book appeared in Rome with the title 'The Gospel of Jesus Christ the Son of God' (Mark 1.1). It is the book we know as the Gospel according to Saint Mark.

How did it come to be written? A full generation had passed since Jesus had died and risen, and in these years many of those who had seen the risen Lord had died, and some had been martyred. It therefore became increasingly important that before all the eye-witnesses passed away, the story of Jesus should be preserved in writing. Besides, the Christians were now being persecuted and had to be reminded of their Lord and his suffering, in order to nerve them to stand fast in their own time of ordeal. So one day a man called Mark procured pen, ink and papyrus and set to work. What was his aim? It was to persuade his readers in Rome that Jesus of Nazareth was the Christ, the Son of God.

1. *The author*

How do we know the name of the earliest evangelist? The answer is that the unanimous tradition of the church in the second century says so, and there is no reason why one who was not himself one of the Twelve should have been named as its author unless it were true.

The earliest statement comes from the first half of the second century, from Papias, Bishop of Hierapolis. He quotes the testimony of 'the Elder' (John): 'Mark, who became Peter's interpreter, wrote accurately, though not in order, all that he remembered of the things said and done by the Lord.'

That testimony is amply confirmed by writer after writer who followed. Thus, Irenaeus Bishop of Lyons, who had himself been in Rome, put it on record: 'And after their (i.e. Peter's and Paul's) death, Mark, the disciple and interpreter of Peter, also handed down to us in writing the things preached by Peter.'

We need not therefore hesitate to date the Gospel soon after AD 65 and ascribe it to Mark, about whom we know quite a lot (Acts 12.12,25; 13.5,13; 15.37,39; Col. 4.10; Philemon 24; II Tim. 4.11; I Peter 5.13).[1]

His full name was John Mark, and he was a native of Jerusalem; for we know that his mother's house was a meeting place for the early church (Acts 12.12) and, very possibly, the house where the Last Supper was held. If Mark was not one of the Twelve, he may well have met Jesus during his last ministry in Jerusalem. Many have, with reason, supposed that he was the 'young man' who fled half-naked from Gethsemane (Mark 14.51), whither he had rushed to warn Jesus of the approach of the arresting posse. This verse would then be his own modest signature in the corner of his Gospel – his quiet way of saying, 'I was there'.

This was in AD 30, the likely year of the Crucifixion. Some fifteen or sixteen years later we have surer information about Mark's movements. The book of Acts (Acts 13.13; 15.36ff.) tells us that he accompanied his cousin Barnabas and Paul on their first missionary journey. Because Mark deserted them at Perga, Paul refused to take him on their second journey, and there was a sharp dispute between the two apostles. But Paul evidently forgave Mark completely; for we find Mark, years later, sharing Paul's imprisonment in Rome (Col. 4.10-12; Philemon 24).

Mark, however, is also linked in history with the other great

[1] Second-century tradition says Mark was known as the 'stump-fingered one'. I see no reason to doubt it. If it had said he was 'tall, dark and handsome', I might.

apostle, Peter. In Peter's First Letter, written from Rome, we find a tender allusion to 'Mark my son' (I Peter 5.13), which suggests that Peter had in fact won Mark for the faith; and tradition, as we have seen, declares that he acted as Peter's 'interpreter', which presumably means that he helped Peter with his Greek.

When, finally, say about AD 65-67, Mark took up his pen, what gospel materials were at his disposal?

First: the story of the Passion plus a general outline of Jesus' ministry derived from Peter's memory of events that preceded the Passion.

Second: the personal reminiscences of Peter. Passages like Mark 1.16-20,29-31; 5.21-43; 9.2-29; 14.26-42,66-72; 16.7 bear the 'Petrine' mark.

Third: many stories about Jesus (e.g. 2.18-20,23-28; 3.31-35 etc.) and sayings of his which were current in the Christian circles in which Mark moved, some of them already grouped in little clusters (e.g. Mark 2.1-3.6; 9.37-50).

With these Mark composed a Gospel which, by the judgment of all save the most sceptical, supplies a reliable (though not complete) picture of Jesus and his ministry which brought him to the Cross. Here is the considered verdict of Vincent Taylor[2] author of the biggest and best modern commentary on the Gospel: 'In Mark we have an authority of first rank for our knowledge of the Story of Jesus.'

2. *Mark's story of Jesus*

This we can divide into three parts: (1) 1.1-13; (2) 1.14-9.1; (3) 9.2-16.8.

1. The first thirteen verses form what we may call 'the Prelude'. As if fulfilling the old prophets (Mal. 3.1; Isa. 40.3), 'John the Baptizer' appears in the desert country down near the Dead Sea, calling Israel to 'return' to God, predicting the advent of a mightier one than himself, and immersing all penitents in the waters of Jordan. Among the crowds who flock to his baptism comes Jesus from Nazareth. As Jesus rises from the water, he sees in vision God's Spirit descending on him, and hears a heavenly voice confirming his divine sonship and calling him to serve as God's Messiah. With psychological fitness, this high hour of revelation

[2] Vincent Taylor, *The Gospel according to Saint Mark*, Macmillan 1952, p. 148.

is for Jesus immediately followed by a time of 'testing' by the devil in the desert.

2. At 1.14f. the *first main section* of the Gospel begins. After the Baptist's arrest by 'King' Herod, Jesus comes into Galilee with the startling news that the appointed time has come and that God's Reign is beginning. Let men turn to God and accept this good news as true. By the lakeside he calls two pairs of brothers from their fishing nets with the promise 'I will make you fishers of men'. Entering Capernaum, he teaches in the synagogue with an authority that astonishes his hearers, he exorcises demons and heals people suffering from various diseases, so that his fame runs like a kindling flame through all Galilee. But his claim to forgive sins (the prerogative of God alone, say his critics), his deliberate association with the social 'down-and-outs', his apparent flouting of the sabbath laws and his 'radiant religion' shock the Jewish churchmen, so that, by and by, he is forced to leave the synagogues and proclaim his good news by the lakeside.

Withdrawing to the hill-country he now appoints twelve men for training as his lieutenants in the work of the Kingdom. (The number symbolizes 'the new Israel' he has in view.) But opposition grows steadily: the scribes, who have come down from Jerusalem, accuse him of being in league with the devil, and some, declaring him out of his mind, cause his family concern.

So the Galilean ministry proceeds; we hear Jesus in parables declaring that God the Great Sower is now at work and will surely bring the seed to harvest; we see Jesus manifesting the presence of God's Reign by mighty works which bring health and healing to the afflicted.

The Twelve, having been to school with Jesus, are now sent forth, in pairs, on a mission to announce God's Reign by word and deed and gather God's people. On their return, Jesus invites them to snatch a rest on the far side of the lake, only to find that the crowds catch up with them and he cannot find it in his heart to send them away. So the Galilean ministry culminates in the Feeding of the Five Thousand, which is a sign and sacrament of the presence of the Kingdom, well re-named the Galilean Lord's Supper.

Here we should note that the Feeding (as John 6.15 makes clear) threatened to spark off a rebellion against Rome, with Jesus as its leader. This hope of 'a Messianic revolt' was utterly at variance with Jesus' own conception of his God-given role. So, to escape the misguided enthusiasm of his followers, Jesus now leads the Twelve beyond the bounds of Galilee to the borders of Tyre, in quest of privacy, a desire frustrated by a Syro-Phoenician woman with a sick daughter. On their return from Tyrian territory, at a place called Caesarea Philippi, in the shadow of Mount Hermon, a decisive stage in Jesus' ministry is reached. In answer to his master's leading question, Peter confesses Jesus to be the Messiah, Israel's long-looked-for deliverer. At once Jesus enjoins silence on the disciples,[3] telling them that the Son of Man (his own title for himself, derived from Dan. 7, and replacing the traditional one of Messiah) must suffer many things and be slain before he triumphs over death. The very idea shocks the disciples; and Peter rebukes Jesus, only in turn to be himself rebuked, 'Out of my sight, you Satan! You think as man thinks, not as God thinks.' From that time on the tension mounts, and the shadow of a cross begins to fall across the story.

3. The *second main section*, which covers chapters 9 to 16.8, carries the story of Jesus down to Calvary and its sequel the Empty Tomb.

Six days after Peter's confession (in what sounds like a historical experience of a visionary kind), Jesus is 'transfigured' on a mountain-top before Peter, James and John, who hear him talking with Moses and Elijah. The Transfiguration is the counterpart in the disciples' experience of the Baptism in that of Jesus; for a heavenly voice authenticates him to them as the Messiah.

Thereafter, with his disciples, Jesus passes through Galilee to Capernaum, and then southwards via Transjordan (where for a time he resumes his public ministry).

Now the march on Jerusalem begins in strong earnest, as a vivid sentence of Mark reminds us: 'They were on the road, going up to Jerusalem, Jesus leading the way, and the disciples were filled with awe, while those who followed were afraid' (Mark 10.32). So they travel on to Jericho, and as they go, Jesus blesses little chil-

---

[3] This is one of many places in Mark where Jesus forbids the disciples and others to make him known as the Messiah, because his own conception of himself as the Servant Messiah ran so completely counter to the popular one. 'The Messianic Secret', so far from being something read back later into the story (as a German scholar has argued), goes back to Jesus himself – is his own doctrine.

dren, challenges a rich young man, in vain, to be his disciple, heals blind Bartimaeus, and all the time prepares his disciples for his approaching Passion. From Jericho they cross the Jordan to Bethany on the outskirts of Jerusalem.

There follow, one after another (with a speed which makes some suspect Mark may have 'telescoped' the actual course of events), the episodes traditionally associated with Holy Week: the triumphal entry, the cleansing of the Temple, a last parabolic appeal to Israel's leaders plus various controversies in the Temple precincts, Jesus' prediction of its coming ruin,[4] his anointing by a woman at Bethany, the defection of Judas.

Finally, on the Thursday evening, Jesus holds the Last Supper with the Twelve, agonizes in Gethsemane, is arrested, tried (first by a Jewish court and then by a Roman) and condemned to death. On Friday morning, at Golgotha, he is crucified along with two 'bandits', and at 3 p.m. he dies. A little later a secret disciple named Joseph from Arimathea, with Pilate's permission, has his body taken down and decently buried in a rock-tomb. It is Friday evening and, to all human seeming, the story of Jesus is over.

But no, there is an astounding sequel. Just after sunrise on the Sunday morning (as we should say), three women, bent on anointing Jesus' body, find the tomb empty, and a mysterious young man tells them, 'He has risen. Go, tell his disciples and Peter that he is going before you into Galilee. There you will see him.' Awestruck, the women flee from the tomb...

Here, with the words 'For they were afraid', the true text of Mark's Gospel ends. The remaining verses, 16.9-20, found in the AV, do not occur in our oldest and best MSS and are by a later hand. They tell how Jesus appeared to various people, commanding them to preach the gospel to all men. There is little doubt that Mark was going on to relate an appearance of the risen Lord in Galilee such as we find in John 21. What has happened to the end of his Gospel? Was he prevented from finishing it? A likelier explanation is that the last papyrus leaf of Mark's Gospel has been accidentally lost. But enough remains to show what the climax of Mark's story of Jesus was.

[4] Mark 13.5-37, sometimes called 'the little Apocalypse', is a *composite* document. That it contains genuine sayings of Jesus nobody denies, but few scholars believe that as it stands it gives a true picture of Jesus' view about the future course of events. See Vincent Taylor, *The Gospel according to Saint Mark*, pp. 636-44.

3. *The style and theology of Mark's Gospel*

Start with Mark's style. Even in an English translation you may see that, if Mark shows little elegance in sentence-building, he is a born story-teller. His Greek is the every-day, colloquial Greek of the time, with, in places, Aramaic idioms glimmering through it and indicating that Greek was not his mother-tongue. Part of the rough vigour of his writing may be due to his love of the adverb 'immediately' (*euthus*, 42 times), or his preference for what the grammarians call 'the historic present' tense (151 times). But more is due to the fact that he is often reporting eye-witness recollections.

His *vivid story-telling* is therefore the first thing that strikes the reader, and the NEB conveys a much better impression of it than the stately English of the AV. Master of graphic detail, he fills his pages with unforgettable pictures suggesting at this point and that the memory of an eye-witness. We see Jesus asleep on the 'cushion' in the stern of the fishing-boat (4.38), taking little children in the crook of his arm (9.36), looking with love on a rich young man who went away with a lowering face (10.21f.), or striding ahead of his disciples, a great lonely figure, wholly absorbed in his coming Passion, on the road to Jerusalem (10.32).

Next, it is the *realism and candour* of Mark which impress us. As no other evangelist quite does, he shows us Jesus not as some kind of demi-god but as 'a real man living on victuals': 'angry' (1.41; 3.5), 'sighing' with dejection (7.34; 8.12), 'filled with compassion' (6.34), stricken with deadly sorrow so that he cries 'My heart is ready to break with grief' (14.33f.). Here is a Jesus never blind to the evil in the human heart, and yet ever gentle with the ignorant and outcast, and believing that 'with God all things are possible' (10.27): in short, a true man, though no ordinary one, so that, as we read his story, we say with Pilate of old, *'Ecce Homo! Behold the Man!'*

Yet if we stopped there, we should have told only half the story – we should have left out the aura of the 'numinous',[5] the *charisma* of the holy and the divine which belongs to this Man. Through Mark's whole story runs a mysterious undercurrent,

---

[5] See R. Otto's book *The Idea of the Holy*, Oxford University Press 1923, for an exposition of the 'numinous'. The fear of the women before the empty grave (16.8) is 'numinous' terror.

reminding us that this is not just the martyrdom of 'the best man that ever lived'. The crowds are quick to perceive that mystery not of this world invests him. 'Amazed', 'astounded', 'awe-struck' are the words used to describe their reactions to what he does. Peter, James and John feel this awe before him on the Mount of Transfiguration (9.6), as do all the disciples on the road to Jerusalem (10.32). They sense that they are in the presence of the uncanny, the awesome, the other-worldly.

Congruous with their sense of the 'numinous' in Jesus is the note of authority – the sense of divine destiny – which informs his words and claims. He does what only God can do – comes forward as the divine pardon incarnate (2.5); he knows that he is God's unique Son and called by him to 'ransom the many' by his sacrificial death (1.11; 12.6; 13.32; 10.45); he declares that, though heaven and earth pass away, his words never will (13.31); in the upper room he speaks of his death as inaugurating a (new) covenant – a new order of relations – between God and man (14.24); and, at his trial, when Caiaphas the high priest asks him, 'Are you the Messiah, the Son of the Blessed?', he answers majestically, 'I am' (14.62).

At the heart of this mystery, therefore, lies Jesus' consciousness of *divine Sonship*, which flames out at certain high and momentous hours of his life (e.g. his Baptism and his Transfiguration), suggesting not only a traffic between two worlds – the visible and the invisible one – but also that unshared and precious communion with 'Abba Father' (14.36) which was the deepest secret of his own life and the source and fount of his authority. When, therefore, we read that the grave could not hold him – 'He has risen; he is not here' (16.6) – we feel that this is the only fitting *dénouement* to his story.

For Mark's story is not that of 'one more unfortunate gone to his death', or even of the supreme prophet sealing his testimony to the truth with his life's blood. Mark's purpose is to record how God's saving rule was inaugurated on earth in his only Son Jesus the Messiah and realized 'with power' (9.1) by his resurrection from the dead: in short, to tell the story of Jesus as the great act of God which enables those who believe to do his will, receive the forgiveness of their sins, and lay hold on eternal life.

For a systematic account of Christ's teaching (here Mark is defective) we shall go to Matthew. For sheer beauty of narrative we shall go to Luke. For profound insight into the meaning of

Christ's coming – 'Word of the Father, now in flesh appearing' – we shall go to John. But for the earliest, simplest and shortest record of how 'the strong Son of God' 'was manifested that he might destroy the works of the devil and make us the sons of God, and heirs of eternal life' (as the Prayer Book collect puts it), there is but one book. Long neglected by the church (which much preferred St Matthew), the Gospel of Mark thanks to modern scholarship, has at last come into its own, and John Mark of the 'stumpy fingers' stands out in history as:

The saint who first found grace to pen
The life which was the Life of men (Laurence Housman).

7

The Gentile-Christian Gospel

What is 'the most beautiful book in the world'? An opinion poll would doubtless award the honour to the Book of Kells, that exquisitely ornate edition of the Latin Gospels, dating from AD 800 and now the chief treasure of the library of Trinity College, Dublin. But if the criterion were not colour but content, many would endorse Renan's judgment that the honour belongs to Luke's Gospel. A late tradition makes Luke a painter. What is indisputable is his literary artistry, and the word-pictures he has given us – from the lowly birth in the Bethlehem stable to the walk to Emmaus at the end – are among the imperishable things in Christian literature.

Two points must be made at the outset about this beautiful book. First, as Matthew's is the Jewish-Christian Gospel, Luke's is the Gentile-Christian one. In it the central figure is more than Jesus the Messianic King foretold by the prophets; he is Jesus the universal Saviour of men. Not by accident does Luke trace Jesus' family-tree back through Abraham to Adam, the father of mankind (3.38). In his song (the *Nunc Dimittis*) Simeon hails the infant Jesus as 'a light for revelation to the Gentiles' (2.32). At the beginning of ch. 3 Luke sets the story he is about to tell against the background of world history, and ends by quoting Isa. 40.5: 'All mankind shall see God's deliverance' (NEB). Later, a Gentile centurion is credited with such faith as Jesus had not found in Israel (7.9), and Jesus declares that 'men will come from east and west, and from north and south, and sit at table in the kingdom of God' (13.29). Fitly, therefore, the Gospel ends with the risen Lord's command to preach the good news of salvation to 'all nations' (24.47).

The second thing to note is that Luke's Gospel is Part I of a two-volume work which nowadays might be entitled 'The Beginnings of Christianity' (in two volumes) by Dr Luke. For Luke's

Gospel and Acts, which between them make up 28% of the whole New Testament, are not two unconnected works: by their style, by their prefaces and by their subject-matter they are bound together. As Volume I recounts 'all that Jesus began to do and teach' (Acts 1.1), so Volume II tells how Christ's apostles, or 'special messengers', carried the good news from Jerusalem to Rome.

But it would be wrong to regard Luke as simply the dispassionate chronicler of the rise and spread of Christianity. As the whole tenor of his work shows, he comes forward as a defender of the faith against contemporary calumniators; and he is concerned to show that Christianity is a creed for all men, as 'Christ is the world's redeemer'. In other words, the two-volume work which nowadays we name for short 'Luke-Acts' is the first great *apologia* for the Christian faith.

1. *Who wrote the Third Gospel?*

Why do we say that the author was Luke 'the beloved physician' (Col. 4.14)?

A study of the Gospel tells us certain things about its author. He was an educated man, with a fine and versatile command of Greek. Next, as already noted, he had a lively interest in the outreach of the gospel to the Gentiles. And, finally, like Christ himself, he had a deep concern for the poor and outcast. Why do we identify this cultured, catholic and compassionate man with Paul's friend and travelling companion? For four reasons:

First: a comparison of the preface to the Gospel (Luke 1.1-4) with the similar preface to Acts (Acts 1.1f.), plus the identity of style in the two books, prove they were written by the same man.

Second: the extracts from a travel-diary in Acts (the so-called 'We passages': Acts 16.9-18; 20.5-21.18; 27.1-28.16) indicate that the writer of the diary and of the two books (their style is indistinguishable) was one of Paul's travel companions during part of his missionary journeys and on his last voyage to Rome.[1] We can thus narrow down the possible diarists to a few names like Demas, Crescens and Luke.

Third: at this point the tradition of the church in the second

[1] Some have supposed that the author of Luke-Acts and the diary writer were two different persons. Were this true, it is passing strange that the writer of Luke-Acts so thoroughly rewrote the diary of another man as to eliminate all traces of its original style, and at the same time so carelessly forget to change 'we' to 'they'.

century comes in to help us to a decision. For church fathers like Irenaeus and documents like the Muratorian Fragment are unanimous that the author was Luke, Paul's travel-companion. There is a strong presumption that the tradition is right. If the Gospel's authorship had been unknown, and the church had been casting about for an author, the odds are they would have hit on someone of apostolic rank and not on a comparatively unknown person like Luke.

Fourth: certain phrases in Luke-Acts (e.g. Luke 4.38; 8.43; 13.11 and Acts 3.7; 9.18; 28.1-10) support the tradition that the author was a doctor. (In 1882 Hobart in his book *The Medical Language of St Luke* found over 400 medical words in Luke-Acts. Though he greatly overstated his case, we may still use the medical argument in a modified form.)

Having stated the argument for Doctor Luke's authorship, we may now note that he is mentioned by name three times in the New Testament (Col. 4.14; Philemon 24; II Tim. 4.11). To these we may add the statement of an ancient prologue prefixed to Luke's Gospel. It says that 'Luke, a native of Antioch in Syria, a physician by profession, who had been a disciple of the apostles and later a companion of Paul', died at the age of eighty-four in Greece. What is certain is that Luke was a Gentile by birth (see Col. 4.11-14), a doctor by profession, a Christian by conversion. and a friend of Paul's by choice. For the rest, if we ask what manner of man he was, the answer is: 'By his books you shall know him.' He was (as an ancient writer put it) 'the scribe of the gentleness of Christ', the Christ who brought God's good news to the poor and outcast, who sovereignly broke the Sabbath to bring pardon to the sinful and healing to the sick, who wept over the doomed city that was soon to crucify him, who, on the cross, prayed, 'Father, forgive them, for they know not what they do', and promised the penitent thief a place with himself in Paradise.

2. *Why, how and when Luke wrote his Gospel*

Luke's preface to his Gospel reads:

'Inasmuch as many have undertaken to compile a narrative of the things which have been accomplished among us, just as they were delivered to us by those who were from the beginning eye-witnesses and ministers of the Word, it seemed good to me also, having followed all things closely for some time past, to write an orderly account for you, most excellent Theophilus, that you may know the truth of the things of which you have been informed' (RSV).

Our first question here is: who was Luke's literary patron, Theophilus? The very respectful form of address 'Your Excellency' (shall we say 'Right Honourable'?) suggests a high-ranking Roman official. As the name was not uncommon, Theophilus may have been his real name, or it may have been a cover-name (literally it means 'friend of God') to hide the identity of one who might land in trouble if his interest in Christianity were made public. It is not certain whether he had been 'informed' about Christianity or actually 'instructed'. The latter seems likelier. In this case Theophilus must have been a Christian catechumen (as we would say), and Luke was writing to assure Theophilus and all like him about 'the truth' of the teaching they had already received.

Next: observe Luke's claim to have done careful research into the work of those who had already sought to write the story of Jesus as attested by original eye-witnesses and servants of the gospel. From our studies in the Synoptic problem we may now indicate what these resources were:

1. The Gospel of Mark, of which Luke used about half.
2. The collection of Jesus' sayings named Q.
3. L: i.e. the tradition about Jesus peculiar to Luke, found in Luke 3-24. This amounts to half of Luke's Gospel and includes many of the finest parables and stories about Jesus. As we have seen, it probably represents the oral tradition Luke had gathered from Palestinian sources in Caesarea during the years AD 57-59.
4. BS: i.e. the birth stories in Luke 1-2. Though they owe their present form to Luke, he must have derived this material from the Jewish-Christian churches in Judaea, and some of it may go back to Mary the mother of Jesus.

How did Luke come to weave these sources into a connected narrative? If you study his Gospel carefully, you will find that he sets matter derived from Mark and non-Marcan matter *in alternate blocks*. (Thus Luke 1-2 is non-Marcan; 3.1-6.19 mostly Marcan; 6.20-8.3 non-Marcan; 8.4-9.50 Marcan; and 9.51-18.14 non-Marcan.) More particularly, matter from Q almost always occurs along with matter from L, and hardly ever in a Marcan context.

This means that Luke combined Q and L matter independently of the linking of either with matter from Mark. These facts led the Oxford scholar B. H. Streeter to frame what is known as 'the Proto-Luke theory'. Here is the gist of it.

During his stay in Caesarea, so much new and precious information about Jesus had come Luke's way that he conceived the idea of writing a Gospel. At Antioch he found Q and combined it with L, the fruit of his own researches, to form 'a mini-Gospel', which Streeter called 'Proto Luke'. Later, in Rome, coming on Mark's Gospel, which was now circulating freely, he fitted extracts from it into his 'mini-Gospel'. Finally, he prefixed the birth stories and wrote the preface.

Streeter's theory has been very ably championed by Vincent Taylor and others; and though it has not commended itself to all scholars, it is a much better explanation of the facts than the older view that Mark's Gospel supplied the framework for Luke's. (The interested reader will find an excellent brief statement of the theory in G. B. Caird's Pelican Commentary on Saint Luke.)[2]

What date may we assign to Luke's completed work? Some time between AD 70 and 80 seems likely. Luke wrote his book after Mark's Gospel had begun to circulate in the church and evidently after Jerusalem had fallen to Rome in AD 70 (cf. Luke 19.43; 21.20-24). On the other hand, Acts, the sequel to his Gospel, shows no knowledge of Paul's letters. Say, AD 75.

The finished Gospel, with its twenty-four chapters, may be divided into five parts:

1. The Birth of the Saviour (chs. 1-2).
2. Prelude to the ministry (3.1-4.13).
3. The Galilean ministry (4.14-9.50).
4. On the road to Jerusalem (9.51-19.10).
5. Death and victory (19.11-24.53).

3. *Luke, historian and theologian*

We have already touched on Luke's literary artistry. This is the best-written of the four Gospels, and the beauty of Luke's style survives in translation. For examples we need only cite the *Magnificat*:

[2] G. B. Caird, *Saint Luke*, Penguin Books 1963, pp. 23-26. If the theory is true, Proto-Luke (i.e. L+Q) and Mark are two independent authorities of roughly the same date for the story of Jesus.

Tell out, my soul, the greatness of the Lord,
rejoice, rejoice, my spirit, in God my saviour (1.47 NEB).

or the perfectly-told tale of the Prodigal Son. In a few vivid verbal strokes he can do a thumbnail sketch of a Zechariah, or describe the visit of Jesus to the Bethany home of Martha and Mary, or relate the memorable encounter, in Jericho, with Zacchaeus the little inspector of taxes. Or he can compose unforgettable narratives like that of the penitent prostitute in Simon the Pharisee's house or the meeting of Cleopas and another with the risen Jesus on the way to Emmaus. Spiritual insight, dramatic power, pathos – all these gifts are Luke's, and to them he adds that economy in words – that 'sweet austerity of art' – we call classical.

But did he add to his gift of style a like concern for historical accuracy?

In the preface to his Gospel Luke explicitly claims to be using reliable traditions about Jesus. As we have seen, these came from the three great centres of early Christianity – Rome (Mark), Antioch (Q) and Caesarea (L). In Mark he had an authority of the first rank for the story of Jesus. For his record of Jesus' words he had Q, a collection of Jesus' sayings resting back on Aramaic originals and probably compiled about twenty years after they were uttered. It is harder to evaluate the worth of L, the materials he had gathered himself at Caesarea; but we may note that at various points it is confirmed by the independent Gospel of John.[3]

Granted, then, that Luke possessed good sources, the question arises: did he use them in a responsible way? That Luke was faithful to the traditions he had received is suggested by two things. (1) We can check how he used Mark. Apart from improving Mark's rough style and abbreviating his narrative, he took few liberties with what he found in Mark's Gospel. This encourages us to believe that he used his other sources with equal fidelity. (2) In his second volume, Acts, modern scholars like Sir William Ramsay and A. N. Sherwin-White have shown that on matters of geography, politics, law and administration Luke was exceedingly accurate.[4] A writer who is thus careful in minute points of detail

[3] Caird, *op. cit.*, pp. 20f.
[4] Sir William Ramsay, *The Bearing of Recent Discovery on the Trustworthiness of the New Testament*, Hodder and Stoughton 1915; A. N. Sherwin-White, *Roman Society and Roman Law in the New Testament*, Oxford University Press 1963.

may be expected to tell his main story in a reliable way.

Being human like the rest of us, Luke may have made occasional mistakes. Some have thought he went astray in the matter of Quirinius and the census (Luke 2.2): but this is by no means proved. That Luke, like his contemporaries, delighted in miracle, is clear and it is possible he may have found a miracle where nowadays we would find none. But if he is less critical of the miraculous than we are in this scientific age, his fault is much less grievous than that of modern scholars who would eliminate miracles altogether from the Gospel record.

Luke's intention, then, was to write history, not fiction; and provided we do not expect from him the standards of a modern scientific historian, we must account him an honest reporter who did not wittingly distort the truth about Jesus as he found it in his sources.[5]

But Luke, as modern scholars are discovering, was *theologian* as well as historian. Perhaps the best way to describe him is historian-cum-evangelist. If he was faithful to his traditions, he gave us his own interpretation of what was significant in them. This does not mean that he read into them what was not originally there. New Testament faith cannot exist independently of its historical basis; and it was Luke's awareness of this that led him to become an evangelist. He could not therefore afford to be careless of historical accuracy. Nevertheless, the way he uses his materials, the things he picks out for emphasis, the features in Christ's ministry he stresses, show him to be a theologian with his own distinctive approach.

His was a theology of salvation which might be best summed up in Jesus' words to Zacchaeus: 'The Son of Man came to seek and save the lost' (19.10). (Of course each evangelist presents Jesus as Saviour, but Luke has his own way of doing it.) The source of this salvation is God the Father. His chosen agent is Jesus the Servant Son of God (his Gospel has at least eight references to the Servant of the Lord as he is portrayed in Isa. 40-66). The ministry of Jesus is, for Luke, the fulfilment of God's saving plan prefigured

---

[5] The birth stories in Luke 1-2 constitute a special case. Three things may be said about them. (1) Luke probably got them from the Jewish-Christian churches in Judea. (2) In them fact is clothed in the language of poetry and devotion. (3) They contain the main themes of Luke's theology – form the overture to the symphony of salvation which follows.

in Old Testament prophecy. For in Jesus' deeds and words the Reign of God, prophesied in such passages as Isa. 40,52 and 61, is inaugurated, and the divine purpose, embodied in Jesus, is the rescue of the outcast, a point magnificently elaborated in the three great parables of the Lost in Luke 15. The burden of the whole central section (9.51-19.10) of the Gospel is the road to Jerusalem. The ministry culminates in Calvary; and for Luke the Cross is the new 'Exodus' (9.31), i.e. the necessary act of deliverance laid on the Son by the Father in his vocation as the Servant of the Lord. And the road to the Cross, as Luke goes on to tell, is the road to victory over death.

Such in brief is Christianity according to St Luke. But as he develops it in telling the story of Jesus, Luke inevitably reveals the features in Jesus' person and work which appeal most strongly to him: Jesus' concern for the underdog; his warm sympathy for womanhood (whether it be the widow of Nain, Martha and Mary, Mary Magdalene, or the women of Jerusalem who wept for him); his constant communion in prayer with his Father (no evangelist oftener shows us 'the kneeling Christ'); or 'the conquering new-born joy' which his coming has brought into the world. There is gladness at the beginning—'Behold I bring you good tidings of great joy' (2.10); gladness – a whole chapter of it (15) – in the middle; and gladness at its ending when the disciples 'returned to Jerusalem with great joy' (24.52).

Surveying the whole story Luke recounts in his two volumes, the great German scholar Harnack wrote: 'What a note of joy, courage and triumph sounds through the whole Lucan story from the first to the last pages! *Vexilla Regis prodeunt!*'

Small wonder that Luke's is still the favourite Gospel of many. Of Doctor Luke the words on the memorial tablet to Henry Blackstone MD in New College Chapel, Oxford, might well have been written: *Et animae et corporis simul medicus*, which may be translated 'physician alike of soul and body'. This is the kind of book to bring spiritual health to distraught and despairing men and women in an age like ours. Its author is still a physician and still beloved.[6]

---

[6] The best commentary on the Gospel for the general reader is G. B. Caird's *Saint Luke* in the Pelican series. The best modern discussion of Luke's two volumes is I. H. Marshall, *Luke, Historian and Theologian*, Paternoster Press 1971.

8

The Jewish-Christian Gospel

Matthew, Mark, Luke, John – in this quaternion Matthew, though not the earliest, has the first place. This order has a certain spiritual logic; for Matthew, with his insistence that Jesus is the fulfilment of Old Testament prophecy, reminds us that it is one purpose of God which runs through both Testaments, one people of God whose story is being told, from Abel to the apostolic age. Moreover, Matthew's Old Testament proof texts (e.g. 1.23; 2.6; 2.18 etc.), designed to prove that Jesus is the true Messiah born of David's line, would not leave his original readers as cold as they sometimes leave us; for Matthew was a Jew writing for Jewish-Christians, and his Gospel is as truly the Gospel for the Jews as Luke's is the Gospel for the Gentiles.

Yet a strange fate has befallen his Gospel. In the second century and long afterwards it was *the* Gospel. Today, if scholars were asked to arrange the Gospels in order of merit, they would probably place it last. Why? Mostly because they now know it to be a *dependent* Gospel – dependent on Mark for 90% of its outline of the ministry of Jesus – and because into Mark's outline, especially near the end, Matthew has inserted some later and less credible stories.

This modern view of Matthew is understandable; but it does less than justice to him and fails to account for that commanding influence down the centuries which led Renan to pronounce it 'the most important book in the world'. Later we shall try to appraise Matthew's distinctive contribution to the church and Christianity. Meantime, think only how spiritually impoverished we should be if we did not possess three things which we owe to Matthew: the Sermon on the Mount, the Great Invitation ('Come unto me, etc.'), and the haunting parable of the Last Judgment.

1. *Who wrote it, when and where?*

Nowadays when referring to the author, we often put 'Matthew' in inverted commas. The explanation is simple; modern scholars do not believe that the apostle Matthew,[1] the ex-tax-collector, wrote the Gospel. We need not here argue the matter at length. Enough to say that they cannot believe that one of the Twelve would have relied so heavily on the work of Mark who was not one of that blessed number, as 'Matthew' does. Why, then, did the early church link the apostle's name with the Gospel? Because they believed he had a connection with it.

Let us recall that Papias (c. 100) was on record as saying: 'Matthew compiled the *Logia* (oracles) in the Hebrew (i.e. Aramaic) language, and each translated them as he was able.' Now Papias cannot have been referring to our Gospel of Matthew which is certainly not a translation from Aramaic. But, as we have seen, Papias's statement fits Q, which is a collection of dominical 'oracles', existed originally in Aramaic, and was translated by various persons.

As T. W. Manson said, 'If we wish to put an author's name on the title page of Q, Matthew is the only candidate in the field.'[2] If this is so, Matthew was a part-contributor to the Gospel which now bears his name, and we may explain how his name came to be linked with it.

The actual writer's name we do not know. What we do know is the kind of man he was, for in his book he gives himself away as truly as Peter did, on a momentous occasion, by his 'north-country accent' (Matt. 26.73). One of the phrases in his own Gospel fits him like a glove: 'a scribe discipled to the kingdom of heaven' (Matt. 13.52). He was a Jewish Christian, possibly speaking Aramaic, perhaps a converted rabbi, with something of the Law and legalism still clinging to him (cf. Matt. 5.18f.), yet no narrow nationalist but a man convinced that Christianity was called to world-mission, charged to 'go and make disciples of all nations' (Matt. 28.19).

Moreover, his book reveals one who was a staunch churchman

[1] Levi (Mark 2.14; Luke 5.27) and Matthew (Matt. 9.9; 10.3) are generally thought to have been one and the same person, 'Matthew' (which means 'gift of God') being the name he got on becoming one of the Twelve.

[2] T. W. Manson, *The Sayings of Jesus*, SCM Press 1949, p.19.

and a skilled Christian teacher, not only convinced that Jesus was the true Messiah of the Jews and the Lord and Judge of all men, but concerned so to set forth Christ's teaching as to promote the worship, discipline and mission of the church he served.

That church was probably in Syrian Antioch. One reason for so saying is that the Gospel shows a special interest in Peter, who had worked in Antioch (Gal. 2.11) and was later said to have been the first bishop of the church in that city. Another reason is that the second bishop of Antioch, Ignatius, calls Matthew's 'the gospel'.

When was the Gospel written? Since Matthew used Mark (AD 65-67), and since Matt. 22.7 ('The king ... sent his troops and destroyed those murderers and burned their city') suggests that Jerusalem had been sacked by the Romans, it must be later than AD 70, when Jerusalem fell to Roman arms. On the other hand, Clement of Rome, writing about AD 95, apparently knew the Gospel. A date in the 'eighties' therefore seems best.

2. 'Matthew' and his sources

'Matthew' employed three sources – Mark, Q and M – this last symbol standing for all the matter peculiar to the First Gospel, some of it possibly derived from a document, some doubtless from oral tradition.

How did he use his sources? First, he *revised* Mark, by improving his rough style, by shortening his narrative, and sometimes by removing phrases likely to give offence. (Compare Matt. 19.17 'Why do you ask me about the good?' with Mark 10.18 'Why do you call me good?'). Second, he *enlarged* Mark: by adding narratives at the beginning and at the end; by incorporating in Mark's outline five great discourses of Jesus (of which more anon); and by inserting Old Testament proof-texts showing how Jesus fulfilled prophecy.

Scholars use the word 'conflation' to describe how 'Matthew' interwove his various sources. If Mark served him as framework, into it he fitted his new materials from Q and M, joining like to like. Thus, Matt. 13, which is based on Mark, sets side by side seven parables of the Kingdom, one from Mark, two from Q, and four from M.

'Special Matthew', or M, comprises both narrative and teaching. Here is a list of its main contents:

The nativity stories (chs. 1-2).

The greater part of the Sermon on the Mount (chs. 5-7).

Much of Christ's charge to his missionaries (ch. 10).

Most of ch. 18, which preserves Christ's teaching about humility, discipline and forgiveness.

Fifteen parables (four in ch. 13 and three in ch. 25).

Three stories about Peter (in chs. 14-17).

The 'Woes' on the Scribes and Pharisees (ch. 23).

Additions to Mark's story of the Passion and Resurrection (chs. 27-28).

Much of Jesus' teaching preserved in M is of priceless worth. Less valuable are some of the traditions with which 'Matthew' has embellished Mark's story of the Passion and Resurrection, e.g. the rising of the Jewish saints from their graves and the portents at the Resurrection (the earthquake and the descending angel). Here 'Matthew' seems to be straying from history into the apocryphal.[3] More significant is the story of the securing of the tomb and the bribing of the guard (27.62-66;28.11-15), which reads like a Christian answer to a Jewish calumny that the disciples had stolen Jesus' body. What it proves is that on the third day the body of Jesus was not found in the tomb.

3. *Contents, Characteristics, Convictions*

The Gospel falls into seven parts:

1. The nativity (chs. 1-2).
2. Preparation for the ministry (3.1-4.11).
3. The Galilean ministry (4.12-13.58).
4. Retirement from Galilee (chs. 14-18).
5. Journey to Jerusalem (chs. 19-20).
6. Ministry in Jerusalem (chs. 21-25).
7. Passion and Resurrection (chs. 26-28).

Matthew has his favourite words like 'righteousness' and phrases like 'the kingdom of heaven' as well as his characteristic formulas, e.g. 'This was to fulfil what the Lord had spoken by the prophet', and 'It happened when Jesus had finished these sayings'. He likes to

[3] 'These are the stories which provide unbelief with its sharpest stones and Hollywood with its brightest inspirations' (Vincent Taylor, *The Life and Ministry of Jesus*, Macmillan 1954, p. 20).

group his materials in threes (three angelic messages to Joseph, three denials by Peter) and sevens (seven parables in ch. 13 and seven 'Woes' in ch. 23). Above all, he *systematizes* Christ's teaching, clearly having in mind the needs of catechumens and being unworried about questions of chronology because, for him, the words that 'will never pass away' have already shaken off the manacles of time.

The attentive reader soon recognizes Matthew's special interests: his stress on the fulfilment of prophecy, his conception of Christ as the new and greater Moses, his sense of the importance of the church in Christ's purpose, his certainty that the Reign of God, now inaugurated, is moving on to Judgment Day.

These special concerns apart, Matthew is as convinced as was Paul that 'God was in Christ'. For proof we need look no further than the beginning and the end of his Gospel. In the story of Christ's birth we read (1.23): 'They shall call his name Emmanuel – God with us.' At the final commission in Galilee the risen Christ says to his disciples: 'And be assured, I am with you always, to the end of time' (28.20 NEB). In other words, Matthew is describing how in the birth, ministry, death and resurrection of Jesus God came to be with men in Christ to the end of time.

Observe that this final commission is addressed to the disciples as the nucleus of a world-wide church. If, remembering this, we go back to the middle of the Gospel (16.13-23), we find Matthew recording, as Mark had done, how the secret of who Jesus was came out at Caesarea Philippi, when Peter said 'You are the Messiah, the Son of the living God'. Thereupon Jesus, after congratulating Peter on his God-given insight, proceeds to say that he must go to Jerusalem to suffer and die before he triumphs over death. That is to say, God wills that Jesus shall be a Messiah after the pattern of Isaiah's Servant of the Lord. But Matthew adds, as Mark did not, a saying of Jesus to Peter: 'You are Peter, the rock, and on this rock I will build my church' (16.18). The point is that the secret of who Jesus is, the secret of his coming victory through suffering, is to find expression in a *new people of God*, dedicated to Christ and living by his grace.

It is for the instruction of this new community that 'Matthew' has set down the teaching of Jesus in the systematic way he has. The church is to continue Christ's work and witness in the world. And if we ask on what principles it is to order its life, the answer

comes in the five great discourses which dominate Matthew's
Gospel.

First, the Sermon on the Mount (chs. 5-7), a masterly com-
pendium of Christ's ethical teaching. Second, Christ's charge to his
missioners (ch. 10). Next, seven parables describing the nature of
God's kingdom, or rule, under which the church lives (ch. 13).
Fourth, the discourse about relations in the Church and how to
discipline sinners in a forgiving spirit (ch. 18). And, finally, Christ's
teaching about the future and the Last Things (chs. 24-25). Put
these five discourses together, and you have what Matthew intended – a description, drawn from Christ's teaching, of what it
means to lead the Christian life.

Of the discourses, the greatest is the Sermon on the Mount. As
once, from Sinai, Moses gave old Israel the revelation of God's
will, so from the Mount, Christ now gives the new revelation of
God's will to the new Israel, which is the church. But 'the new law
of Christ' goes deeper, as it makes far higher demands than the
Law of Moses. Whereas the Law of Moses prescribed what must be
done in each and every situation, 'the law of Christ' provides direction rather than directions: it sets forth the divine ideals towards
which Christians, even if in this life they never attain them, must
strive. Thus, these teachings of Christ remain at once a judgment
on ourselves and our sins, and a perpetual challenge to nobler
Christian living. But, observe, the lofty moral principles of the
Sermon are meant for men and women who have already accepted
the good news of God's grace and forgiveness in Christ, and are
promised his continual presence and power, through the Holy
Spirit, in their effort to shape their lives by them.

If this is a fair account of what 'Matthew' designed his book to
be, it is quite unfair to dismiss him simply as a reviser and enlarger
of Mark. He had his own distinctive contribution to the story of
Jesus and its meaning for his followers, the members of his church.

In 'Matthew's' day the church needed a 'Life of Christ' which
would show that the new Israel was the true heir of old Israel, and
yet give Christians a real sense of the newness of the Gospel. It
needed the assurance that, despite all setbacks, God's rule moved
to its consummation. It needed to be shown how the words and
works of Jesus could feed faith, guide worship, and supply a design
for Christian living. It needed to know how grace and discipline
could go together in a Christian fellowship. And it needed to be

summoned to the high task of world evangelization. These were
the needs 'Matthew' sought to meet. Concerned to serve Christ
and to promote his work through the church, he gave Christendom
what has been called 'the ecclesiastical Gospel'.[4] Though he wrote
nearly two thousand years ago, he did his work so wisely that his
Gospel continues to shape the life of Christ's followers in a world
which, though vastly changed from his, still needs to hear the good
news of Jesus, the first-born son of Mary, the true Messiah of
David's line, Emmanuel – God with us. And though centuries
divide them, Matthew would have said Amen to G. K. Chesterton's
prophecy:

> To an open house in the evening
> Home shall men come,
> To an older place than Eden,
> And a taller town than Rome,
> To the end of the way of the wandering star,
> To the things that cannot be and that are,
> To the place where God was homeless,
> And all men are at home.

---

[4] Not only is Matthew's the only Gospel containing the word 'church'
(16.18; 18.16f.); but in it we may trace the influence of the church's *liturgy*
in Matthew's version of Jesus' sayings over the bread and the cup (cf. Matt.
26.6-9 with Mark 14.22-25), and of the church's *discipline* in his account of
what Jesus said about divorce (Matt. 5.31f.; 19.9). Only Matthew among the
evangelists has the words 'except for unchastity'. 'Here we see the beginning of the development of ecclesiastical law, based on the teaching of Jesus,
but allowing, under the guidance of the Holy Spirit, for exceptions in hard
cases' (A. W. Argyle, *Matthew*, Cambridge University Press 1963, pp. 4-6).

9

The Spiritual Gospel

'The spiritual Gospel' Clement of Alexandria called it, noting that
it was a Gospel with a difference. The most obvious difference is
that it opens differently – not at Jordan or at Bethlehem but in
eternity. 'In the beginning was the Word, and the Word was with
God, and the Word was God ... all things were made through him,
and without him was not anything made that was made ... and
the Word became flesh and dwelt among us, full of grace and truth.
No man has ever seen God; the only Son, who is in the bosom of
the Father, he has made him known.' What a tremendous start it
is! Years ago, on BBC radio, the Brains Trust, being asked, 'What
is the finest beginning in literature?' answered, 'The Prologue to
John's Gospel'.

Yet the Prologue (1.1-18) has mystified many. I recall a conversation I once had with the then Lord Provost of Aberdeen, a good
man, something of a poet and a student of scripture. When our
talk turned to John's Gospel, he said, 'It's the philosophy at the
beginning which puzzles me'. What was John seeking to say in his
opening 'philosophy'? There is a little-known saying of Karl Barth,
greatest of modern theologians: 'God loves the world. He has said
Yes to it in Jesus Christ.' By this Barth meant that in the man Jesus,
God has spelt out his nature and purpose to men, and it is one of
grace. John, I suggest, was saying the same thing.

But the Fourth Gospel's difference does not end with the beginning. John tells the story of Jesus' mission differently, recording a
preliminary ministry in Judea before the Galilean one began
and an extended one in Jerusalem when the Galilean one was
over. True, John tells some of the stories found in the first three
Gospels, like the Feeding of the Five Thousand and the anointing

of Jesus at Bethany; but he omits the Temptation, the Transfiguration, and the founding of the Lord's Supper; while he tells new stories about Jesus, how he talked with Nicodemus or with a Samaritan woman by Jacob's Well, how he healed a Bethesda cripple, raised Lazarus from the dead, washed his disciples' feet in the upper room, and appeared to Mary Magdalene in the garden on the first Easter morning.

Moreover, he dates the crucifixion a day earlier than the first three evangelists. Finally, his account of Jesus' teaching differs in both manner and matter. Parables are fewer and the discourses of Jesus longer; and the burden of Jesus' good news is God's gift to men of eternal life in himself rather than the advent of God's reign in his own mission.

One reason for these differences is that John possessed much ancient and independent tradition about Jesus. This is something that has only recently been demonstrated. Thirty years ago scholars agreed that John knew and used both Mark and Luke. The discovery of John's 'independence' – a British discovery, though it is now 'majority opinion' even in Germany – explains, among other things, the new stories about Jesus and the new light on the course of his ministry.[1]

The other reason is that John, seeking *rapport* with a wider world of readers, aimed to tell the story of Jesus *in depth*, and so reveal its ultimate meaning. This is why he begins it in eternity: 'When all things began, the Word already was' (John 1.1). This is why he calls Jesus' miracles 'signs', i.e. symbolic pointers to who and what Jesus really is. This is why he represents the Cross as the place where the glory of God is supremely revealed. Divine glory is divine love suffering in Christ for the sins of the world. But of all this more later. First, we must ask and try to answer the questions: Where was the Gospel written? When? And by whom?

1. *Provenance, date and authorship*

Tradition going back to the second century says the Gospel was written in Ephesus and links the book with John the apostle, whose long residence in Ephesus is attested by men like Justin Martyr and Polycrates who had lived there. There is no good reason for doubting that the Fourth Gospel was written in Ephesus.

[1] See my *According to John*, SCM Press 1968.

When was it written? The discovery in 1920 of a papyrus fragment of the Gospel, belonging to the first half of the second century, proves that the Gospel was circulating in Egypt c. AD 130 and must – if we allow a generation for the book to travel to Ephesus – have been written not later than AD 100. Since the Gospel is independent of the Synoptic Gospels, we do not need to date it after them. It may have been written about AD 80 or even earlier.[2] More important is the evidence we now have that the historical tradition preserved in it goes back to Palestine before the outbreak of the war with Rome in AD 66.[3]

But who was John? The early church had little doubt that he was the son of Zebedee. Thus Irenaeus, Bishop of Lyons, testified: 'John the disciple of the Lord, who also leaned upon his breast, himself issued the Gospel while living in Ephesus.' What makes the bishop's testimony very strong is the fact that as a boy Irenaeus had heard his friend Polycarp tell of his conversations with 'John the disciple of the Lord'.

Now consider what we may learn from the Gospel itself. A study of the Dead Sea Scrolls shows the background of the Gospel to be genuinely Jewish. The writer's Greek is that of a man whose mother-tongue was Aramaic. He apparently knew the geography of Palestine at first hand, describing it accurately, as though he moved about in a country he knew. He possessed ancient tradition about Jesus going back to, say, the years AD 40 to 60. All this encourages us to pursue a connection between the Gospel and 'John the disciple of the Lord'.

But it is not all. The Gospel claims to preserve eye-witness testimony. Thus, in 19.34f., after describing the issue of blood and water from the pierced side of Jesus, the evangelist adds: 'This is vouched for by an eye-witness, whose evidence is to be trusted.' Again in 21.24 which sounds like a certificate of the church leaders at Ephesus we read: 'It is this same disciple (the beloved disciple) who attests what here has been written.'

Who was the 'beloved disciple' (13.23; 19.26; 20.2ff.; 21.7,20)? The evidence points strongly to the son of Zebedee. (1) Except in 21.2, the son of Zebedee is not mentioned in the Gospel. A very

[2] 'Not much later than 70' (R. M. Grant, *A Historical Introduction to the New Testament*, Collins 1963, p. 159). F. C. Grant (his father) dates it c. 120!

[3] Here the decisive discussion is C. H. Dodd's *Historical Tradition in the Fourth Gospel*, Cambridge University Press 1963.

odd state of affairs – unless in fact his name is hidden in the phrase
'the disciple whom Jesus loved'. (2) The close association in the
Gospel of the beloved disciple with Peter fits nobody as well as
John.[4] (3) Only the Twelve were present at the Last Supper. Among
them the closest to Jesus were Peter, James and John. But in John
13.23f. Peter is clearly distinguished from the beloved disciple;
and (Acts 12.2) James had been slain by King Herod about AD 44 –
many years before the Gospel could have been written. So we are
left with John.

It is not surprising that many believe that the Gospel was actually
written by the apostle John. But there are one or two difficulties in
the way. Is it likely that John would have styled himself his master's
'favourite pupil'? If the writer was in fact John, should we not have
expected him to report Jesus' sayings in a form more like that
found in the first three Gospels? Besides, there is evidence (see
John 4.2 and 21.24) that the Gospel underwent some editing before
being 'issued'.

The solution which best fits all these facts is that John the
Apostle was the *source* of the tradition behind the Gospel, and the
actual writing was done by a close disciple. This makes the apostle
the 'authority' behind it. Who, then, did the actual writing? If
style and theology are any guides, he was 'the elder' who wrote the
three Epistles of John. Now Papias (AD 60-130) knew of two
eminent Johns in the early church: one John the apostle and the
other 'the elder John'. Moreover, according to tradition there were
two tombs in Ephesus bearing the name John. Not unreasonably,
therefore, many conclude that 'the elder John' was the Fourth
Evangelist and the close disciple of the apostle John. If this is so,
it is the Gospel of John the elder according to the teaching of John
the apostle.

2. *John's readers and purpose*

In John 20.21 John states his purpose in writing. 'These things,' he
says, 'are written that you may believe that Jesus is the Christ the
Son of God, and that believing you may have life in his name.' If
we ask whom John meant by 'you', the answer would seem to be:
all interested people, Jews and Greeks, Christians and non-Christians, in Ephesus.

[4] In the Synoptic Gospels Peter and John appear regularly together, as
they are paired in Acts 3-4.

His use, in his very first sentence, of the term *Logos*, or Word, confirms this. A word is an uttered thought, and John proceeds to say that the whole creation is a revelation of the thought, or purpose, of God, before he finally declares 'the Word became flesh', that is, the thought of God expressed itself in a human life. Now this kind of beginning was calculated to appeal to both Greeks and Jews. Had not their philosophers (especially the Stoics) taught the Greeks about the *Logos*, the soul of the universe, the divine principle pervading all things? And had not the Jews learned from their scriptures about 'the Word of God' which meant God showing himself in his power, wisdom and love, God's saving purpose in action? When John began by telling how the Word of God became flesh, he was using language that would be meaningful to all his readers, Jews and Greeks. It was a language that went straight to the heart of reality and set the coming of Christ in eternal focus. John's purpose was therefore to suggest to his readers that the ensuing story of Jesus was the ultimate truth about God – the word 'God' spelt out in terms of a human life.

The treatment of the story which follows agrees with this. John tells the story of Jesus in such a way as to appeal to any who might declare an interest in Christianity but who might be puzzled by such Jewish phrases as 'the kingdom of God'. Such people were asking different questions. What place did Jesus have in the saving ways of the Almighty with men? What was the chief blessing which his Gospel offered believers? And how did this Jesus who had been crucified almost half a century before remain, as he incontrovertibly did, a living and vital force in the world? It is questions like these which John answers. He says that Jesus is the saving purpose of God expressed in a human life. He says that the blessing which the Gospel offers is eternal life – real life, divine life, life with the tang of eternity about it. And he says that Jesus, before his departure to the Father, promised his disciples the Holy Spirit to be his 'other self', guiding them into all the truth of his gospel.

John's supreme gift is therefore as an interpreter of the meaning of Christ's coming. Let us develop this point. We may begin by noting that *it is always hard at the actual time to discern what is going on in what is taking place*. The Indians have a wise proverb, 'There is always a shadow under the lamp', that is, you can be too close to a thing to see its significance. Take an example from British history. What took place at Runnymede in 1215 was that King John very reluctantly signed the Magna Carta. When the King put pen to paper, a few may have dimly surmised what was really going on. But the modern historian, with the help of hindsight, sees clearly that what was being inaugurated was the birth of British Parliamentary democracy as we know it.

Now apply all this to the story of Jesus. If one of the Twelve, say, in AD 31, had tried to set it down in writing, he certainly would not have fully understood what had been going on in Galilee and Judea between AD 28 and 30. But John, writing, say, forty-five years later, saw clearly what had been going on in what had taken place. Why? Because he had the help of hindsight and (as he would certainly have claimed) the guidance of the Holy Spirit.

Not that the earliest evangelist was blind to all this. Even in Mark certain episodes like the Baptism and the Transfiguration are attempts to suggest, in Oriental imagery, a traffic between two worlds, the heavenly world breaking through into this one. But they occur here and there, like breaks in the cloud revealing glimpses of the infinite blue vault beyond. John saw the whole story of Jesus thus. For him it is 'an earthly story' – and he will have no truck with those who deny this – but 'an earthly story with a heavenly meaning'. This 'heavenly meaning', however, is not something superimposed on a plain tale which would be better told without it. It is the true meaning of what God did when he sent Jesus. And the proof of this is that John's Gospel does make sense of the earlier Gospels – is, as John Calvin rightly said, the key which unlocks their secrets. Down the centuries thousands upon thousands of readers, high and humble, have found that for them John brings out the eternal dimensions of the story of Jesus. What John has done for them must have been his main purpose when he wrote his Gospel in Ephesus long ago.

Before we evaluate the Gospel, let us recall that the two themes which form its ground base are the Word of God and eternal life. That is, the Gospel is the record of how God in Jesus spelt out his saving purpose for men, and so made possible a new divine life which is mediated to us through the life-giving Holy Spirit, 'the life of God in the soul of man'.

We may divide the contents of the Gospel into six parts:

1. The Coming of the Word of God in Christ (ch. 1).

2. His Revelation to the World (chs. 2-12).
3. His Revelation to the Disciples (chs. 13-17).
4. The Conflict of Light with Darkness (chs. 18-19).
5. The Dawn (ch. 20).
6. The Final Commission (ch. 21).

3. *The value of the Gospel*

This is twofold: (*a*) the new historical light it sheds on the ministry of Jesus; and (*b*) the profound reading of what was going on in what was taking place.

Not long ago when scholars undertook to write the life of Christ they commonly set aside John's Gospel, holding it to be dependent on the Synoptic Gospels, late in date, and more interested in theology than history. Recent studies have changed all this. We now see that at this point and that John illuminates and supplements the earlier story of Jesus. It tells, for example, how John the Baptist and Jesus conducted concurrent ministries in Samaria and Judaea before the Galilean ministry (3.22-30). John's account of the Feeding of the Five Thousand and what followed it (ch. 6) enables us to understand better Peter's confession of Jesus as the Messiah. Chs. 7-12 contain much credible tradition about Jesus' ministry in the south after he left Galilee for good, and before he returned to Jerusalem for the fatal Passover. John's account of the Passion, which is independent, contains much good history. Finally, it is to John we owe the record of how the risen Lord appeared to Mary Magdalene in the garden and to seven disciples, including the sons of Zebedee, by the lakeside in the grey of a Galilean dawn.

What of the sayings of Jesus in John? True, they are often coloured by John's own style; but they are not his free inventions. The Gospel contains at least ten short parables which have every claim to authenticity, besides many pithy sayings which have the ring of truth. Often the words of Jesus in John simply spell out fully what we find in the earlier Gospels. A good example is Jesus' sense of unique divine Sonship. Take the Q saying: 'All things have been delivered to me by my Father; and no one knows the Son except the Father, and no one knows the Father except the Son, and any one to whom the Son chooses to reveal him' (Matt. 11.27; Luke 10.22). Now compare what we find in John: 'The Father loves the Son and has given all things into his hand' (3.35);

'The Father knows me and I know the Father' (10.15); 'No one comes to the Father, but by me' (14.6). Even long discourses like that on the bread of life in John 6.26-51 may claim to be substantially authentic.[5] Finally, though there is nothing quite like it in the Synoptic Gospels, Jesus' farewell discourse in John 13.31-14.31 is surely true to the mind of Jesus. Is it incredible that on their last night together Jesus should have spoken to his disciples about his death and its sequel, comforted them with an assurance of a Father's house with 'many rooms', reiterated his law of love, insisted on obedience to his commands as the true test of their continuing allegiance, promised them the help of the Holy Spirit, and bequeathed to them his peace: 'Peace I leave with you; my peace I give unto you; not as the world giveth, give I unto you. Let not your heart be troubled, neither let it be afraid'?

No book in the New Testament has influenced the faith and life of Christians like this one. John's Gospel has become 'the textbook of the parish priest and the inspiration of the straight-forward layman' (Hoskyns). Wherein lies its appeal? On the first reason we have already dwelt. This Gospel depicts the person and work of Jesus in depth, shows what was really going on in what was taking place while Jesus walked the dusty roads of Palestine. God the Father was spelling out in Christ his Son his saving purpose for the world.

Next: John's Gospel is pre-eminently the Gospel of Life. Its keyword is 'life' or 'eternal life'. If, as Sabatier said, 'all religion is a prayer for life', it is John's claim that in him who 'came that men may have life and have it more abundantly' (10.10), that prayer is answered. For the blessing *par excellence* which Christ offers during his earthly life and makes effectual by his death and resurrection is life that is life indeed, life lived in fellowship with God through Christ, life informed by love because it begins in

[5]Once, according to Luke 4, in the Nazareth synagogue, Jesus took the lesson for the day, Isa. 61, and expounded it in terms of himself and his mission. According to John 6, in the Capernaum synagogue (6.59) and at Passover time (6.4), Jesus spoke of the bread of life. Now we know that at Passover time the two chief synagogue lessons were the stories of the manna (Exod. 12; Num. 11) and the tree of life (Gen. 3). According to John, Jesus spoke of the manna (6.31) and claimed to be the bread of life (6.35). If we allow Luke 4.16-21 to be historical in substance, must we not admit that John 6.26-51 is the same?

On the whole question of the Johannine sayings of Jesus see my *According to John*, SCM Press 1968, chapters 8 and 9.

God's love once supremely manifested on a Roman cross, outside Jerusalem, on an April morning in AD 30, life which, because it is God's own life, is everlasting.[6]

Third: the Gospel presents the challenge of Jesus *existentially*, that is, in terms of a life-or-death situation calling for decision. So it is in the most famous verse John wrote: 'God so loved the world that he gave his only Son that whoever believes in him should not perish but have eternal life' (3.16). 'Life' or 'perishing' – such are the alternatives. God's purpose of love is to save men: but men may, by rejecting his Christ, forfeit for ever their chance of salvation.

A like existential note rings through this Gospel's teaching about judgment. This is not simply something that happens at a great end-of-the-world assize, but something happening here and now, as God is

> sifting out the hearts of men
> Before his judgment seat.

Men judge themselves by the response they make to Christ who is the incarnate truth of God (John 3.18ff.; 5.22; 9.39ff.). In short, John depicts Christ not as a figure in an antique story but as our eternal contemporary; and it is not from first-century Palestine only but here and now that he is to be encountered and his challenge heard, for weal or for woe. To the modern enquirer, as long ago to the would-be follower, Christ cries, 'Follow me. If any man wills to do his will, he shall know of the doctrine whether it be of God' (7.17). So he sets his followers today to the tasks which he has for them, assuring them that if they obey him, they shall learn, in the joys and sorrows they pass through in his service, who and what he is. 'But the final word of the Gospel is that "only those who love will ever understand". Today, as nineteen hundred years ago, the disciple who loves his Lord and is loved by him, will discern his face through the morning mist. And now, as in the days of old beside the Galilean lake, the ardent defender of the

---

[6] John uses 'life' and 'eternal life' interchangeably. 'Life' occurs 19 times in his Gospel, and 'eternal life' 17 times. Only once, in 17.3, does John define it. It is knowing the only real God through Jesus Christ his messenger to men. Such knowledge is not theological learning or mystical contemplation. It is fellowship with God through Christ who is 'the only true and living Way' to the Father (14.6). This knowledge begins here and now, but is only to be perfected in his Father's house with its many rooms in heaven (14.3).

cause of Christ is still met by the thrice-repeated challenge, "Lovest thou me?".[7]

NOTE

Two technical points need to be noted. (1) John 7.53-8.11 in the Authorized Version, the story of the woman taken in adultery, though a genuine piece of tradition, is no real part of the Gospel of John. The story, which is one of the most wonderful of all, is absent from our oldest MSS; its style resembles that of the Synoptic Gospels; and indeed it occurs in some MSS attached to Luke 21.37. For its meaning see my commentary on St John's Gospel in *The Cambridge Bible Commentary*, 1965, pp. 199ff.

(2) John 21 may have been added at a later date to the Gospel, for it looks as if originally the evangelist meant to end at 20.30f. But this extra chapter is by the same hand as wrote the rest of the Gospel. What was its purpose? To tell another and vivid story of the risen Lord? Yes, but this cannot be the whole reason. To clear up some misunderstanding in the early church about the destiny of the beloved disciple? Verses 21-23 lend colour to such a view. But may not the most probable reason be that the evangelist wished to indicate the very different tasks Christ designed for Peter and for the beloved disciple? In this Gospel the beloved disciple (i.e. John the apostle) is depicted as the apostle of *insight* (see John 13.23-26; 20.8; 21.7), whereas Peter is the man of *action*. Therefore in chapter 21 the practical oversight of the flock is given to Peter ('Feed my sheep'); whereas the beloved disciple's task is to be theological rather than pastoral. He is to be the witness and guardian of the Lord's revelation and 'the truth of the Gospel. And such in fact he became by his testimony preserved in a book which, by the judgment of countless Christians down the centuries, is the profoundest record of how the love of God opened up the way of real life to men.

[7] W. F. Howard, *The Fourth Gospel in Recent Criticism*, Epworth Press 1955, p. 244.

PART THREE

The Early Church and Saint Paul

10

How They Brought the Good News
from Jerusalem to Rome

Every schoolboy knows Browning's poem, 'How They Brought the Good News from Ghent to Aix', with its electric beginning:

I sprang to the stirrup, and Joris, and he:
I galloped, Dirck galloped, we galloped all three.

If you change the place-names in the title, and for Ghent and Aix write Jerusalem and Rome, you have an apt description of the Acts of the Apostles. It is the story of how, in 'three crucial decades' (AD 30-60), the apostles[1] brought the Gospel from the Holy City to the capital of the world.

1. *The author and his book*

As we have seen, the man who wrote Acts was the author of the Third Gospel, Luke 'the beloved physician'; and Acts is the second volume of his work on 'The Beginnings of Christianity'. Volume I had recounted 'all that Jesus began to do and teach' (Acts 1.1). But the risen Lord had promised his disciples divine power to enable them to witness to his salvation among the nations (Luke 24.48f.), and in Volume II Luke tells how the apostles, or 'special messengers', of Christ, empowered by the Holy Spirit, brought the good news through Samaria and Syria and across the Mediterranean to Rome.

'His excellency Theophilus', to whom Luke dedicated both his

---

[1] Of the original apostles, Peter apart, we do not hear a great deal. The 'big six' in Acts are Peter, Barnabas, Stephen, Philip, James the Lord's brother and, of course, Paul.

books, was probably a Roman of high rank, and typical of the readers – educated Romans? – whom Luke wished to reach. His aim was to give them a trustworthy account of the new religion, in hope of bringing them to full belief on the basis of a reliable record of the facts. But, besides this evangelistic purpose, he had a secondary apologetic one. A study of Luke-Acts (as we call it nowadays) shows Luke eager to vindicate Christianity in the eyes of his Gentile readers, to convince them that it was no threat to the *pax Romana*, as its enemies were insinuating. This is why in Luke-Acts we find a tendency to absolve the Roman authorities from guilt, first in their treatment of Jesus[2] and then in their treatment of his apostle Paul.[3]

What sources did Luke have when he began to write Acts? For his Gospel he used Mark plus Q and L. In Acts it is much harder to be specific. To be sure, in the second half of Acts most of what Luke records came either from his own travel diary (the 'We Sections') or from Paul and his companions. But when we look for Luke's sources for the church's story in its earliest days, they become harder to pinpoint. Since these earlier chapters sometimes show Semitic idioms in Luke's Greek, some have thought he used a written Aramaic source, or sources. What is certain is that he had access to the local traditions of three great centres of early Christianity: Jerusalem, Caesarea and Antioch. Why make him free of these traditions? The stories about the mother church in Jerusalem may well have come to him from Mark 'the cousin of Barnabas' (Col. 4.10-14; Philemon 23), for he was a native of Jerusalem and a friend of Luke's. Those about Caesarea probably came from Philip the evangelist,[4] in whose home at Caesarea Luke lodged when accompanying Paul on his last visit to Jerusalem (Acts 21.8ff). Those about Antioch could have come from three different sources – from Barnabas (who knew Antioch well), from Paul, or even from his own researches, if Luke, as a good ancient tradition says,[5] was himself an Antiochene.

As Luke's purpose in his Gospel was to describe the saving ministry of Jesus, so in Acts he undertook to tell how the church continued to proclaim and confirm the salvation Jesus had brought.

[2] Luke 23.4,14,22.
[3] Acts 18.14; 23.29; 26.31.
[4] Not to be confused with the Philip who was Jesus' disciple.
[5] The 'Anti-Marcionite' Prologue to Luke's Gospel, dated about AD 170, which begins 'Luke was an Antiochene of Syria, a physician by profession'.

Volume II must therefore have come after Volume I, though not necessarily long after. But when? An early date (say, about AD 64) is excluded by the fact that Luke used Mark's Gospel (AD 65-67) when composing his own. On the other hand, those who would date the book of Acts late – say, about AD 95 – assume that Luke had read, or rather misread the *Antiquities* of Josephus the Jewish historian, which appeared about AD 93. This is not proven and seems very unlikely.[6] On the whole a date about AD 80 seems likely.

2. *The contents of Acts*

Acts has twenty-eight chapters, covering the years 30-60. It falls into four parts:

1. Introduction (ch. 1).
2. The Church in its Jewish-Christian Setting (2.1-9.31).
3. The Founding of the Gentile Mission (9.32-15.35).
4. Paul Apostle to the Gentiles (15.36-28.31).

The Introduction relates Jesus' leave-taking of his disciples and the election of Matthias to fill Judas's place.

Chapter 2 describes the church in Jerusalem on the day of Pentecost when the promised Holy Spirit descended on the waiting disciples. The faith begins to spread in and around Jerusalem, with Peter as the church's acknowledged leader. At first, there is no open breach with Jewry, but by and by the new wine of the gospel begins to burst the old wine-skins. Stephen, the first to grasp the essential newness of the faith, by his bold speech incurs the wrath of the Jews, and is stoned to death. Thereupon persecution breaks out; and with the dispersal of the church the circle of the gospel's influence widens to Samaria (through Philip) and then to Damascus, where the foremost persecutor is dramatically converted to the faith (2.1-9.31).

Part 3 tells how the Gentile mission began in real earnest. At Caesarea Peter is given unmistakable evidence that the gospel is for Gentiles as well as Jews. The good news spreads north to

---

[6] The important passage here is Acts 5.36ff., where Gamaliel refers to a Jewish insurrectionist named Theudas and then proceeds: 'After him Judas the Galilean arose in the days of the census.' The historical order here is Theudas-Judas. In Josephus it is Judas (about AD 6) and later Theudas (about AD 46). On the whole question see F. F. Bruce, *The Acts of the Apostles*, Tyndale Press 1951, pp. 24f.

Syrian Antioch, the third city of the Roman Empire, which is destined to become the base of operations for 'the thirteenth apostle' (as he has been called). Soon he and Barnabas are setting out on a mission to Cyprus and then Asia Minor, and its success leads to the first apostolic council in Jerusalem (probably AD 49), to decide on what terms Gentiles are to be admitted to the church (9.32-15.35).

Part 4 tells how Paul spearheaded the gospel's advance through Asia into Europe; and how in Macedonia, Athens and Corinth the gospel was proclaimed.

Paul's third missionary journey sees the gospel firmly planted in the great pagan city of Ephesus before he again sets foot in Europe. Then Luke's story moves to its climax. Returning to Jerusalem, Paul is attacked as a renegade by the Jews, and put under arrest by the Romans. As a Roman citizen, he appeals to Caesar for justice. For two years he lies in prison in Caesarea; then he is taken by sea to Rome, and the book of Acts ends with Paul still a prisoner – in a sort of free custody – awaiting the Emperor's verdict.

> He stayed there for two full years at his own expense, with a welcome for all who came to him, proclaiming the kingdom of God and teaching the facts about the Lord Jesus quite openly and without hindrance. (Acts 28.30f. NEB.)

'The victory of the Word of God,' commented the old German scholar Bengel, 'Paul at Rome, the culmination of the Gospel, the conclusion of Acts. It began in Jerusalem: it finishes at Rome' (15.36-28.31).

Some people have thought it odd that Luke did not go on to record the result of Paul's appeal to Caesar. They have supposed that he was contemplating a third volume to round off his work.[7] But (as Bengel suggests) probably Luke felt that, having described 'the last lap – how we came to Rome', he had completed what he planned – to describe the gospel's 'road to Rome' – Rome, the very centre of civilization as Luke knew it, symbol of the world as it is, and of man in need of salvation.

---

[7] Cf. Acts 1.1. 'The first book' does not necessarily imply that Luke designed a trilogy. Strictly the Greek *prōtos* means 'first' and not 'former', which is *proteros*. But, like ourselves, the Greeks often loosely used 'first' for 'former'.

3. *Luke, historian, evangelist and writer*

Our study of his Gospel revealed Luke as a historian evangelist – a man bent on commending Jesus as Saviour on the basis of the best historical sources available. In his second volume his aim is the same; only now he stands on the far side of the Resurrection, and he is recording how the little people of God whom Jesus had created went forth from the upper room, 'conquering and to conquer'.

How does Luke impress as a guide to the truth about the early church? Two things strike the careful reader. In the second half of Acts where he is describing events in which he himself partly shared, his narrative is more graphic and circumstantial than in the first, where he is relating things that happened before he came personally on the scene. (Thus the tale of Paul's escape from shipwreck in ch. 27 is more vivid and credible than that of Peter's escape from prison in ch. 12.) Second: in his account of the church's earliest days Luke is obviously not trying to tell the whole story, but selecting characteristic episodes to serve his main purpose, which was to describe the breaking down of the barriers between Jew and Gentile as the church moved outwards in the power of the Spirit.

How reliable then is Acts as history? Recently some radical German scholars (e.g. E. Haenchen and H. Conzelmann) have argued that Acts is a book written primarily for the edification of the church, and its author a theologian who manipulated the historical facts to suit his purpose, being not above inventing when it suited his purpose.[8] This is in sharp contrast to the views of Luke's trustworthiness held earlier in the century by such great scholars as the German Adolf Harnack and Sir William Ramsay of Aberdeen. Did Luke really subordinate history to theology? Or was he both historian and theologian – a man composing his book on the basis of real history but so using the historical facts as to preach the gospel of salvation through Christ? The latter is undoubtedly the true view. Luke set out to write history, not fiction. Where he is relating events which happened long before he came himself to the scene, he may, occasionally, have got his facts mixed. (Thus, in Acts 2, he may have thought the phenomenon of Pentecost was the

---

[8] In a sense they are reviving the views about Luke held by the Tübingen school in the middle of the last century. Well does Stephen Neill say that 'no ghost in German theology is ever truly laid'.

gift of speaking in foreign tongues when it was 'glossolaly', that
ecstatic utterance under the stress of religious emotion with which,
as I Cor. 12-14 shows, Paul had to cope in Corinth.) But to suggest
that Luke dreamed up history to suit his theological purpose is to
traduce 'the dear doctor'.

Here the massive testimony of Anglo-Saxon scholars to Luke's
reliability shows how absurd is this German view. All may be said
to have started in 1848 when the English yachtsman James Smith,
in his book *The Voyage and Shipwreck of St Paul*, proved that
Acts 27 must be the work of an eye-witness. At the beginning of
this century Sir William Ramsay's diggings in Asia Minor and his
study of inscriptions showed how accurate even in the matter of official titles Luke was: 'proconsuls' in senatorial provinces like Cyprus
and Achaia (13.7; 18.12), 'praetors' in Philippi (16.20); 'politarchs' in
Thessalonica (17.6) and 'Asiarchs' in Ephesus (19.31).[9] In 1927 the
American H. J. Cadbury[10] noted how precise Luke was in his geographical locations: 'Perga in Pamphylia' (13.13); 'Philippi, a city of
the first rank in that district of Macedonia, and a Roman colony'
(16.12); Fair Havens in Crete, 'not far from the town of Lasea' (27.8);
'Phoenix, a Cretan harbour exposed south-west and north-west'
(27.12); etc. Finally, in 1963, A. N. Sherwin-White's book *Roman
Society and Roman Law in the New Testament* confirmed that
Luke was well-versed in the intricacies of Roman Law (e.g. in
what he has to say about Paul's trials before Gallio, Felix and
Festus). A man who was so conversant with the political and legal
institutions of the first century AD, whose geography of the Mediterranean world was so accurate, and whose details – geographical,
legal and administrative – can be verified, never wittingly played
fast and loose with his historical facts.

On the other hand, Luke may also claim to be a *theologian* in
his own right, and no mere historian. Indeed, in one respect he is
unique among New Testament writers. All the others stand on
one side or the other of the great watershed which is marked by the
life, death and resurrection of Jesus. Mark does not go beyond it,
and Paul starts where it stops. But Luke stands on *both* sides of
the great divide. Consider his unique position *vis-à-vis* the Ascen-

---

[9] See Ramsay's *The Bearing of Recent Discovery on the Trustworthiness
of the New Testament*, Hodder and Stoughton 1915.
[10] *The Making of Luke-Acts*, SPCK 1924.

sion. With that event he ends his Gospel; with it he begins Acts. The Ascension is the end of the earthly life of Jesus and the beginning of the life of the church. In Luke's view, therefore, Jesus does not stand at the end of time but *in its middle*. True, for the New Testament generally, the time after the Resurrection is the last time. But, whereas for Paul and John, the stress is on the last, for Luke this last chapter of history is also a new chapter of history. Jesus is at once the end and the beginning; not the close of all history, but the starting-point of a new kind of history – church history. (The hope of Christ's final coming in glory has not been given up, but the question of when it will happen has ceased to matter.)

The man who saw things thus was not an untheologically-minded physician. He was the first in a long line of doctors who have found in Jesus, the Great Physician, their Saviour and Lord, and seen God and the world through Christian eyes. His is a theology of salvation in which 'the Word of God' centres in Jesus as Saviour, now the exalted Lord of the church, in whose name the forgiveness of sins is offered to men; and the power by which his messengers witness to that salvation is the Holy Spirit which so dominates the book of Acts that it has been called 'The Book of the Holy Spirit' (the Spirit is really the exalted Christ in action, as in the Third Gospel Jesus' ministry is God in action).

Of course Luke is not a great creative Christian thinker of Paul's stature. Yet on the fundamentals they are at one – that the salvation prefigured in the Old Testament has been fulfilled in Christ, that it is for Gentiles as well as Jews, and that the apostles' task is to confirm it, build up the church, and carry the gospel to the ends of the earth.

But if Luke is historian-cum-theologian, he is also in Acts, as in his Gospel, a literary artist. Acts abounds in memorable narratives: the martyrdom of Stephen (chs. 6-7); Paul and Barnabas at Lystra (ch. 14); Paul and Silas in gaol at Philippi (ch. 16); the riot in the theatre at Ephesus (ch. 19); Paul's defence before King Agrippa (ch. 26); the storm and shipwreck on the voyage to Rome (ch. 27). In scene after scene we watch the gospel going forward against all the forces of paganism bigotry and superstition. And with what splendid figures Luke crowds his chapters: Stephen the first martyr, dying, like his Lord, with a prayer for his enemies on his lips; Peter now much more like a 'rock' than when Jesus had nicknamed him so; James now a staunch believer in his divine brother; Apollos the eloquent preacher from Alexandria; Priscilla and Aquila, that fine Christian couple (with, we surmise, 'the grey mare the better horse'); not forgetting lesser figures like the excited little maid in Mary's house, the honest gaoler at Philippi and Eutychus of Troas who dozed off during Paul's long sermon and nearly died as a result.

And besides these Christian men and women, what a varied collection of non-Christians who, in one way or another, came within the orbit of the advancing gospel: Gamaliel the sage rabbi at whose feet Paul had once sat; Simon the sorcerer who thought to buy the gift of the Holy Spirit; the effete intelligentsia of Athens who dismissed Paul as a 'dabbler'[11] (*spermologos*) in strange divinities; Demetrius the trade-unionist at Ephesus; the Roman proconsul Gallio, tutor of Nero and brother of Seneca the Stoic philosopher, who turned away his dainty nose lest the breath of the ghetto should come between him and his dignity.

4. *The Value of Acts*

We can hardly overrate the importance of Acts for our knowledge of the origins of the Christian church. Lacking it, how little we should know about the immediate sequel to the Resurrection! Without it, we should be largely ignorant of the events which led to the writing of the New Testament epistles. Acts is the link which holds together the Gospels and the rest of the New Testament.

But there is another side to its importance. For many the value of the book is that it forms a bridge between the days of Christ's ministry and ourselves. There are always people who suppose that belief in Christ is harder for us than for those who knew Jesus in 'the days of his flesh', saw him heal the sick, heard him utter the Beatitudes. Their unspoken cry is:

> Oh, had I lived in that great day
> How had its glory new
> Filled earth and heaven, and caught away
> My ravished spirit too![12]

But this nostalgic longing for a figure in past history is not Christianity. We worship not a dead hero but a living Lord. When

---

[11] Ronald Knox's translation.
[12] Matthew Arnold, *Obermann Once More.*

James Denney wrote 'No apostle ever *remembered* Christ',[13] his paradox was profoundly true. The first Christians never thought of Christ primarily as a person in past history, they had no wish to turn back the clock and relive the dear dead days in Galilee. For them, the paramount miracle was not Jesus, a hero in past history, but Christ the Lord, present now with them, through the Holy Spirit's working; and following Christ meant living in a quite new fellowship – the company of those in whom the living Christ moved and worked.

Now it is just here that Acts helps us to a true view of what Christianity is. For in this book we see men and women who, though Christ's bodily presence is no longer with them, know that he lives and reigns and that, through the Holy Spirit, his help is available for them in all the changing scenes of life.

In Masefield's play *The Trial of Jesus* the Roman centurion who stood at the foot of the cross and whom tradition names Longinus, is heard talking with Procula, Pilate's wife, after the crucifixion. 'Do you think he is dead?' she asks. 'No,' lady, I don't.' 'Then where is he?' 'Let loose in the world, lady, where neither Roman nor Jew can stop his truth.' It is that Christ – the living Christ of men from Paul of Tarsus to Grenfell of Labrador, from John of Patmos to George MacLeod of Iona – who is the chief figure in the book of Acts, as he remains the central figure in the lives of all who try to follow in the steps of 'the glorious company of the apostles'.

Note on the Speeches in Acts

Ancient historians often freely composed the speeches in their books (though a great one like Thucydides tried to 'adhere as closely as possible to the general sense of what was actually said'). Did Luke in Acts use this freedom and write the speeches out of his own head?

That the speeches of Peter, Stephen, Paul and the rest bear many marks of Luke's own style is not to be denied; yet they are not his free inventions. Study Peter's sermons from that on the day of Pentecost to that addressed to Cornelius at Caesarea, and you will find in them Semitic-sounding Greek, very early conceptions of Christ's person and work (Jesus described as 'the servant of God' or 'the righteous one' or his cross called 'the tree') and a liberal use of *testimonia*, i.e. OT proof texts showing the fulfilment of prophecy in Jesus and the church. All this suggests 'traditional' material. Luke never 'made up' Stephen's speech (ch. 7) with its sharp attack on the Temple and its highly individual line of argument. If Paul's speech at Pisidian Antioch (ch. 13) resembles the style of Peter's *kērygma*, we should remember that they did not differ in their preached gospels (see I Cor. 15.11), and that

[13] James Denney, *Studies in Theology*, 1894, p. 154.

Paul's characteristic doctrine of 'justification by faith' appears in Acts 13.38f. But is not Paul's speech on Mars' Hill (ch. 17), with its affinities to Stoic thought, very uncharacteristic of Paul? No, it is in line with Paul's theology in his letters and has much that comes from the Old Testament and Jewish tradition. (Hellenistic Jews were wont to argue that the Divine Being of the Greek philosophers was the one living God of Hebrew revelation; and passages like I Thess. 1.9f. and Rom. 1.19ff. show that Paul, when addressing Gentiles, proceeded from 'natural theology' to 'revealed religion'.) There are many parallels in Paul's letters to the speech he made to the Ephesian elders (ch. 20), which Luke himself heard (20.15). And if we ask how Luke knew what Paul said to the people of Jerusalem (ch. 22) or to King Agrippa in Caesarea (ch. 26), were there not many witnesses who could have given him reports? In short, if the speeches in Acts are not verbatim accounts of what the apostles said (and only a dyed-in-the-wool traditionalist would claim this), they admirably fit the different audiences addressed and are probably summaries giving 'the general sense' of what Peter, Paul and the others actually said. (See C. F. D. Moule, 'The Christology of Acts', in: L. E. Keck and J. L. Martyn (eds.), *Studies in Luke-Acts*, SPCK 1968; B. Gärtner, *The Areopagus Speech and Natural Revelation*, Acta Seminarii Neotestamentici Upsaliensis, Uppsala 1955.)

11

Paul

Of all the great men of antiquity there is none we know better than Paul. Where many others are mere shadows, he stands before us as a living man. Not only do we have in Acts a reliable (if incomplete) record of the most important part of his life, but we possess at least ten of his letters (on the problem of the Pastoral Epistles see ch. 21). And what revealing documents they are! All Paul's faith, fervour and passion went into his writing. True, he could be obscure, abrupt, abrasive. But these are mere spots on the sun – the faults of a man in great haste on the King's business. (You do not stop to polish your prose when your converts are 'resiling' from the grace of God, as in Galatia, or getting drunk at the Holy Communion, as at Corinth.) And when he is most inspired, as in Rom. 8 or I Cor. 13 and 15, it is not because he has spent hours prettifying his periods, but because he is overmastered by his theme, and it cries out for sublime expression. Of all this more later: meantime, with Luke's record in Acts and Paul's letters we must sketch his life.

Saul or Paul – one was his Jewish, the other his Gentile name – was born, the Hebrew son of Hebrew parents (Phil. 3.5), in the city of Tarsus, the capital of Cilicia. 'No mean city' Paul justifiably called it (Acts 21.39). About forty years before Paul's birth Cleopatra attired as Venus had sailed up its river, the Cydnus, to meet Mark Antony. The weaving of linen and tent-making made up its main industries; and it was an important seat of learning which had produced not a few notable philosophers, including Athenodorus, the tutor of the Emperor Augustus.

Paul's parents were Pharisees – the Puritans of Judaism – and they reared their son in the strict tenets of the Jewish faith. Its staple was the Law, both written and oral; and if Paul's was a narrow education, it was a thorough one. From his father he inherited the proud privilege of Roman citizenship (Acts 22.28). Like every Jewish lad, he had to learn a trade – in his case, tent-making, a skill that was later to serve him well (Acts 18.3; 20.34; I Cor. 4.12). The other thing worth noting is that cosmopolitan Tarsus brought the young Paul into close contact with the Greek world, and his resultant knowledge of it – note how many of his metaphors are drawn from the Greek games – was a vital element in the training of one destined to be 'the apostle to the Gentiles'.

Evidently it was his parents' ambition that Paul should become 'a doctor of the Law'; and in his early teens he must have sailed for Jerusalem to study the Law under one of the very great Jewish rabbis, Gamaliel. All we know of Gamaliel from the New Testament and the Talmud proclaims him a man of liberal and catholic mind, and his teaching must have deeply influenced the young Tarsian at a most malleable period of his life.

So Paul grew to manhood and (as he says in Gal. 1.14) 'advanced in Judaism beyond many of my own age among my people, so extremely zealous was I for the traditions of my fathers'. The future pattern of his life seemed settled – the career of a distinguished rabbi.

But 'just when we're safest...'. When Browning tells how the unexpected event can change the whole course of a life, he instances, among other things, 'someone's death'. So it was with Paul. In the year AD 30 a young Nazarene called Jesus had been crucified in Jerusalem. He had affronted the majesty of the ancient Law, had claimed a knowledge of God that to the Pharisees seemed blasphemous, and by word and deed towards the end of his career had suggested that he was the Messiah. But, at last, he had paid the penalty which every such pretender deserved, by dying on a gibbet – a death which, according to Jewish law, proved him under God's curse (Deut. 21.23).

But if Paul and his friends supposed that the crucifixion was the end of the pretender, they were mightily mistaken. A few days later his followers were filling Jerusalem with the news that God had raised Jesus from the dead, and on the day of Pentecost their leader, a Galilean fisherman named Peter, was declaring that God had made this Jesus 'both Lord and Messiah'. To Jews like Paul this was blasphemous nonsense. Yet the heresy spread

like wildfire, and in a year or two the followers of 'the Way' (as
they were called) had so multiplied that Paul and his friends grew
alarmed. One of the ablest of them, Stephen, a Greek-speaking
Jew, even dared to assert that Jesus Christ had superseded the
Law and the Temple (Acts 7). This was the last straw. So 'they
stoned Stephen' as he prayed, 'Lord Jesus, receive my spirit', and
cried, 'Lord, do not hold this sin against them'. 'And the witnesses laid down their garments at the feet of a young man named
Saul' (Acts 7.58ff.). Paul never forgot that day, or that prayer. 'If
Stephen had not prayed,' said St Augustine, 'the church would not
have had Paul.'

Stephen's martyrdom sparked off a bitter persecution of the
Christians in Jerusalem (Acts 8.1). Many of them fled the city,
some going to Damascus, others as far as Antioch, the great city
three hundred miles to the north. Paul, resolved that he could best
serve God by stamping out the heresy and armed with the high
priest's commission, set out for Damascus, midway between
Jerusalem and Antioch. What happened on the road to Damascus
is history. The form of the glorified Jesus flashed before Saul's
eyes; the spirit of Jesus spoke to his heart, 'Saul, Saul, why are you
persecuting me?' So after all, Stephen had been right. The crucified 'pretender' was indeed the Lord of heaven. (See Acts 9; 22; 26,
and compare Gal. 1.16f; I Cor. 9.1; 15.8.; Phil. 3.12). So Paul became a Christian.

No doubt his conversion was in some sense the last explosive
stage in a long process of inner search. His haunting sense of failure
to win peace of mind by observance of the Law (cf. Rom. 7.7-20)
was one factor in his conversion. No doubt the impression made
on him by the triumphant death of Stephen was another. Perhaps
his journey to Damascus was a desperate endeavour to stifle his
doubts by action. But all attempts to rationalize the actual experience by calling Paul an epileptic and explaining his *volte face* as
'the discharging lesion of an occipital cortex', utterly fail to account
for something which transformed Saul the persecutor into the
dynamic apostle of Christ. For the experience Paul himself had but
one explanation. 'I was arrested by Christ Jesus' (Phil. 3.12); 'he
appeared to me also' (I Cor. 15.8).

Doubtless it took time for the full meaning of his 'arrest' to
become clear to him. But we may fairly say that it brought three
decisive consequences. First, it meant that Jesus was indisputably

alive – alive by the power of God who, by the Resurrection, had set his seal on the deed of the Cross. Second, the Cross itself, which had been for Saul the persecutor the sign of God's curse (Gal. 3.13), became for Paul the place of revelation – the revelation of God's sacrificial love for sinners (Rom. 5.8). And, third, it revealed to Paul the purpose for which God had called him – to be the apostle to the Gentiles (Gal. 1.16).

Paul was received into the Christian fellowship at Damascus through the agency of Ananias. What followed it is not quite clear; but, by combining the data supplied in Acts 9 and Gal. 1, we may suppose that he first retired to Arabia – the country just south of Damascus – to think out the meaning of his conversion and to begin missionary work, before returning to Damascus where he began to proclaim Jesus as the Messiah (Acts 9.22). Eventually Damascus grew too hot for him, and his friends were forced to smuggle him away over the city wall in a basket (Acts 9.25; II Cor. 11.32f.).

So, three years after his conversion – probably in AD 36 – he paid his famous fortnight's visit to Jerusalem to see Peter (Acts 9.26; Gal. 1.18-24). What a historic meeting that must have been! Ah, if only we had a tape-recording of these conversations! For we may presume that they did not spend all their time talking about the weather. If Paul had much to tell Peter, Peter had a lot to tell Paul.

Then (Acts 9.30), perhaps on the advice of his friends who feared for his safety, Paul retired to his native Tarsus, and for about ten years – the 'hidden years' of Paul's life (say, AD 36-46) – he disappears from our view. To those years must belong many of the sufferings listed in II Cor. 11.23-27, as also the mystical experience 'fourteen years ago' related in II Cor. 12.2ff.

Paul reappears in Antioch, the capital of Syria. After the outbreak of persecution in Jerusalem, it had become the second great centre of Christianity. Hither the mother church had sent Barnabas to report on what was happening and especially on the admission of Gentiles to the church. What he saw convinced Barnabas that Paul must be recalled from Tarsus; and off he went to find him (Acts 11.25). Paul had found his life's work. After a year's collaboration in Antioch, Barnabas and Paul were sent on a special mission to Jerusalem. (We here assume that the visit of Acts 11.30 is that described by Paul in Gal. 2.1-10.) A famine was threatening

Judaea and the two delegates from Antioch took with them a relief contribution for the poor brethren of the Jerusalem church. The year was probably AD 46. On this occasion Paul, who was still suspect in the eyes of many, submitted his gospel to Peter, James and John, the leading apostles in Jerusalem. Not only did they endorse it; but they 'accepted Barnabas and myself as partners, and shook hands upon it, agreeing that we should go to the Gentiles while they went to the Jews. All they asked was that we should keep their poor in mind, which was the very thing I made it my business to do' (Gal. 2.9f. NEB).

The first journey: AD 47-48 (Acts 13-14)

Paul started on his first missionary journey with Barnabas and his cousin Mark as their assistant. From Antioch they sailed to Cyprus, of which Barnabas was a native. After a short mission in the island they crossed the sea to Asia Minor where, at Perga, Mark left them and returned to Jerusalem. Moving inland to Antioch in Pisidia, they began work in the local synagogue. (It was Paul's usual practice to start in the synagogue, which generally had an outer fringe of Gentile adherents:[1] then, when Jewish hostility forced him out, to take with him the nucleus of a small Christian community.) They continued to proclaim the gospel in Antioch till Jewish antipathy expelled them from the district; whereupon they moved along the Roman road to Iconium, Lystra and Derbe. There much the same thing happened. Then, turning back in their tracks, they appointed leaders in the new congregations, and returned by sea to Syrian Antioch, only to learn that a crisis was brewing in the church, which deeply concerned them.

The trouble was a threatened split in the church over the policy to be adopted towards Gentile converts. For the Jewish party, the gospel was primarily a Jewish affair. If Gentiles were to be admitted to the church, they said, they must be circumcised and made to keep the law of Moses. To the advanced wing in Antioch, led by Paul and Barnabas, faith in Christ was the one *sine qua non* for salvation, and to impose on Gentiles all the burdens of the Law would be a fatal mistake.

So, in AD 49, Paul, Barnabas and some others were despatched

---

[1] The so-called 'God-fearers', i.e. devout Gentiles who professed monotheism and accepted the Jewish moral code but, understandably, fought shy of circumcision.

from Antioch to Jerusalem where the first great council of the church was held to settle this problem. The result, predictably, was a compromise embodied in a decree (Acts 15.20). It had three main points. Gentile Christians were required to avoid all that savoured of idolatry, to reject meat from which the blood had not been drained, and to conform to the high Jewish code of sexual relations.

We need not suppose that Paul found the decision unacceptable: where no compromise of principle was involved, he could be the most conciliatory of men. In this case, he evidently interpreted the decision as giving him all the freedom needed for his work.

The second journey: AD *50-52 (Acts 15.36-18.22)*

Paul had not long returned to base at Antioch when he was proposing another mission to Barnabas. But when Barnabas wanted to take the 'deserter' Mark with them, Paul demurred and the two friends quarrelled. Barnabas went off with Mark to Cyprus, and Paul, choosing Silas (Silvanus), began his second journey.

Setting off overland, they visited the cities of South Galatia where they delivered the council's decisions about Gentiles, and enlisted Timothy. The trio then travelled west-north-west to the seaport of Troas, near ancient Troy. There Paul had a vision in which a man from Macedonia seemed to implore him, 'Come over and help us'. So Paul and his friends took ship for Macedonia – and Europe. (Sir William Ramsay made the suggestion that the Macedonian was in fact Luke. At any rate, at this point in the narrative [16.10] we find the first 'We passage'. Here, we infer, Luke had joined the company.)

They began their mission in Philippi, a Roman colony, where Paul's cure of a clairvoyant slave-girl led to their being clapped by the magistrates in prison. Released after an earthquake they now pushed westwards to Thessalonica (modern Salonika), where they must have spent some time. Once again their preaching roused Jewish rancour, and they had to go on to Beroea where the same thing happened. So, leaving his two colleagues to settle affairs in the young churches, Paul went south to Athens. Here he had little success. The Athenians were in no mood to listen to the little Jew who seemed to be 'dabbling' in strange divinities, and his address to the court of the Areopagus got a mixed reception.

And now Paul struck west to the great commercial city of Corinth. Here he fell in with Aquila (a tent-maker like himself) and his wife

Priscilla, who had been very recently expelled along with other Jews from Rome by the Emperor Claudius.[2] Eighteen months he stayed in Corinth: in spite of opposition his work prospered; and he was rejoined by Silas and Timothy with news of the church in Thessalonica which moved him to write the two *Epistles to the Thessalonians*. When in AD 51 (a date we know from an inscription found at Delphi) the new Roman governor Gallio arrived in Corinth, the Jews tried to accuse Paul before the authorities;[3] and though the governor sent them about their business, Paul left Corinth taking with him Aquila and Priscilla. Halting briefly at Ephesus, where he left his friends, he sailed back, via Caesarea, to Antioch, his base.

The third journey: AD 53-57 (Acts 18.23-21.17)

Before long Paul was on the road again. He had promised to revisit Ephesus, and thither he now went, after revisiting his churches in Galatia. Here he spent almost three years. During this time disturbing news from Corinth made him write *The First Epistle to the Corinthians*. In Ephesus itself his labours bore rich fruit; the gospel spread to the country all round Ephesus, and even penetrated to Colossae and Laodicea in the Lycus valley. But again trouble arose – this time from the local silversmiths whose revenues had suffered from Paul's polemic against idolatry. (Ephesus with its temple was the centre of the cult of Artemis, an Asian fertility goddess, and Demetrius and his fellow-tradesmen got their living by making and selling little silver statues of her.) That Paul's life was in grave danger at this time is clear (see II Cor. 1.8ff.); and it is just possible that he underwent an imprisonment here of which Acts says nothing, and that one or more of the Prison Epistles came from Ephesus, and not, as tradition says, from Rome.

Paul left the city, went north, and crossed to Macedonia and Greece on a tour of inspection. While in Macedonia he wrote *The Second Epistle to the Corinthians*, having heard that things in Corinth had taken a turn for the better. Then he proceeded in person to Corinth for a three months' stay. It was during this stay

[2] 'Claudius', says the Roman historian Suetonius, 'banished the Jews from Rome when they made a constant rioting at the instigation of Chrestus.' The year was AD 49, and the reference probably to the rioting which ensued when some men preached the good news about Jesus to the Jews of Rome.

[3] The *bēma* (tribunal) on which Paul appeared (Acts 18.12) has been discovered – a high broad platform, made of white and blue marble.

that, his thoughts turning westwards, he wrote *The Epistle to the Romans* in order to pave the way for his long-cherished visit to the capital.

Meanwhile, however, a debt of honour remained to be paid. For some time he had been making a collection among his Gentile churches for the poverty-stricken mother church; and he now resolved to accompany the delegates to these churches to Jerusalem, hoping hard that this gesture of goodwill would mollify his enemies there. Returning, therefore, via Philippi and Troas, he had a poignant meeting with the Ephesian elders at Miletus (see Acts 20) before resuming his journey by sea to Caesarea and Jerusalem.

The last journey: Jerusalem, Malta, Rome, AD *57-64* (*Acts 21.18-28.31*)

Though warned at Caesarea by Agabus of the risk he was taking, Paul went up to Jerusalem. When James, the Lord's brother, and now head of the mother church, advised him to conciliate the Jews who were out for his blood, he obeyed: but some Jews from Asia, alleging that he had desecrated the Temple, attacked and would have killed him but for the intervention of the commander of the Roman garrison. A speech by Paul failed to pacify the angry mob, and when next day he appeared before the Sanhedrin, the only result was a quarrel between the Pharisees and the Sadducees, and Paul found himself again in the Roman barracks. At last, the commander, hearing from Paul's nephew of a plot against his life, packed Paul off under escort to Felix the Roman governor at Caesarea. His accusers followed him there, but when they failed to convince Felix, the governor deferred judgment indefinitely, and kept his prisoner in gaol for two years until his successor Festus arrived (probably in AD 59).

The new governor's arrival encouraged Paul's enemies to try to have him transferred to Jerusalem for trial. Realizing that this could mean only death for him, Paul played his last card: 'I appeal to Caesar.' 'You have appealed to Caesar,' replied Festus, 'to Caesar you shall go' (Acts 25.11f.).

'I must see Rome also,' Paul had once said (Acts 19.21). His wish was now to be fulfilled, though in circumstances far other than he had expected. En route for Rome, the ship carrying him ran into a heavy storm off Crete, and after being tempest-driven in the Adriatic Sea was shipwrecked on Malta. Three months they wintered there, and then proceeded by stages to Rome. But Caesar was in no hurry to judge Paul, and for two years kept him in open confinement in Rome. According to tradition – and we should not reject it unless there is strong evidence that it is wrong – it was during these two years that he wrote the Prison Epistles: *Colossians*, *Ephesians*, *Philemon* and *Philippians*.

Here Luke closes his narrative. Paul's end is uncertain. One tradition declares that at his trial he was acquitted and on release, resumed his travels, only to be re-arrested.[4] (To this period would belong the Pastoral Epistles, if they are, in whole or in part, the work of Paul himself.) It is perhaps likelier that at the end of the two years mentioned in Acts 28.30 there came that change in Roman policy towards the church which culminated in the Neronian persecution, and that Paul was a victim of the ensuing 'purge'. Tradition has it that he died at a place called 'Three Fountains' on the Ostian Way. (A stately basilica, 'St Paul's outside the Walls', now marks the spot.) There one swift sword-stroke, and the apostle to the Gentiles left for ever what he called 'our lowly body' (Phil. 3.21) to be 'at home with the Lord' (II Cor. 5.8).

Such is the life of Paul. A second-century writer[5] describes him as short and balding, with beetling brows and an aquiline nose. He may well have been so. What none may dispute is his exceptional toughness (witness the catalogue of sufferings in II Cor. 11.22-27), his indomitable courage and his single-minded devotion to the conquest of the Roman world for Christ.

No man ever packed more achievement – more thinking and doing and suffering – into his earthly span. So unprejudiced a judge as Lord Birkenhead once declared that beside the achievements of Paul of Tarsus the work of Alexander the Great or of Napoleon 'pales into insignificance'. Paul the tent-maker from Tarsus, pupil of Gamaliel, *civis Romanus*, apostle to the Gentiles, first of Christian mystics, most dynamic of Christian missionaries, supreme servant and interpreter of Christ, the most illustrious name in the roll-call of the saints.

[4] Clement of Rome (I Clem. 6.4) says Paul 'reached the farthest bounds of the west' before he was martyred. This certainly suggests Spain.
[5] The writer of the apocryphal *Acts of Paul and Thekla*.

Note on the Chronology of Paul's Life and Letters

The Life

The Crucifixion of Jesus	AD 30
Paul's conversion	33
His fortnight's visit to Jerusalem (Acts 9.26; Gal. 1.18)	36
Second visit to Jerusalem (Acts 11.30; Gal. 2.1-10)	46
The third ('council') visit (Acts 15.2)	49
Arrival at Corinth	50
Third journey (in Ephesus 53-56)	53
Arrest	57
Arrival in Rome	60
Martyrdom	64-5

The Letters – Chronologically Arranged

Time	Letter	Place of Writing
49 (?)	Gal.	Antioch (?)
50-51 (II)	I and II Thess.	Corinth
55-56 (III)	I and II Cor.	Ephesus and Macedonia
57 (III)	Romans	Corinth
60-61	Col., Eph., Philemon	Rome
62 (?)	Phil.	Rome (or Ephesus, c. 55)

Paul's Ephesian ministry

We have assumed, following tradition, that Paul's Prison Letters came from Rome. But is it possible Paul wrote them from a prison in Ephesus? Some modern scholars like Deissmann and G. S. Duncan have thought so.

How do they state their case for Ephesus against Rome? First, they weaken the link with Rome by asking whether it is likely that the ten friends of Paul named at the end of Col. and Philemon all followed him to Rome. Their next point is that Ephesus, only 100 miles from Colossae, was a likelier refuge for the runaway Onesimus than Rome, 800 miles away. True, but Luke says nothing in Acts about an imprisonment of Paul in Ephesus. Yet Luke's narrative is far from exhaustive, and odd bits of evidence in Paul's letters suggests that 'the half has not been told'. Consider, for example, passages like I Cor. 15.32, 'I fought with wild beasts at Ephesus', and II Cor. 1.8, 'the affliction we experienced in Asia ... we despaired of life itself'. Add to these the Marcionite Prologue to Colossians: 'Paul, now in bonds, is writing to them from Ephesus.'

Suppose, then, a *prima facie* case for Ephesus has been made out. Do the contents of the Prison Letters themselves favour it?

What about Colossians and Philemon? Luke was with Paul when he wrote these two letters. We know that Luke was with Paul in Rome, but we cannot be certain he was with Paul in Ephesus. So the case for linking these two letters with Ephesus is thereby weakened. A better case can be argued for Philippians.

1. We can no longer say that the references to the Praetorium (Phil. 1.13) and 'the saints ... of Caesar's household' (Phil. 4.22) necessarily mean Rome. 'Praetorium' often means 'government house', and 'Caesar's household' was a kind of imperial civil service. Ephesus had both of these.

2. The frequent 'to-ings' and 'fro-ings' between Paul's prison and Philippi (see Phil. 2.25ff) may be said to suit Ephesus better than Rome. Rome to Philippi took about sixty days, Ephesus to Philippi about ten.

3. The travel-plan coincidence of Phil. 2.19 and Acts 19.22 appears to tell in favour of Ephesus. In the first passage Paul plans to send Timothy to Philippi in Macedonia; in the second, he sends Timothy to Macedonia.

But argument (1) does not tie Phil. to Ephesus. It could apply, e.g., to Caesarea, where Paul certainly was imprisoned.

Argument (2) can be effectively countered. Paul was imprisoned for *more than two years* in Rome – ample time for the frequent comings and goings of Phil. 2.25ff.

And the two arguments may be thrown in on the side of tradition.

1. There is in Phil. no reference to the collection for the poor Christians of Jerusalem which Paul was organizing among his Gentile converts during his stay in Ephesus.

2. Paul could not have been in danger of a death sentence at Ephesus, because, as a Roman citizen, he could always appeal to Caesar, as he finally did.

Though attractive in the case of Phil., the Ephesian theory remains an unproved hypothesis because (*a*) some of the arguments for it weaken upon examination, and (*b*) because we do not certainly know that Paul was ever imprisoned in Ephesus. Since, in cases like these, the burden of proof rests with the innovator, we may be content – unless and until further evidence is produced – to follow tradition and assign all the Prison Letters to Rome.

12

The Gospel According to Paul

What is the most profound work ever written? It is a question which would be answered very differently by different people. S. T. Coleridge, who had one of the most powerful minds in the nineteenth century, answered it by choosing a book of the New Testament. 'I think,' he declared, 'that the Epistle to the Romans is the most profound work in existence.'[1] Luther called it 'the chief book in the New Testament and the purest Gospel'. And in our day a distinguished American Christian thinker, John Knox, has pronounced it 'unquestionably the most important theological book ever written'.[2]

These are very bold claims to make for a letter written nineteen centuries ago, in a back street of Corinth, by a little Jewish tentmaker. Yet history supports them; for in century after century 'Paul to the Romans' has been the flame at which one great Christian leader after another – Augustine, Luther, Calvin, Wesley and Barth – has kindled his own torch to the revival of the church and the enrichment of Christendom. Paul wrote *urbi* – to the city called Rome; unwittingly, he wrote *orbi* – to the world, and to posterity.

What is Romans, and why should it have exerted so enormous an influence? It is the mature answer to the question, 'What is Christianity?', by the ablest mind in the early church. Later we shall consider the substance of Paul's answer. Meanwhile let us dispose of the usual 'introductory' questions.

1. *Writer, readers, date and purpose*

No one has ever doubted that Paul wrote Romans. It bears his mark

[1] S. T. Coleridge, *Table Talk*, Oxford University Press n.d., p. 232.
[2] *The Interpreter's Bible*, Vol. 9, Abingdon Press 1954, p. 355.

as surely as an essay of Lamb's or (to take a modern example) a letter of Alistair Cooke's bears his. Nor are Paul's addressees in doubt: 'All of you in Rome whom God loves and has called to be his dedicated people' (Rom. 1.7 NEB).

Nobody knows who founded the church in Rome. On the day of Pentecost there were 'visitors from Rome' (Acts 2.10) in Peter's audience; and doubtless it was men like them who first brought the gospel to the capital. What is certain – witness the statement of the Roman historian Suetonius[3] – is that the gospel had reached Rome within twenty years of the Crucifixion. About eight years later the church there had so grown that Paul could write, 'All over the world they are telling the story of your faith' (1.8 NEB). And when in 64 Nero began to persecute the Christians in Rome, they were, according to Tacitus, 'a huge multitude'; one which, to judge from Paul's letter (Rom. 1.5f.,13; 11.13; 15.15f.), contained more Gentiles than Jews.

The date of the letter was probably AD 57. The evidence for this comes from combining Acts 20.2f. with Rom. 15.17ff. It was written towards the end of Paul's third journey. He wrote it during his three months' stay in Corinth before he went up to Jerusalem with the fund raised in his Gentile churches for the poor of the mother church.

Rom. 15.18-33 tells us why he wrote it. Paul felt that his work in the east was done. Now he was turning his gaze west – was projecting a journey to Rome and then to Spain. Only too well he knew he was suspect in many circles, especially Jewish ones. So he wrote to Rome not only to pave the way for his visit there by establishing 'contacts' in the capital, but also to explain the Christian faith as he understood it. It was to prove *ein Schicksal-brief* – a letter of destiny. But we may doubt whether his secretary Tertius (16.22), or even Paul himself, had any guess how its message would reverberate down the centuries.

Note on problems raised by Rom. 15 and 16

1. Were there two editions of Romans? There is evidence that the letter circulated in two versions, the shorter of which lacked the last two chapters. Thus some early Latin chapter-headings imply a version which lacked 15-16. The doxology (16.25-27) occurs in some MSS at the end of 14. And the words 'in Rome' (1.7,15) are wanting in some of our best MSS. Either, then, Paul wrote the shorter version (1-14) as a circular letter and later expanded it

---

[3] Quoted in ch. 11, p. 89.

for Rome; or somebody, for reasons we can only guess at, abridged it. The latter seems likelier. For (a) Rom. 14.23 makes an uncharacteristic ending; and (b) Rom. 1.8-17 does not read like a circular letter: it is *ad Romam* stuff.

2. But was Rom. 16 really meant for the Christians in Rome? Some hold it was a separate letter to Ephesus commending Phoebe 'the deaconess' (16.1). They argue that Paul cannot have known so many people in Rome as are named in ch. 16; that Aquila and Priscilla, when last heard of, were in Ephesus (I Cor. 16.19); and that the phrase 'Epaenetus the first convert to Christ in Asia' (16.5) and the sharp warning against mischief-makers (16.17-20) suit Ephesus better than Rome.

Their case is not made out. (1) Paul did not usually single out individuals for special greetings in churches he knew well (as he certainly knew that in Ephesus). He did not know the congregation in Rome personally and was anxious to make as many 'contacts' in it as he could. (2) Aquila and Priscilla may well have returned to Rome after the relaxation of the imperial decree against the Jews. Many Jews did.

Against the Ephesian theory we may set three considerations. (1) It is hard to regard Rom. 16 as a complete letter. (2) Many of the persons named in the greetings can be connected with Rome. (3) Rom. 16.16 suits Rome better than Ephesus. When writing, Paul was in touch with the churches of Galatia, Asia, Macedonia and Achaia over the business of the relief fund for the mother church. What more natural than that he should mention these churches in order to buttress his appeal to Rome?

We conclude that Rom. 16 is an integral part of Romans.

2. *Contents of Romans*

The letter falls into five parts:

1. Paul and his readers (1.1-16).
2. The gospel according to Paul (1.17-8.39).
3. The purpose of God in history (chs. 9-11).
4. The Christian ethic (12.1-15.13).
5. Plans and greetings (15.14-16.27).

Obviously sections (2), (3) and (4) are the important ones. It will simplify matters if, before we study Paul's gospel and ethic, we consider his 'philosophy of history' in chapters 9-11. Paul may have written this section earlier, as a separate discussion of a vexed question. It forms a continuous whole and may be read without reference to the rest of the letter.[4]

God's purpose in history

A friend of mine, an orthodox Jew, told me that, on being appointed to a famous Oxford chair, he was welcomed by his Gentile

[4] C. H. Dodd, *The Epistle of Paul to the Romans*, Fontana Books 1959, p. 161.

predecessor in these words: 'So you're one of the people who missed the bus 1900 years ago.' It was a maladroit way of raising a question over which Paul had agonized and to which we have his answer in Rom. 9-11. 'Why have the chosen people rejected their Messiah and apparently been excluded from God's grace?'

First (ch. 9) Paul looks at the matter from the divine side. The Jewish nation as a whole, he says, was never able to claim God's promise of blessing. Right through their history God is to be seen *selecting* – choosing one, rejecting another. And if we ask why, the answer is that God, as the Lord of history, acts as he wills, and it is not for the creature to criticize his Creator. Moreover, if some Jews have apparently fallen out of God's favour, God always planned to include Gentiles among his people, as he is doing now.

Next (9.30-10), he considers the problem from the *human* side. Israel, he declares, has gone about salvation the wrong way – sought it by works of Law instead of by faith in Christ. But, someone may protest, the Jews have never had the chance of accepting Christ by faith. This is not true. The heralds of the gospel have gone everywhere. No, Israel's failure is due not to ignorance but to that old recalcitrancy of which the prophets spoke.

But Paul cannot rest in this sad conclusion. And so, lastly (ch. 11), Paul affirms that God has not *finally* rejected Israel. Even now there is a faithful remnant; the lapse of the rest from grace has in fact led to the conversion of the Gentiles; and when God has completed his saving purpose, for Israel also will dawn the day of God's mercy.

The gospel according to Paul

Now we may take chapters 1-8 and 12-15. In the first sixteen verses Paul greets his fellow-Christians in Rome and tells them of his long-cherished plan to visit them. He is not ashamed of the gospel; for it is God's power for saving sinners, and Rome has no lack of these. Then begins his exposition of Christianity which falls into three parts:

1.17-3.20   the sin of man
3.21-8.39   but the grace of God
12.1-15.13   therefore the Christian Ethic.

The sin of man

In the gospel, Paul begins (1.17), 'the righteousness of God is revealed through faith for faith'. 'The righteousness of God', be it noted, is one of Paul's key-phrases and – as the NEB makes clear ('Here is revealed God's way of righting wrong') – we must understand it dynamically, as a divine *activity*. It means 'God putting things right' for men, by delivering them from their enemies and their sin. Through the centuries Israel had prayed that God would so intervene in men's affairs and put things right. Now, Paul says, in the event of the gospel story he is to be seen doing it.

But why is 'the righteousness of God' needed? Because of the *unrighteousness* of men. All mankind, Jews and Gentiles alike, have sinned by breaking God's law. Take the Gentiles first (1.18-32). They have had a revelation of God's nature and will in his created world, but they have deliberately refused it and relapsed into futile speculations and darkness. One need only look at pagan society, worshipping its man-made gods and sunk in moral pollution, to see how God's retribution has fallen on its sin. Lose the true God, and that is the morass of depravity into which men sink. (It is still true today.)[5]

But the Jews are not one whit better. They have enjoyed God's special revelation of his nature and will in the Law of Moses; yet they have flouted and disobeyed it. Thus all men, Jews and Gentiles without distinction, are guilty at the bar of holy God, as the scriptures say (3.10-18). Such is the disease – the sin of man.

But the grace of God

But now, Paul says (3.21), here is God's remedy. Quite independently of law, God has begun to put things right for sinners. No man can by works of Law – by his own moral achievements – set himself right with God. But in Christ God has provided a way for sinful men to be 'justified', that is, to get right with God. In the gospel God declares his gracious will to forgive men and set them right with himself. He has made Christ's cross the appointed means of that forgiveness, and what God requires on man's part is faith, which is trust and obedience. As long ago Abraham, when God spoke to him, took God at his word and obeyed, so Christian faith

---

[5] Here we break a lance with the humanists. As Paul sees, in the great scale of things, religion and morality hang together. A man's morality – or a people's – is determined by what he worships. It is no accident that in our day and society when so many have jettisoned the Christian faith, we are witnessing a widespread collapse in moral standards.

is taking God at his word in Christ. When sinners so put their trust in God's Christ who has died for their sins, God forgives them and sets them in a new relationship with himself (3.21-4.25).

Then (in chapters 5-8) Paul describes what follows from 'justification' – peace with God and the hope of glory, so that our very hardships now take on new meaning. (In 5.12-21, he pauses to explain how the work of Christ the Second Adam has more than undone the evil brought on the race by the first man's disobedience.)

By baptism (6.1ff.), which admits us into the new divine community, we die in union with Christ to our old evil ways and rise into new life, and we are called to become what we potentially are, men dead to sin and alive to God.

Freed from the slavery of sin and the Law's deadly grip, we may now serve God in a new way. Thus, in his Son, God has done what the Law could not do – broken the power of sin in our fallen nature – and we now have the Holy Spirit helping us to live as God wills and promising us life that can never die. Adopted into our heavenly Father's family, we are fellow-heirs with Christ of God's glory, provided that we are ready to suffer with him.

Yet the suffering which we endure is not worth comparison with the glory God has in store for his children. Meanwhile, with the Holy Spirit to aid our weakness, we hopefully await the time when we shall be fully 'shaped to the likeness of God's Son' (8.29).

God is on our side, Paul triumphantly concludes. The Christ who died for us and rose again, now pleads our cause at his right hand. If God spared not his only Son in order to save us, we may trust him to give us all we need, and nothing in the world or out of it will be able to separate us from that strong love of God in Christ.

This is the gospel as Paul understands it; but for the apostle 'truth is always truth *in order to goodness*'. Or, to put it another way, if the gospel has a 'believing' side, it has also a 'behaving' side. To this we now turn.

Therefore the Christian ethic

'In the New Testament,' said Erskine of Linlathen,[6] 'religion is grace and ethics is gratitude.' True of the New Testament gener-

---

[6] Thomas Erskine (1778-1870) of Linlathen, near Dundee, was a layman of deeply spiritual insight, the friend of F. D. Maurice, Carlyle and others.

ally, it is specially true of Paul. So, having in 3.21-8.39 expounded the grace of God, in chapters 12-15 he describes the grateful response in living which those who have experienced this grace ought to make. Here, he says, is the way forgiven men must behave. What kind of behaviour does he proceed to outline?

It is a life 'in Christ', i.e. a life lived in that fellowship of which Christ is the living head, and we are limbs in that organism which may be called his body. It is a life whose master-principle is that selfless love (*agapē*) which is the fulfilling of the Law (13.10). Christians should be law-abiding citizens of the state, owing no debt but the debt of love which they must always be paying. In fact, their whole behaviour should be patterned on Christ's design for living. (Note how chapters 12-14 are shot through with echoes of Christ's teaching as we have it in the Gospels: Rom. 12.14,17,21; 13.7,8; 14.4,10,13,14; 16.19.) There must be no paying back of evil for evil, no censorious judgment of our brothers, no putting of stumbling-blocks in others' way. Always we should be trying to show special consideration for the weak and building up the common life of the church. So (Paul concludes) may the God of hope fill them with all joy and peace in believing and cause them, by the Spirit's power, to overflow with hope.

Such is Christianity according to St Paul in Romans. First, the diagnosis of man's condition; then the prescribing of God's remedy for his disease; and finally the charting of the way in which the 'renewed' man should walk, with the hope of glory at journey's ending.

3. *The relevance of Romans*

Luther once said that 'the Christian should not only have every word of Romans by heart, but should take it about with him every day as the daily bread of his soul'. But how many modern Christians have ever read the letter even once? Why do people who will study the Gospels boggle at Romans? One reason is that even in a modern translation Romans makes tough reading. Another is the dark suspicion (totally unjustified in the light of modern scholarship) that Paul was the pernicious perverter of an originally simple gospel of God's Fatherhood and man's brotherhood. And another is the widespread impression that Paul is an 'old fogey' out of the Bible, dealing in issues now as dead as the dodo. How could Karl Barth say that 'if we rightly understand ourselves, our problems are the problems of Paul', and that, 'if we be enlightened by the brightness of his answers, those answers must be ours'?[7]

Consider, first, what Paul says about 'our human predicament'. He diagnoses its cause as 'the unrighteousness of men'. He believes in original sin – that sin is not an accident but a state, and a racial state at that. Without exception, we are all involved in it: like runners in the strawberry-bed, we are all connected up through a common life-root, and through that life-root flows evil. Now we need not accept all that Paul says about Adam to see that his diagnosis is well-founded.[8] For all the amazing strides made in modern science, medicine and other fields of human activity, mankind remains the *verdammte Rasse* (as Frederick the Great called it), the same 'perishing human race', the same sin-sick, unhappy proposition that Paul knew, and one which all our higher education, political panaceas and improved psychological techniques seem powerless to cure. The sins of our ancestors form a baleful heritage which affects our lives and determines our character. Moreover, the experience of the last fifty years has taught us, in blood and tears, how dread a laboratory of good and evil is the heart of man. In the event, does not Paul emerge as a better diagnostician of our human predicament than all those sky-blue optimists like H. G. Wells who, at the beginning of this century, were telling us so confidently that 'man was out of the woods at last' and marching irresistibly to perfection and paradise on earth?

What then of the divine remedy? Can the gospel of God's grace in Christ, which in the first century turned bad men into good ones, do the same for us today who live in quite different times and are vexed by so many problems which never came within Paul's purview?

James Denney once said that what was needed for understanding Paul's gospel was not higher criticism but *despair*. Wherever and whenever that condition exists, Paul's gospel can speak. For the heart of it is that what we men, because of indwelling sin, cannot do for ourselves, is done for us by God – through Christ. In Jesus Christ incarnate, crucified, risen, regnant and now present with us through the Holy Spirit, God has bridged the awful gulf

[7] Karl Barth, *The Epistle to the Romans*, Oxford University Press 1933, p. 1.

[8] Richard Crossman has recently said that there is more evidence in the world today for the Christian doctrine of original sin than for the Marxist doctrine of the classless society.

between divine holiness and human sin. To the man with a sense of his own sin upon him and a willingness to cast himself unreservedly on heaven's mercy, God, through Christ's cross, provides forgiveness and offers a new start in life, enabled by the Spirit, and the blessed hope of everlasting life.

Does this divine remedy still retain its virtue and power? You cannot demonstrate the truth of Paul's gospel as you would demonstrate a proposition in Euclid. You can prove its truth only *by experiment* – by finding the gospel to be God's saving power in your own life. Now countless Christians down nineteen centuries have made that experiment and found that God in Christ can

> break the power of cancelled sin
> And set the prisoner free.

What Kingswood colliers found in the eighteenth century has been authenticated for themselves by a multitude of men and women, from Augustine and Bunyan to John Wesley and Thomas Chalmers. And still today, in their moral despair and defeat, men and women venture themselves on that unchanging grace of God in Christ and find afresh that it is God's power for saving sinners of which Paul speaks in Romans 3-8.

Nor is Paul's Christian ethic less usable by us than by his first readers. Romans 12, for example, remains a noble expression of Christian character and conduct.[9] True, with the advance of civilization since Paul's day, moral problems have often changed their shapes. Yet Paul's pattern for Christian living, so firmly based (as we have seen) on Christ's design for life, has not become outdated with the lapse of centuries. The principles of Christian behaviour which he lays down in Rom. 12-15 are capable of endless re-application to the moral issues which perplex us today, whether they are those of law and liberty or drink and drugs. When we are tempted to pass censorious judgment on others, we need his reminder that 'none of us lives to himself' and that we have a Christian duty to abstain from anything which causes our brother's downfall, that brother for whom Christ died. Above all, Paul's insistence on the primacy of Christian love (*agapē*) remains as challenging and relevant as ever. In our complex modern world the law of love will often be hard to apply. As Reinhold Niebuhr has said, 'love

[9] Splendidly translated in the NEB. Less famous than I Cor. 13, it is worthy to stand beside it and rank among Paul's greatest chapters.

is always relevant but never a simple possibility'. Yet it remains the supreme standard of Christian action. The will of God is love, and 'when this is done, all is done'. No less than those far-off Christians in first-century Rome we are called, in our situation, to make our love genuine, to bless those who persecute us, to render to no man evil for evil, but to overcome evil with good.

So Karl Barth is right. Paul's problems are our problems and Paul's gospel in Romans is not outdated. To be sure, if Paul's message is to come home to us today, it will often need to be translated into modern words and idioms. Here the *New English Bible* and books like J. B. Phillips' *Letters to Young Churches* can show us how it is to be done. Again, we are not required to accept everything that Paul says. Indeed, occasionally we may find ourselves disagreeing with him, and like Martin Luther, when he came across an unconvincing argument, crying, 'Brother Paul, this does not hold'. (A case in point is Paul's analogy of the pot and the potter in Rom. 9.20f. It is not a happy one. A man is *not* a pot. He will cry, Why did you make me thus? And he will not be bludgeoned into silence.)

Nevertheless, to dismiss Paul's gospel as so much theological 'old hat' because, for example, we cannot accept today what he says about Adam and the Genesis story, would be the profoundest of mistakes. Real and abiding issues underlie the problems Paul discusses in Romans, above all the question of salvation by faith or by works. The almost universal desire to run our own lives and earn our own salvation shows that it is still a live issue. If it was the grand assumption of Judaism in Paul's day, it is still the grand assumption of all systems of ethical self-culture in ours. But it is wholly mistaken. It cannot work, cannot bring the peace of mind it promises, because it has never plumbed the depths of our human predicament or taken the measure of original sin. Thus Paul's argument never loses its force, as his remedy for man's predicament remains available and relevant. 'Miserable creature that I am,' he cries, 'who will rescue me from the body on which sin has laid its death-grip?' And he answers, 'God alone, through Jesus Christ our Lord' (Rom. 7.24f.).

Finally, if we grant what may be called Paul's major premiss (which as Christians we can hardly avoid doing) that there is a living God, who shapes the course of history, and once broke openly and decisively into it in Jesus of Nazareth, then the main outlines of his theology stand firm, and we no less than his first readers may make it our own:

> Long long ago the Truth was found,
> A company of men it bound.
> Grasp firmly then – that ancient Truth.

13

The Church of God in Vanity Fair

Nowadays any schoolboy interested in etymologies associates Corinth with currants. But nineteen hundred years ago it was not currants but courtesans which the name suggested. In its temple, where Aphrodite was worshipped, there were a thousand priestess-prostitutes, and to 'corinthianize' was polite Greek for following what Shaw calls Mrs Warren's profession.

The other thing to note about old Corinth was its cosmopolitan character. Situated on the Isthmus of Corinth, it was the capital of the Roman province of Achaia, contained half a million inhabitants, and was a great commercial city. In it dwelt men of all races, bond and free – Greeks, Romans and 'barbarians' – all sorts of trades prospered, and many cults and religions had their devotees. It has been called 'a compound of Newmarket, Chicago and Paris', with perhaps a bit of Port Said thrown in. To the Christian community in this very pagan city – 'the Church of God in Vanity Fair', as someone has called it – Paul wrote *First Corinthians*.

1. *Paul's contacts and correspondence with Corinth*

We have reason to believe that Paul paid *three* visits to Corinth and wrote *four* letters to the Christians there.

(a) *The First Visit*. Acts 18.1-18 tells how Paul, on his second journey, founded the church in Corinth, and after almost two years' work there returned to base in Syria.

(b) *The Previous Letter*. During his third journey he went to Ephesus where he ministered for three years. It was from Ephesus that he wrote his first letter to Corinth – let us call it 'the previous letter'. Its existence we infer from I Cor. 5.9. 'I wrote to you in my letter,' Paul says, 'not to associate with immoral men.' A fragment of it possibly survives in II Cor. 6.14-7.1, a section which seems out of place in its present context.

(c) *First Corinthians.* The Corinthians sent Paul a rather complacent reply, in which they asked his advice about certain church problems (cf. I Cor. 7.1: 'Now concerning the matters about which you wrote'). About the same time some persons called 'Chloe's people' (servants of a business woman in Corinth who had possibly become a Christian) reported to Paul the outbreak of party strife and immorality in the church at Corinth. To this letter and report Paul replied in *First Corinthians.*

(d) *The Painful Visit and the Severe Letter.* Later events are obscure; but probably the situation worsened and Paul paid the Corinthians what is known as 'the painful visit', hoping to clear matters up. This visit, not recorded in Acts, is inferred from II Cor. 13.1ff. ('This will be my third visit to you'). Humiliated, Paul returned to Ephesus and wrote 'the severe letter'. This letter's existence we infer from II Cor. 2.4,9 and 7.8 ('Even if I did wound you by the letter I sent'). A fragment of it may survive in II Cor. 10-13.

(e) *Second Corinthians.* Better news came later from Corinth, through Titus, to Paul in Macedonia (II Cor. 2.13; 7.13). Paul then decided to visit Corinth a third time and from Macedonia wrote a letter of reconciliation, sometimes called 'the thankful letter': our Second Corinthians, or possibly II Cor. 10-13.

(f) After a short interval Paul did arrive in Corinth (Acts 20.2).

Thus the first three Corinthian letters came from Ephesus, the fourth from Macedonia, probably in the years AD 55-57.

I Corinthians falls within situation (c) in our scheme. Paul is in Ephesus when the report and the letter arrive. His work will not permit him to leave Ephesus at once (I Cor. 16.5-9) and, as matters are urgent, he must deal with them by letter. So, first, he takes up the disorders in Corinth reported by Chloe's people; then he discusses the problems raised in the Corinthian letter.

We may analyse I Corinthians thus:

1. Greeting and thanksgiving (1.1-9).
2. Unity and order in the church (1.10-6.20).
3. The Christian in a pagan society (chs. 7-11).
4. Spiritual gifts (chs. 12-14).
5. Life after death (ch. 15).
6. Business and closing messages (ch. 16).

2. *The letter itself*

After a greeting to 'the church of God which is at Corinth' and a thanksgiving, Paul turns to the three reported disorders – party strife, a case of incest, and 'litigiosity'. To begin with, factions and schisms had arisen in the church at Corinth. Some swore allegiance to Paul, others to Apollos, others to Peter; while some, despising all human intermediaries, styled themselves 'the Christ party'. Here were unhappy divisions indeed. Paul has to remind them that they have but one Saviour and that apostles are but servants of Christ. Never think of us, he says in effect; remember your common Lord. Keep your unity in Christ (chs. 1-4).

Then he adverts to the case of incest – a Christian man living with his father's wife – which the Corinthians had condoned (5.1-13; 6.12-20). He bids them excommunicate the offender and forbids association with all immoral Christians. The third matter was the fondness of the Corinthians for law-suits (6.1-11). Why must you, Paul asks, take your quarrels before heathen judges? Are there no Christian judges fit to settle your disputes? Better still, as Christians you ought to suffer wrongs without thought of redress. He ends with a stern warning against sexual sin (chs. 5-6).

At ch. 7 Paul comes to the six issues raised in the Corinthian letter: marriage problems, the eating of sacrificial food, the veiling of women at public worship, behaviour at the Lord's Supper, the exercise of spiritual gifts and the Christian hope.

To marry or not to marry when the world's end might not be far away? Might a Christian seek divorce, if one of the partners were a pagan? What about 'spiritual marriages' (7.36-38)? (This was the curious custom whereby a man and woman lived together as brother and sister and not as man and wife.) Paul's answer to these questions may be summed up thus: 'Remain unmarried if you can. If you cannot then marry. Divorce, followed by remarriage, is not permitted. If a widow must be remarried, let it be to a Christian' (ch. 7).

The next question was about eating sacrificial food. Most of the meat on sale in the markets[1] must have been of this kind. The Corinthians were asking: May a Christian eat meat which has

---

[1] Archaeologists have discovered in the ruins of Corinth an inscription referring to the *makellon*, or 'meat-market', possibly the one Paul had in mind.

been consecrated to heathen deities? And may he accept invita-
tions to pagan supper-parties? Paul answered: 'All things are
lawful for a Christian, but not all things are advisable. Of course,
as some of you enlightened Christians[2] in Corinth are saying, these
heathen idols are not really gods. Yet you would be wise to forgo
your Christian rights if the exercise of them leads astray your
weaker brothers' (ch. 8).

He goes on (in chs. 9 and 10) to tell how he himself had renounced many of his rights 'rather than put an obstacle in the way
of the gospel'. Let them not imagine that, because they have the
Christian sacraments, they can go anywhere or do exactly what
they like. The Jews in the wilderness had their sacraments also;
yet this did not prevent God punishing their wickedness. Participa-
tion in pagan supper-parties is fraught with dangers. Christians are
not free to do as they like. Always they must seek by their actions
to build up the life of the community.

The next question (11.2) was: Should women be veiled in
church? Paul replies that it is generally agreed in Christian circles
that they should be. Then he turns to the reported scandals at the
Lord's Supper. At this church supper, which was a common meal
culminating in Holy Communion, the richer members were gorging
themselves and getting drunk while their poorer brothers were
going hungry – and this at what should have been a time of sacred
fellowship. This, Paul sternly reminds them, is the Lord's Supper.
not an orgy! It goes back to what happened in the upper room on
the night when the Lord Jesus was betrayed. Unless you keep a
reverent sense of what you are doing at this meal, you sin against
the Lord himself and will incur God's judgment (ch. 11).

In chs. 12-14 Paul turns to the 'spiritual gifts' of which the
Corinthians were inordinately proud. Evidently there was much
debate about the relative merits of the various manifestations of
spiritual power: teaching, preaching, healing, speaking with
tongues, etc.

All such gifts, Paul tells them, proceed from the one Spirit who
dwells in the one body, which is the church of Christ. In a human

---

[2] In I Cor. 8.1 Paul says: 'Knowledge (*gnōsis*) puffs up but love (*agapē*)
builds up. If anyone imagines that he knows something, he does not yet
know as he ought to know.' Paul is referring to some Corinthians whose
Christianity had been adulterated with 'Gnosticism', that queer theosophy
laying claim to esoteric revelation (*gnōsis*) which made its devotees believe
they were specially enlightened people who could do as they liked.

body no rivalry exists among the various limbs and organs; all act together for the common good. So it should be in Christ's body. All gifts, even the less showy and spectacular ones, have their place in the church (ch. 12).

But of all the gifts incomparably the finest is love. Lacking it, the rest are worthless. Other gifts will pass away; it alone will last on, for love is the life of heaven (ch. 13).

What, then, about 'prophecy' (inspired preaching) and 'speaking with tongues' (ecstatic speech addressed to God under the stress of strong religious emotion)? Prophecy, Paul says, is much to be preferred, because it builds up the Christian community, as 'tongues' do not. The numbers of those who prophesy and those who speak with tongues must be strictly limited at public worship, and one at a time must be the rule. Women should not address the meeting. 'Let all things be done decently and in order' should be their guideline in such matters (ch. 14).

The last topic Paul handles is life after death. Apparently the Corinthians' chief difficulty was about the resurrection of the *body*. After quoting the historical evidence for Christ's Resurrection (and it is the earliest and best we have) Paul points out that, if resurrection of the body is an impossibility, Christ himself cannot have been raised. But it is the very keystone of Christian faith that God *did* raise Christ, and his Resurrection is the pledge that those who are in faith-union with him will also rise. What sort of 'body' will Christians have in the after-life? Paul makes it clear that he does not believe in 'a resurrection of relics' (15.50). His answer, based on the analogy of the seed in nature, is that, as man has now a 'natural' (or 'animate') body, so hereafter he will receive from God a 'spiritual' body – a body adapted to the conditions of the next world as his present body of flesh and blood is adapted to this one.[3] All will take place at Christ's advent in glory when death is swallowed up in victory. No longer does 'the last enemy', death, have the last word. Because God has given us the victory through our Lord Jesus Christ, our labour in the Lord can never be lost (ch. 15).

Then, after a reference to the collection he was raising among

---

[3] 'Body' (*sōma*) for Paul is not a synonym for 'flesh' (*sarx*). *Sōma*, as the principle of individuation, signifies the whole man, the self, the personality. It persists through all changes of substance. Now it has a 'fleshly' expression; hereafter it will have a 'spiritual' one.

the Gentile churches for the mother church, a promise to visit them soon, a commendation of Stephanas, he ends with a handful of greetings (ch. 16).

3. *The value of the letter*

If Romans reveals Paul as the theologian, I Corinthians reveals him as pastor and administrator. No letter better illustrates his own phrase 'the daily pressure on me of my anxiety for all the churches' (II Cor. 11.28). Preachers sometimes bid us look back to the glorious days of the early church. Glorious indeed they were, but they held 'headaches' aplenty for those who, like Paul, were spearheading the gospel's advance into 'that hard pagan world'. And certainly in Corinth's ultra 'permissive society' it must have been desperately hard to lead a truly Christian life. What Paul's letter shows is the impact of the gospel on the low morality of that city, and the many temptations that faced the members of Christ's church in that ancient Vanity Fair.

But this letter also reveals one with an indomitable belief in the adequacy of the gospel to match the situation. To the Corinthians' questions Paul offers answers according to the light given him. Let us be honest and say that they do not always convince us in this twentieth century. Certainly modern youth will never agree with Paul that 'flowing locks disgrace a man' (11.14). We no longer think it shameful for a woman to appear bare-headed in church, or even to lift up her voice in its councils. Again, we may well feel that Paul, as a bachelor, never quite knew what a happy Christian marriage could be, or what blessing a Christian family could bring.

Nonetheless, we cannot read I Corinthians without marvelling at the Christian wisdom which Paul brings to the solution of problem after problem. Take the party strife at Corinth, for instance. Christ cannot be divided, Paul tells the rival factions, as if to say, 'Can't you see he can never be parcelled out as you are doing with him, as if he were the private treasure of one little clique or conventicle?' Can we not hear Paul crying down the centuries to us Christians in our unhappy divisions, one saying 'I am of Calvin', another, 'I am of Luther' and yet another 'I am of Wesley'?

Or consider what he has to say about the matter of eating sacrificial meat. 'See that this liberty of yours does not become a pitfall for the weak' (I Cor. 8.9). The fact that this is no longer a live issue does not invalidate the important rule for the guidance of the Christian conscience which Paul gives us here. We, too, may harm other people by doing something that is not really wrong. Thus, for a Christian who has worshipped God in the morning, it is not really wrong to play golf on a Sunday afternoon. But suppose you play your golf under the eyes of some sabbatarian fellow-Christians, will not this exercise of your Christian freedom cause them pain? (We may add that by the evidence of Col. 2.16, 'Allow no one to take you to task ... over the observance ... of the sabbath', Paul was no sabbatarian. But if he had ever been tempted to play games in Jerusalem on the sabbath, he would certainly have refrained.)

Or consider what Paul has to say on the exercise of spiritual gifts: 'All of these must aim at one thing: to build up the church' (I Cor. 14.26). 'Does it build up the church?' is the one question that matters. Should not this be our touchstone still when we seek to evaluate, say, revivalist preaching, or appraise the worth of the Pentecostal movement,[4] which in the last fifty years has spread so dramatically in Latin America and parts of Africa?

The principles, then, which Paul lays down in his letter are capable of wide application to the problems of our day. Moreover, it is worth observing how often, when handling matters of Christian practice, Paul lets theology come breaking in. As for example in 1.22f., where, talking about their party strife, he brings them to the heart of his gospel, the Cross of Christ:

Jews demand signs and Greeks seek wisdom, but we preach Christ crucified, a stumbling-block to Jews and folly to Gentiles, but to those who are called, both Jews and Greeks, Christ the power of God and the wisdom of God.

Or again in 6.19f., where he is rebuking some libertarian Christians who evidently regarded all things as lawful and sins of the body as not really sins at all:

Do you not know that your body is a temple of the Holy Spirit within you, which you have from God? You are not your own; you were bought with a price. So glorify God in your body.

But, these passages apart, the two shining glories of this letter come in chapters thirteen and fifteen. The first is Paul's famous

[4] See W. J. Hollenweger, *The Pentecostals*, SCM Press 1972.

hymn in praise of the love that 'suffers long and is kind' and will
endure when prophecy and tongues are no more. The other chapter
preserves Paul's words about the Christian hope. They are founded
on the unshakable conviction that God raised Christ from the
grave and that he now lives and reigns till he 'has put all his
enemies under his feet' and God the Father consummates his
kingdom in glory.

One final comment on the letter as a whole. It is Christian
doctrine, supremely exemplified in the Cross, that God can bring
good out of evil. Wickedness like that in ancient Corinth is never
to be welcomed. But was it not almost worthwhile to have so
much wickedness in Corinth and all those schisms, questionings
and doubtings, in order to evoke from Paul those salutary words
on Christian unity, that call to curb one's Christian freedom if it
causes a weaker brother's downfall, that solemn reminder of the
original meaning of the Lord's Supper, that Song of Songs in
praise of Christian love, and those great and comfortable words
about the Christian hope?

Let us, as we close our study, hear some of them again:

What is sown is mortal,
What rises is immortal.
Sown inglorious,
It rises in glory;
Sown in weakness,
It rises in power;
Sown an animate body,
It rises a spiritual body ...

For this perishable nature must put on the imperishable, and
this mortal nature must put on immortality. When the imperishable puts on the imperishable, and the mortal puts on immortality, then shall come to pass the saying that is written: 'Death
is swallowed up in victory.' Thanks be to God who gives us the
victory through our Lord Jesus Christ (I Cor. 15.42-44,53-56).

14

The Trials and Triumphs of an Apostle

The letter is II Corinthians, but we might also have entitled it, more tersely, 'Apostolic Autobiography', for no letter of Paul's – not even Galatians – tells us more than this one about Paul himself. 'Here broken sharply off, with none of the jagged edges filed down, is a chunk of Paul's life – authentic, uncensored, bewilderingly complicated, but amazingly interesting.'[1] But, as the same writer, R. P. C. Hanson, says, reading II Corinthians is like turning on the radio in the middle of a difficult play. Characters are speaking, things are happening, but we cannot always be sure who the people are – the 'baddies' particularly – or what precisely is going on. Nevertheless, we are not wholly in the dark, for the letter itself lets fall a number of clues, and by a little detective work we can solve most of the major problems.

To begin with, we must recall and amplify what was already said about Paul's contacts and correspondence with Corinth. I Corinthians was written from Ephesus about AD 55. From Acts 20.1-3 we know that Paul later visited Corinth before going up to Jerusalem with the collection he had been making among his Gentile churches for the needy Christians in Judaea. But the clues in II Corinthians show that, between the writing of I Corinthians and that Acts 20 visit, Paul not only visited Corinth again but wrote at least one letter to it.

This is evidently what happened. After the receipt in Corinth of I Corinthians (and because of it?) some sort of rebellion against Paul's leadership broke out in the church of Corinth. It was led by some Jewish Christians (11.22f.) who called themselves 'apostles' (11.5; 12.11) and came with 'letters of introduction' (3.1). The

[1] R. P. C. Hanson, *II Corinthians*, SCM Press 1954, p. 7.

situation grew so bad that Paul was compelled to hurry from Ephesus to Corinth (2.1; 12.14; 13.1f.). But his visit was a very 'painful' one (2.1) and he had to return without quelling the revolt. Back in his base at Ephesus he resolved to see what writing could do; so he sent a 'severe' letter, ordering the Corinthians to mend their ways and deal with the rebels (2.3,4,9). His friend Titus carried this letter; and Paul, waiting anxiously for the result, moved from Ephesus to Troas and across the Aegean sea to Macedonia. There (2.13 and 7.13) Titus turned up, and the news he brought from Corinth sounded very reassuring. The situation had greatly improved. The Corinthians had punished a local trouble-maker (2.5-11), and rebellion had been replaced by genuine sorrow for what had happened. So Paul sat down and wrote a thankful letter to Corinth. This is our II Corinthians – or possibly II Cor. 1-9.

Why this hesitation? We spoke a moment ago of a 'severe letter'. Has any of it survived? Nobody who reads II Corinthians attentively can fail to note the abrupt change of tone that comes over the letter after the ninth chapter. Up till then Paul's tone has been one of thankful reconciliation. But with chapter 10 the thankfulness changes to a fierce defence of his apostleship and an equally fierce denunciation of some men as 'sham apostles' (II Cor. 11.13) and agents of the devil. If these four fierce chapters (10-13) were part of the thankful letter, must they not have defeated the eirenic purpose of the first nine chapters?

Accordingly (though there is no MS evidence for it), some hold that II Cor. 10-13 are a part of the 'severe letter' which followed the 'painful visit'. (The alternative explanation is that there was a break in the writing between chapters 1-9 and 10-13. The bitter tone of the last four chapters would then be explained by Paul's later receipt of bad news from Corinth.) If we take the first view, both the 'severe letter' and the 'thankful letter' must have been written fairly close to each other – let us say in the year 56.

II Corinthians may be analysed as follows:

1. Greetings and thanksgiving (1.1-11).
2. Paul's relations with the Corinthians (1.12-7.16).
   (a) Defence against the charge of fickleness (1.12-2.17).
   (b) The glory of the apostolic office (3.1-6.10).
   (c) Paul's reconciliation with his converts (6.11-7.16).
3. The collection for Jerusalem (8-9).

4. Paul's defence of his character and work (10.1-13.10).
5. Farewell and blessing (13.11-14).

Paraphrase

Dear people of God in Corinth:

God be praised for comforting us in all our troubles, and especially for delivering me in Asia when I despaired of life itself. You think me fickle because I had to change my plans for visiting you? Before God I protest I am not a man to say Yes or No in the same breath. (Christ, God's Son, is the Yes to all his promises.) Not fickleness but the wish to spare you a second painful visit made me change my plans (ch. 1).

My severe letter was really prompted by my love for you. The offender (the ringleader in the Corinthian revolt) I forgive, and I hope you will do so also – you have punished him enough. How worried I was when I reached Troas and found no Titus there! So on I went to Macedonia – and now I feel like singing a *Te Deum* to God who always leads us in triumph (ch. 2).

I need no letters of introduction, as some do. You Corinthians are my testimonials – a living letter written not with ink but with the Spirit of the living God, not on stone tables but on human hearts. God has made us ministers of a new dispensation, one of the Spirit, not of the letter, whose splendour quite eclipses the old one's. But, alas, when the scriptures are read, a veil still covers Jewish minds, for it has never dawned on them that in Christ the old covenant is done away (ch. 3).

In this ministry we toil bravely and honestly. It is a ministry of light against darkness – the light of God's splendour which once shone at creation and now shines in the face of Jesus Christ. Fragile folk the bearers of this gospel may be, but this only shows that its power is God's, not man's. Killing work it is, but God sustains us, even in the most desperate situations; but if in our bodies we show Christ's dying, we share the hope of the Resurrection, assured that present brief affliction preludes eternal glory (ch. 4).

A heavenly dwelling is prepared for us; but, whether at home with the Lord, or absent from him, our aim is to please him, remembering that he is to be our judge. Christ died in love for us all; in Christ God was reconciling the world to himself; and we are called as his ambassadors to preach his reconciling grace to all men (ch. 5).

So accept God's grace now, as you see how we apostles endure all kinds of suffering for your sake. Our heart is open to you. Won't you open yours to us? [Avoid sinful ties with unbelievers; keep yourselves from all that defiles flesh or spirit (6.14-7.1).][2] Open your hearts to us! We have wronged nobody, and you know how proud we are of you. How comforted I was when Titus met me in Macedonia, with all his good news from Corinth. Now I have no regrets about my severe letter – it made you repent and revived your zeal, and the joy of Titus confirmed my confidence in you (ch. 7).

Now about the collection. Despite their poverty the congregations in Macedonia have contributed splendidly. See that you do so, too. Remember how our Lord gave up his heavenly riches for your sake, and give all you can. You made the promise a year ago: well, fulfil it now, according to your resources. Titus and the two others who are going with him to Corinth have my full backing (ch. 8).

'Achaia has been ready since last year,' I have been telling the Macedonians. So have your gift ready before I come, and let it be generous. God loves a cheerful giver; and by this service you will glorify him, and the recipients will thank God for you (ch. 9).

Please don't force me when I come to deal sternly with my opponents. I am neither a coward nor a worldling as they say, but a spiritual warrior capturing every human thought for Christ. Are they saying, 'Paul can write powerful letters, but he has no personality and can't preach.' Then they will find out when I come that my presence can be as formidable as my pen. Are they saying that I am trespassing where I have no right? On the contrary, I keep to the sphere God gave me at Corinth (ch. 10).

Bear with me. My jealous love for you makes me fear you may be seduced from your single-minded devotion to Christ. How easily you let yourselves be hoodwinked by these superlative apostles! The fact that I supported myself in Corinth and sponged on no one shows up these charlatans in their true colours. You take so much abuse from them that you cannot object to a little bravado from me. Well, then, I am as good a Jew as they – and who among them can boast a record of beatings and dangers for the gospel like mine (ch. 11)?

[2] Possibly a fragment of the 'previous letter' mentioned in I Cor. 5.9.

On this business of boasting, I could tell you of my rapture, fourteen years ago, into the third heaven, when I heard words not to be repeated by human lips; but I prefer to tell you how the Lord used my thorn in the flesh to lead me into a deeper knowledge of his grace. Yet you forced this bragging on me; for if ever a man did the work of a genuine apostle among you, that man was I. Now, ready for my third visit to Corinth, I protest my honesty and my love for you; though I fear I may find the same old sins rife among you (ch. 12).

On this third visit I warn you that I will discipline all offenders, and you will find Christ's power as well as his weakness in me his servant.

All God's people here greet you, and may Christ's grace, God's love, and the Spirit's fellowship be with you (ch. 13).

Despite its difficulty, this letter has its great moments. Some of them come in chapters 4 to 6 where Paul describes the griefs and glories of the apostolic ministry. Here we see what suffering may mean to one who finds the key to the world's riddle in Christ, and who knows that God works with him for good even in the bitterest experiences. Paul sees the killing strain of this ministry as the life of the Crucified One extended in the suffering of his servant. The result of suffering so borne is as sure as what happened on the first Easter morning. The God who raised Jesus from the dead will raise us also. So *nil desperandum*! Our brief affliction preludes an eternal weight of glory, of which the Holy Spirit in our hearts is the first instalment. Christ's love has us in its grip. If any man is 'in Christ', he is a new being. Christ died, the sinless one, by God's appointing, to reconcile a sinful world, and we are his ambassadors calling men to be reconciled to him.

Paul wrote many fine passages but this one just summarized (4.7-5.21), must rank among his greatest. No less magnificent are the words in which he describes all that is involved in being a servant of God and an apostle of Christ:

Honour and dishonour, praise and blame, are alike our lot: we are the impostors who speak the truth, the unknown men whom all men know; dying we still live on; disciplined by suffering, we are not done to death; in our sorrows we have always cause for joy; poor ourselves, we bring wealth to many; penniless, we own the world (6.8-10 NEB).

15

Christian Freedom

'The Epistle to the Galatians', said Martin Luther, 'is my epistle; I have betrothed myself to it; it is my wife.' It is not hard to understand Luther's affection for this short, passionate and difficult letter. Like Paul, Luther was a liberator; and when you pierce down beneath the historical accidents to the essentials, you discover they were fighting much the same battle – a battle for Christian freedom. The issues in that battle will become clearer as we proceed.

Nobody has ever doubted that Paul wrote this letter. But our learned men still do not agree on two points: who the Galatians were, and precisely when the letter was written.

The older view, still held by many, is that Paul uses the word 'Galatia' (1.2) in its *geographical* sense. (Here the reader must pause and get a map of Paul's world open before him.) The modern view, associated with the name of Sir William Ramsay, is that he uses the word in its *political* sense. If the first view is right, Paul was addressing Christian communities in places like Ancyra (modern Ankara) in the old northern kingdom of Galatia where some roving Gauls had settled in the third century BC. If the second view is right, by 'Galatia' Paul means the Roman province of that name, founded in 25 BC, which included, besides the old kingdom, parts of Lycaonia, Pisidia and Phrygia. In the south of this province lay Antioch, Iconium, Lystra and Derbe, evangelized by Paul and Barnabas during their first missionary journey (Acts 13-14).

We cannot settle the matter by appealing to the two passages in Acts (16.6 and 18.23) which describe Paul's visits to the regions of Galatia; for both parties – the 'North Galatianists' and the 'South Galatianists', as they are called – can plausibly interpret them to

suit their own views. The question must be answered on the basis
of other considerations.

How do the 'North Galatianists' support their case?

1. For Luke, in Acts, Pisidia, Phrygia and Lycaonia are
geographical terms. *Ergo*, in Paul's letter Galatia must be the
same.

2. In Acts, Luke does not call Antioch, Lystra and Derbe cities
of Galatia. So why should Paul have done so?

3. The fickleness of the Galatians, as evidenced by Paul's letter
(1.6, etc), agrees well with their Gallic origin.

The 'South Galatianists' advance the following arguments:

1. There is no clear evidence that Paul ever went to the old
kingdom of Galatia – a wild country with poor communications
and hardly open enough for Paul's opponents to have dogged his
footsteps there.

2. In his letter (2.1,9,13) Paul assumes that Barnabas was well-
known to his readers (as he was to the cities of South Galatia); and
it is possible that Gal. 4.14 ('You welcomed me as if I were an
angel of God') refers to the incident at Lystra recorded in Acts
14.12.

3. Paul, the Roman citizen, usually thinks in terms of Roman
provinces, and must be doing so in this letter.

The question is not finally settled, but the evidence for the
'South Galatian' view is undoubtedly the stronger.

Still harder to settle is the date of the letter. On the 'North
Galatian' view, it was written after the visit of Acts 18.23, i.e.
during Paul's third missionary journey (AD 53-56). On the 'South
Galatian' view, it could have been written either before or after
the apostolic council of Acts 15 (probable date AD 49). Those who
put it after, and date it about 55, stress the theological similarity
between Galatians and Romans written from Corinth about 57.
This is a dubious argument. True, in both Galatians and Romans
Paul teaches justification by faith, not by works of the Law. But
the discussion of it in Galatians sounds like 'fighting talk' when
the battle was fiercest. In Romans the heat has gone out of the
argument and Paul expounds his doctrine in measured tones.

But the really strong argument for putting Galatians before the
council is the letter's complete silence about the apostolic decree
of Acts 15. This settled the point at issue in Galatia, viz. that
Gentile converts need not be circumcised. If Paul had been writing

after the council, all he needed to do was to quote the council's decision and end the controversy.

Our view is therefore that Paul was writing *before* the council. If this is right, the letter is to be dated 48-49. It may have been written at Antioch, or even on the way up to Jerusalem for the council. It would thus become the earliest of Paul's letters.

The occasion of the letter is not doubtful. Since Paul had left Galatia, certain 'Judaizers' (Jewish Christians anxious to preserve Jewish customs) had appeared there and were persuading Paul's converts that circumcision and observance of the Law of Moses were essential to Christianity. This flatly contradicted Paul's gospel; so the Judaizers were at pains to vilify Paul's credentials as an apostle, by saying that he was a trimmer or, at best, a second-hand apostle who had learned everything from Peter and James. Paul wrote at once, and in great passion, to counteract this Judaizing propaganda, to assert his apostolic independence, and to explain the deepest principles of his gospel. These were, as the New English Bible rightly says, 'faith and freedom'.

1. *The letter paraphrased*

(*Chs. 1-2 contain Paul's declaration of his apostolic independence.*)

Paul, an apostle by God's appointment, not man's, to the congregations in Galatia.

How quickly you have gone back on your call and exchanged the gospel of God's grace for another! A curse on all who pervert it! (Are these the accents of a trimmer?) My gospel was no human invention – it came to me through a revelation of Jesus Christ. I was a perfervid Jew persecuting the church till God revealed his Son to me. Did I then consult the Jerusalem apostles? No, I went to Arabia, and it was three years before I paid a fortnight's visit to Jerusalem, where I met only Peter and James the Lord's brother. Then I was off to Syria and Cilicia (ch. 1).

Fourteen years after, with Barnabas and Titus, I again visited Jerusalem and submitted my gospel to the authorities. (If Titus was circumcised, I made no sacrifice of principle to the false brethren.) The pillars of the mother church approved the gospel that I preach; indeed, James, Peter and John gave us their blessing, and agreed that, while they worked in the home field, Barnabas and I should go to the foreign. One request they made, that we should remember their poor, a thing I made it my business to do.

Later, at Antioch, I openly opposed Peter. At first he had fra-
ternized with Gentile Christians, but he drew back when James's
men arrived from Jerusalem. I said to him, 'If you, a Jew, live
like a Gentile, why do you compel Gentiles to live like Jews?'.
Jews though we are, we know that acceptance with God comes
not by doing the Law but by believing in Christ. Doing the Law
will never put a man right with God. For myself, I have done with
the Law, and my life is one of trust in God's Son who died for me
(ch. 2).

You senseless Galatians, tell me what produced your Christian
experience. Was it observance of the Law or faith in Christ?
Faith of this kind is as old as Abraham. Because Abraham took
God at his word and obeyed, God accepted him; and, as we have
a faith like this, we are Abraham's true sons. The Law, which
nobody can fully keep, exposes us to God's curse. But Christ's
death has delivered us from it, and God's blessing is now open
to the Gentiles.

A human will and testament cannot be set aside once it is rati-
fied. No more can God's covenant with its promise. His covenant
with Abraham had Christ in view, and cannot be annulled by a
law which came 430 years after it. The purpose of the Law, a
temporary measure, was to make wrong-doing a legal offence; but
it was impotent to give life. Custody under the Law was a stage on
the way to the realization of God's promise which makes us all
alike, in Christ, God's sons and heirs (ch. 3).

Once, we resembled children under guardians and trustees; now,
our minority at an end, we have, through God's gift of his own
Son, been adopted into God's family. Why then do you want to
revert to your old religious slavery, with all its fussing over special
days and seasons?

Take my line, I beg you. How kind you were to me, a sick man,
on my first visit! Why have you now left me for these false
flatterers? See, I am like a mother in labour with you over again
till you take the shape of Christ.

Why, the very Law you rely on shows you wrong. You remember the Genesis story of Abraham's two sons? Sarah and her son
(Isaac) prefigure the religion of freedom; Hagar and hers (Ish-
mael), the religion of slavery. Like Isaac, you are children of the
promise and meant for freedom (ch. 4).

(*In chs. 5-6 Paul comes to the practical issues.*)

Christ set us free, to be free men. Freedom then, but not licence to indulge your lower nature! Live not by that nature but by the Spirit – you will know them by their fruits. Those who indulge their lower nature can never be saved; so let the Spirit bring forth in you its harvest of love, joy, jeace and all the rest (ch. 5).

Please restore an erring brother very gently, and by bearing each others' burdens fulfil the law of Christ.[1] Give yourselves no airs, and test your own work. Let the catechumen share his material blessings with his teacher. God is not to be fooled: a man reaps what he sows; so cultivate the harvest of the Spirit, and not that of your lower nature. One brings life, the other death. And let us never tire of doing good to all, especially the members of God's family.

Mark my big letters! I am now writing to you in my own hand. The circumcisers are interested only in externals. Why, they do not even keep the Law themselves. All they desire is to glory in your flesh. But all I want to glory in is the Cross of Christ which has changed everything for me. What matters is not marks in the flesh but the making of new men. Peace and mercy be on all who take this way, and on the whole Israel of God.

As for my troublers, let them note the marks of Christ's ownership branded in my body. I defy them all.

The grace of our Lord Jesus Christ be with you (ch. 6).

2. *The message of Galatians*

The question handled in Galatians is this: What makes a man a Christian? Is it circumcision and keeping the Law, or faith in Christ? Paul's answer is in 5.6: 'External things like circumcision do not matter. What matters is faith in Christ that works through love.'

This is part of the bigger question. How is a man to get right with God? Is it by keeping the Law – in modern terms, by keeping the Ten Commandments and living according to the Sermon on the Mount, etc., etc.? No, these things we ought to do, but we never fully can. No man can, by his own moral exertions, put himself right with God. The way to acceptance with God is not by 'works' – what we might call 'ethical heroics' – but by faith in Christ who has

[1] That is, the design for Christian living Christ gives us in his teaching.

died for our sins. And real goodness is the *result*, and not the pre-requisite, of our faith. The Christian life is not the punctilious observance of a mass of rules but living according to 'the law of Christ', by the help of the Spirit.

The precise issues of Galatians – 'except you be circumcised you cannot be saved' – are long dead ones; but the message of the letter is not out of date. Whenever any religious rite is made co-ordinate with faith in Christ as the condition of salvation, this letter becomes a sword of the Spirit to strike down the error. Salvation is by faith in Christ alone. Small wonder Galatians has been called 'the epistle of Christian freedom' and 'the Magna Carta of evangelical Christianity'.

16

The Glory of Christ in the Church

Were an opinion poll held to decide the greatest of Paul's letters, though most would choose Romans, some would plump for Ephesians. Calvin called it his favourite epistle; Coleridge pronounced it 'one of the divinest compositions of man'; and in our day Dr John Mackay of Princeton has confessed, 'To this book I owe my life'.[1]

1. *The authenticity of the letter*

After these tributes, it is a shock to some when they learn that a number of modern scholars refuse the letter to the one man in the early church apparently capable of writing Ephesians, and ascribe it to an imitator of Paul's – a 'Paulinist', as they call him. Why has Paul's authorship of Ephesians been doubted?

First, because of its style and vocabulary. Ephesians contains some 90 words not found elsewhere in Paul. When it is replied that the shorter Colossians (generally admitted to be Paul's) has 56 such words, they retort that the writer of Ephesians uses words like 'body', 'fullness' and 'mystery', which occur also in Colossians, in a different sense. When this is challenged, they point us to its long involved sentences which, they say, are uncharacteristic of Paul. (Have they forgotten say, Rom. 3.21-26; Col. 1.3-8 or Philemon 8-14, or considered that the language of prayer and meditation – such as we find in Ephesians – inevitably differs from the more direct question-and-answer style of, say, I Corinthians?)

Since the test of style is admittedly inconclusive, the doubters turn next to the *theology* of Ephesians. Here, they say, we have

[1] See his book *God's Order*, Nisbet 1948, where he expounds the message of Ephesians in modern terms.

the doctrine of the church universal and ecumenical, something beyond Paul's spiritual ken. But is it? Are there not anticipations of it in I Cor. 10.32; 12.28; 15.9, as well as in Colossians? Paul undoubtedly held and taught the doctrine of the church's universal mission. What we have in Ephesians is the natural and logical development of his earlier thinking.

Finally, the doubters appeal to the *literary links* between Colossians and Ephesians. More than one third of the words and phrases in Colossians reappear in Ephesians, and this or that passage in Ephesians seems patterned on a corresponding one in Colossians. Here they invite us to see the copying hand of a disciple of Paul's. But the alleged copying is done with such freedom and subtlety that other people draw the opposite conclusion – in favour of Paul's authorship. (How many modern theological writers or preachers, being invited to write or speak on a subject they have handled in an earlier book or sermon, 'fall back on former trains of thought', yet vary their treatment to suit the new occasion!) Besides, say the defenders of Paul's authorship, if Ephesians was written soon after Colossians (and Tychicus carried both letters), would not the phrases of his earlier letter have still been running in Paul's head?

At this point we may state the positive case for the defence. First, we may ask the deniers of Paul's authorship what is the point of the reference to Tychicus (Eph. 6.21f.; cf. Col. 4.7; Acts 20.4)? It has all the marks of genuineness. Second, out of 618 short phrases in Ephesians, no less than 550 have parallels in the other Pauline letters. Third, if Paul does not in Ephesians stress the importance of the Jewish-Gentile controversy, this is because he is addressing largely Gentile readers (see Eph. 2.11-13). Fourth, let us remember the complete unanimity of the early church about Paul's authorship. The doubt is quite modern. And, fifth, if the letter is not Paul's we must posit the existence in the early church of 'a great unknown' who was Paul's spiritual peer. (We are almost left in the position of the schoolboy who was being introduced to the Homeric question and said that, as far as he could see, Homer was not written by Homer but by another man of the same name – and the same genius.)

The American scholar H. J. Cadbury has summed up the whole debate in one question: 'Which is more likely – that an imitator of Paul in the first century composed a writing ninety or ninety-five per cent in accordance with Paul's style, or that Paul himself wrote a letter diverging five or ten per cent from his usual style?'[2] The burden of proof lies with those who deny Paul's authorship. Since they have failed to prove their case, we do well to follow tradition and ascribe the letter to Paul.

But was Ephesians really addressed specifically to the Christians in Ephesus? The question is raised by two features in the letter itself. First, our oldest and best MSS omit the words 'in Ephesus' (1.1). Second, the writer does not seem to know his readers personally (Eph. 1.15 and 3.2), as Paul knew the Christians in Ephesus. The natural explanation is to see in Ephesians a *circular letter* sent by Paul to the Gentile churches in Asia. This would explain the lack of the words 'in Ephesus' in the oldest MSS, and the absence of personal greetings to individuals at the end. In the original letter Paul would leave a blank space in the salutation, and it would be the duty of Tychicus, who carried the letter, to fill in the appropriate place-names, as he took it round the various churches.

2. *The letter itself*

Few of Paul's letters are easier to analyse than this. It falls into two parts, the first theological, and second ethical, thus:

Salutation (1.1-2).
Doctrinal section (1.3-3.21). Here the theme is God's eternal purpose for man manifested in Christ and the church.
Ethical section (4.1-6.20). Here we learn what church membership means for daily living.
Conclusion (6.21-24).

The ordinary man who reads this letter in the Authorized Version will undoubtedly find it 'hard going'. To get the hang of it, he should therefore use a modern translation like the NEB; for the long sentences and the archaic diction of the King James Version make up a pretty daunting combination. To take one example only: the opening doxology ('Blessed be the God and Father of our Lord Jesus Christ, etc.') has no fewer than 258 words, with phrases in it like 'the dispensation of the fullness of times' and 'the redemption of the purchased possession', well calculated to bewilder him. Let him turn to the NEB, and he will find that drawn-out doxology split up into seven short sentences and a phrase like 'the fullness

[2] *New Testament Studies* 5, 1959, pp. 91ff.

of times' simplified into 'when the time was ripe'.

The other service we can do the ordinary reader is to try to put Paul's thoughts into modern terms (mostly those of the NEB), and this we now propose to do.

In II Cor. 5.19 Paul had summed up the purpose of God's sending Christ to men in the words, 'In Christ God was reconciling the world to himself'. In Ephesians Paul spells out God's plan for the world in Christ and the church.

'In Christ ... a plan ... to unite' (Eph. 1.9f. RSV). These six words from the opening doxology sound quite modern and ecumenical. As they stand, they might suggest the theme for a conference on how to heal our unhappy denominational divisions, which so weaken the witness of Christ's church to men. But Paul is thinking of something bigger, about God's plan for humanity's reunion in Christ – what Tennyson prayed for in his *In Memoriam*, 'the Christ that is to be'. God's purpose in Christ, Paul says, is a unity designed to embrace not only the world but the whole universe (cf. 3.10).

But now to God's plan itself as outlined in Ephesians. We have already noted that of the letter's six chapters, the first three supply the theology, the last three the ethics. The theology may be summed up in one sentence of C. H. Dodd's: 'It is the glory of the church as the society which embodies in history the eternal purpose of God revealed in Christ.'[3] Can we make this still clearer by teasing out the thought of Eph. 1-3 in three paragraphs, using many of Paul's own words?

(*a*) The ultimate reality is the 'one God and father of us all'. Through Christ he 'has destined us in love to be his sons' (1.5), and he purposes community for all his creatures (1.10). But the world – and indeed the cosmos – has a great rift at its heart, with sinful men at odds with each other and desperately divided, and superhuman forces – demonic 'principalities and powers' – disrupting the order which God intended for his creation. That fatal rift – that estrangement and hostility – in the universe man cannot himself repair. Only God can, and it is his purpose to subdue all evil forces – human and superhuman – so as to create a great unity.

(*b*) This plan is *centred in Christ*. The gospel is the good news of God's 'mystery', or unveiled secret (1.9 etc.), i.e. the hidden

[3] F. C. Eiselen, E. Lewis and D. G. Downey (eds.), *The Abingdon Bible Commentary*, Epworth Press 1929, p. 1222.

purpose of God now disclosed. It is embodied in Christ, who is not only the Messiah of the Jews but God's reconciling agent for the whole human race. When 'the time was ripe' (1.10). God put his plan into effect by sending Christ to die for men's sins, raising him from the dead and enthroning him in heaven where he now reigns above all possible authorities and powers (1.20f.). What God planned in Christ was nothing less than the reconciliation of all his rebellious subjects to himself, and to one another.

(c) It is *through the church* that God's plan is now being realized (3.9f.). The church, which draws its life from Christ its ascended head (1.22; 4.15; 5.23), is his working body (1.23; 4.12; 5.23) – the society meant to execute God's saving purpose among men. What God wills in Christ, through his church, is fellowship – belongingness in the same body. In that fellowship 'the middle wall of partition' (2.14),[4] i.e. the Jewish Law which once separated Gentiles from Jews, has now been broken down by Christ's sacrificial death (2.13,16): with the enmity between them killed, Gentiles, once 'far off' in 'a world without hope and without God' (2.12), are now 'no longer aliens in a foreign land, but fellow-citizens with God's people and members of God's household' (2.19). But this healing of an age-old rift is a prelude to something still vaster – the movement under God of the whole universe to an ultimate unity in Christ (1.10). When this comes to pass, there will be 'a single new humanity' (2.15), enjoying access through Christ to the Father (2.18) and forming a great living temple for 'a habitat of God through the Spirit' (2.22).

The bulk of this sublime theology comes in the first two chapters. In the third, after touching on the grace of God which granted him 'the privilege of proclaiming to the Gentiles the good news of the unfathomable riches of Christ' and God's great plan disclosed in it, Paul ends with a noble prayer for his readers:

> With this in mind, then, I kneel in prayer to the Father, from whom every family in heaven and on earth takes its name, that out of the treasures of his glory he may grant you strength and

---

[4] In the Temple area at Jerusalem stood a stone fence, five feet high, separating the Court of the Gentiles from the inner precincts. Notices on it, one of which was discovered in 1871, warned the intruding Gentile that, if he crossed it, he was liable to death. That fence symbolized the hostility between Jew and Gentile.

power through his Spirit in your inner being, that through faith Christ may dwell in your hearts in love. With deep roots and firm foundations, may you be strong to grasp, with all God's people, what is the breadth and length and height and depth of the love of Christ, and to know it, though it is beyond knowledge. So may you attain to fullness of being, the fullness of God himself (3.14-19 NEB).

But truth in the New Testament is always 'truth in order to goodness'. So, in the second half of his letter, Paul tells his readers (and us) how they are to conduct themselves if they are to 'live up to their calling' (4.1). The church's marching orders are in fact four, and we may apply them to ourselves.

First: By Christian gentleness and forbearance, and by the use of the various gifts the ascended Christ has given us, we are to 'build up the body of Christ' (4.12) so that 'we all at last attain to the unity inherent in our faith and our knowledge of the Son of God' who is the head of the church and on whom the whole body depends (4.13ff.).

Second: We are to 'give up living like pagans with their good-for-nothing notions', and, as renewed men, forgive one another as God in Christ forgave us, seeking always as God's dear children to live in self-spending love like Christ's (4.17-5.1).

Third: We are to build Christian homes – homes where 'reverence for Christ' will produce among the members of the household (husbands and wives, parents and children, masters and slaves) that deference, honour, obedience, service and forbearance which will make the family a little miniature of the church (5.21-6.9).

Fourth: In the struggle confronting the church in the world we must put on the spiritual armour which God supplies – the belt of truth, the chain-mail of integrity, the shoes of the gospel of peace, the shield of faith, the helmet of salvation, the Word of God which the Spirit supplies – these, with the power of prayer, are the weapons to equip Christians to fight the battle of the Lord against the devil and all his minions. And the end in view is nothing less than a Christian empire growing under God until it unites all men under the sovereignty of Christ the Lord (6.10-20).

Thus Christ's 'ambassador in chains', as Paul calls himself, draws his letter to a close. No book in the New Testament is more relevant to the task which confronts the church in the world today in its fight against all the devilries abroad in the earth. It holds out the vision of a united church being truly the working body of Christ, and of its mission to bind all nations in a brotherhood of worship and of love under 'the God and Father of our Lord Jesus Christ'. It calls to men cowering behind their ideological iron-curtains and living a kind of barbed-wire existence, 'Unite – or perish'. And to those who fight under Christ's banner it says, 'Onward Christian soldiers'.

17

A Paean from Prison

About thirty years ago, just after Martin Niemöller had been thrown into a concentration camp because he chose to obey God rather than Hitler, I was privileged to hear a letter which he wrote to an Oxford friend. One sentence of it stuck in my memory: 'In the old days I used to be a bearer of the gospel,' wrote Niemöller, 'now that gospel is bearing me.' That sentence and the serenity of the whole letter are all I remember. But when I first heard it, it reminded me of nothing so much as Paul's Letter to the Philippians.

This was not surprising, for the circumstances which led to the writing of both letters were similar. The place of writing was in each a state prison, as the writers of both letters were ambassadors of Christ imprisoned for their loyalty to their Lord.

It is the earlier letter, probably written about AD 62,[1] that forms the subject of this chapter. In some ways Philippians is the most beautiful of his letters. It is also one of the simplest, and anyone who wishes to make a study of Paul's letters might well begin with this one.

1. *How the letter came to be written*

A glance at the map will show that Philippi is a town of Macedonia in north-east Greece. A famous town, too. Named after Philip of Macedon, father of Alexander the Great, it had been the scene of

---

[1] See the earlier discussion (pp. 92f.) of the Ephesian theory concerning the prison Epistles. Personal allusions in Phil. like, 'To live is Christ and to die is gain' (1.21), or, 'If my life blood is to crown that sacrifice which is the offering of your faith' (2.17 NEB), Paul's retrospect on his life as a Christian (3.7-14), and the reference to what he has learned from experience (4.11-13), all suggest that the letter comes from a late date in Paul's ministry.

one of the decisive battles of history. My map has crossed swords on it at the spot and the words 'Death-bed of the Roman Republic'. There, in 42 BC, the Republicans, Brutus and Cassius, who had murdered Caesar met their doom at the hands of the man who was destined to be Roman Emperor when Christ was born, Augustus. Not long after the battle, the victors had turned Philippi into a Roman colony (cf. Phil. 3.20: 'We are a colony of heaven' – Moffatt) and settled many of their veterans there. But,

> The tumult and the shouting dies
> The captains and the kings depart,

and no fanfare of trumpets heralded the arrival there, some ninety years later, of a little man known today to thousands who may never have heard of Philip or Augustus.

It was in the course of his second missionary journey that Paul and his coadjutors crossed the Aegean Sea and landed in Europe, not far from Philippi. The story of how Paul began work in Philippi is told in Acts 16. The narrative, which is one of Luke's best, culminates in the imprisonment of Paul and Silas in the local gaol, their providential release by an earthquake, and the conversion of their gaoler. Thus Paul sowed the seed of the gospel in Philippi, and a fine harvest it was to yield. In a few years there had sprung up a congregation which Paul called 'My joy, my crown' (Phil. 4.1).

So the years went by; once again Paul visited Philippi (Acts 20.1,6); and though the young church did not escape persecution (1.29f.) or trouble-makers (3.2ff.), the cause of the gospel prospered. At length Paul was arrested in Jerusalem, and, after two years' detention in Caesarea, was sent to Rome to stand his trial before Caesar. Even in that ancient world, without a decent postal service, news travelled fast, and one day the Philippian Christians heard with dismay of Paul's plight. So 'they put the hat round for him', as we would say, and not long after there arrived in Rome a Christian called Epaphroditus with news from Philippi – and a present for Paul. 'It was kind of you to share my trouble,' he said gratefully (4.14). Unfortunately, Epaphroditus fell seriously ill and he had to stay on in Rome. When he recovered, Paul wrote a letter of thanks for the messenger to take back to Philippi. This is the letter we are now studying.

2. *The letter*

Let us paraphrase it briefly.

My dear fellow-Christians in Philippi, with all the office-bearers there, Timothy and I send you greetings. Grace and peace be with you from God our Father and the Lord Jesus Christ.

I never say my prayers without thanking God for you and your fellowship in the gospel. God knows how I am longing for you all and praying that you may grow in love and wisdom.

You ask for news about myself. Strangely enough, my imprisonment has meant the progress of the gospel and more preaching of Christ. True, not all are doing it from the purest of motives, but the main thing is that it is being done. I believe I shall be released. But what matters is that Christ shall be honoured in my person – whether in life or in death. I am torn two ways and don't know which to prefer. To die and go to be with Christ would be better for me, to stay on in the body would be better for you. And this, I think, is what will happen, and you will see me again. However, whether I come or not, you must live worthily of the gospel, standing firmly together for the faith and undismayed by your foes. Like myself, God has granted you the privilege not only of believing in Christ but of suffering for his sake (ch. 1).

Now a word about these little rifts in your fellowship. By all your best Christian instincts I urge you to fill my cup of joy full by agreeing among yourselves. Think of others and be truly humble – like Christ himself who freely gave up the glory of heaven and chose the path of earthly humiliation, even to death on a cross. Therefore God highly exalted him and gave him the name above all other names.

Work out your own salvation; God is with you in it all. On judgment day I shall be proud of you. Even if I have to sacrifice my life now, I rejoice and I bid you do likewise.

Now about my plans. Timothy I hope to send to you soon. He is devoted to you, and I have no trustier friend. But I am confident I will come myself ere long. With this letter I am sending back your messenger Epaphroditus. How worried he was when you heard he was ill! But God mercifully spared him. Give him a worthy welcome, for he risked his life to render me the service you could not give (ch. 2).

Finally, brethren, rejoice! I was about to close but will repeat what I said before. Beware of these dogs of Judaizers who would like to have you circumcised! Outward marks and privileges are what they take pride in. If it came to that, I could brag about my privileges as a member of the chosen people as much as anyone. But when I became a Christian, I gladly forfeited them all. To know the power of Christ's risen life and share his suffering is the supreme blessing. Not that I feel myself already at the goal, but my one aim is to win the prize of God's high calling in Christ.

So follow my example. Christ has many enemies, sensual and earthly fellows whose doom is ruin. But we are a colony of heaven, and we wait for our Saviour Christ to transfigure our lowly bodies into heavenly ones like his own (ch. 3).

Stand firm, my dear people, in the Lord. Make it up, you two quarrelling women! Rejoice in the Lord! I will say it again, rejoice! Be forbearing to all; have no anxiety; bring all your needs to God in prayer, and give him thanks. His peace shall guard you. Lastly, take account of what is noble wherever you find it.

I was greatly heartened by your practical remembrance of me. Not that I ever complain of want; for no matter what the circumstances, I have learned the secret of contentment, and in union with Christ I am able for anything. Yet thank you for your gift – not the first you have sent me. With it I have enough, and more than enough. My God shall supply all your wants.

Give my greetings to each one of God's people. The brothers here, especially those who belong to the imperial establishment, send their greetings.

The grace of our Lord be with you all (ch. 4).

PAUL

3. *The value of the letter*

Philippians is full of good things: great utterances about the faith, and intimate little touches which reveal the man Paul.

'For me to live is Christ,' he says, 'and to die is gain' (1.21). This is how the world and life and death appear to this Christ-captured man. Or he will invest the lowliest Christian virtue with the loftiest of sanctions – the example of Christ, who though he was rich for our sakes became poor (2.6-11).[2] Or in a couple of verses (3.20f.)

---

[2] It is now widely held that Phil. 2.6-11 is an early – perhaps the earliest – Christian hymn. See my *Paul and His Predecessors*, SCM Press 1961, pp. 39-44.

he will express the Christian hope: 'Our commonwealth is in heaven, and from it we await a Saviour, the Lord Jesus Christ, who will change our lowly body to be like his glorious body, by the power which enables him even to subject all things to himself.' Or – possibly in answer to the Philippians who had asked what should be their attitude to what was good in the pagan society around them – he will write a golden sentence like this: 'All that rings true, all that commands reverence, and all that makes for right; all that is pure, all that is lovely, all that is gracious in the telling; virtue and merit, wherever virtue and merit are found, take these things into your account' (4.8: Knox).

But the dominant note of the letter is joy. As Bengel said, 'The sum of the epistle is: I rejoice; do you rejoice.' No fewer than sixteen times do the words 'joy' or 'rejoice' occur in it. It is a paean from prison. If, as Baron von Hügel once told the Quaker Rufus Jones, the supreme mark of the saint is 'radiance amid the strain and stress of life', no man has a better right to the title than Paul.

Note on the unity of Philippians

Up to 3.1 Paul's tone is conciliatory and encouraging. But here two things give us pause. First, Paul writes 'finally', as though closing his letter. And, second, he explodes into a denunciation of the Judaizers. Some scholars therefore hold that Philippians contains bits of two letters. 3.2-4.23 is a letter of warning and thanks which Paul sent to Philippi soon after the arrival of Epaphroditus. 1.1-3.1 is the letter Paul gave him to take back home to Philippi. But this theory of partition is hardly necessary. The Greek words (*to loipon*) rendered 'finally' may be merely a phrase of transition: 'And so'. In the second place, sudden changes of tone in a letter of Paul's are not unparalleled. All we need to explain Paul's 'explosion' here is the receipt of bad news about the work of the Judaizers in Philippi. The case for partition is not proved. We may well maintain the unity of the letter.

18

The Cosmic Christ

Christ the divine centre and spiritual end to which the whole evolving cosmos is moving – this, briefly, was the creed of that remarkable scientist-priest, Teilhard de Chardin (1881-1955), whose books, banned by his church while he lived, are now being read all over the world. For Teilhard, the risen and ubiquitous Christ was the unifying principle of all movement and the goal and crown of the evolutionary process. But the man first to express this 'Christo-cosmic' view of the world was Paul writing to the Colossians. In Christ 'the image of the invisible God', he said, 'all things are held together: the whole universe has been created through and for him' (Col. 1.15-17 NEB). Under the providence of God, heresies can have their happy by-products; for it was the outbreak of heresy in Colossae that led Paul to give Christ the freedom of the universe, to set him forth as the cosmic Christ.

To start with, however, we had better concentrate not on the cosmos but on Colossae. If you locate Ephesus on the map and then let your eye travel inland a hundred miles due east, you will find the towns of Laodicea, Hierapolis and Colossae, all lying in the valley of the river Lycus. Hierapolis and Laodicea, both mentioned in Col. 4.13, stood on either side of the valley, with the river between. A dozen miles up river, and straddling it, lay Colossae, with a population mainly Gentile, though it also had many Jews.

The founder of the church there was probably Epaphras (1.7; 4.12). The result of Paul's three years' work in Ephesus had been to create what we should call a diocese rather than a congregation. And doubtless it was men from the Lycus valley, converted by Paul's preaching, who had started the little Christian communities inland. But Epaphras was not Paul's only friend in Colossae. Philemon lived there, and Archippus was evidently one of the local pastors (Col. 4.17; Philemon 2). Thus, though Paul had never set foot in Colossae (Col. 2.1), he was deeply interested in the church there, as also in the sister-church at Laodicea (4.16).

One day, while he lay in his Roman prison (AD 60-62), Epaphras arrived reporting the outbreak of serious heresy in the Colossian congregation. From the clues Paul supplies in his letter the general nature of the heresy may be inferred. It was a theosophy in which Judaism, Gnosticism (the pagan 'higher thought' of the time) and Christianity were blended in a strange hotch-potch. The heresy had Jewish features, because we read about a preoccupation with new moons, festivals, sabbaths and angel-worship (2.16,18). Equally, it had Gnostic traits, since Paul speaks of a pernicious 'philosophy' (2.8) trafficking in 'delusive speculations' and concerned with 'the elemental spirits of the world'. Moreover, the heretics' stress on 'self-mortification' and 'severity to the body', i.e. asceticism (2.20-23), suggests the Gnostic doctrine that matter is something evil with which God – or his worshippers – can have no contact. (Note: if you believe that matter, and therefore your bodies, are intrinsically evil, you may take one of two ways. Either you keep your body in check by rigorous asceticism, or you argue that, since the body is evil, it does not matter what you do.) Hence the heretics seem to have 'dreamed up' a hierarchy of spirit-mediators, or powers, strung out between the high God and the world – a system in which Christ had a place, but not the supreme one.

The errors of the heretics were therefore christological and ethical. On the one hand, they were scaling down the person and work of Christ, robbing him of his uniqueness. On the other, they were forcing on their fellow-Christians a false asceticism accompanied by futile food taboos – 'Do not handle this, do not taste that, do not touch the other'. So, in the first and christological part of his reply, Paul had to tell his readers that Christ was the totality,[1] or complete fullness, of God, and had done all that was needed for their saving: and, in the second and ethical part, that the Christian life means not a despising of God's good gifts but a clean break with the bad old pagan life and a new one in union with the risen and regnant Christ.

[1] Greek: *plēroma*, probably one of the words used by the heretics.

We may analyse the letter thus:

1. Salutation and thanksgiving (1.1-12).
2. The person of Christ and his work (1.13-2.7).
3. Warning against heretics (2.8-23).
4. The new life in Christ (3.1-4.6).
5. Greetings and blessing (4.7-18).

1. *The letter paraphrased*

Paul and Timothy to the Christians at Colossae: I thank God for your Christian faith and love founded on the heavenly hope of the gospel, now spreading in all the world. Epaphras has told us of your love, and I pray that you may grow in goodness and live worthily of him who rescued us out of the domain of darkness into the realm of his dear Son.

Christ, the image of the unseen God, was in being before creation; the visible and the invisible worlds owe their being to him, as creation was through and for him. Moreover, as death's first conqueror, he is head of the church, which forms his body. God in his fullness chose to dwell in him and, by means of the Cross, to reconcile all warring elements in the universe. Once estranged from God, you share in that reconciliation – provided that you hold fast your faith and hope.

So I rejoice to have my part in the sufferings of Christ for his church. God has revealed to me his long-hidden secret – I mean, 'Christ in you, the hope of glory to come'; and into that secret I labour to initiate every man (ch. 1).

My concern is that you and the Laodiceans (though we have never met) should grow in love and grasp God's secret – the Christ who embodies all God's treasures of wisdom and knowledge. So I beg you not to fall prey to all that man-made teaching based on elemental spirits, and not on Christ. Christ has all you need for salvation. The true circumcision is that which he made possible – that severance with your old lower nature, when you died and rose with him in baptism. When you were dead in sin, God made you alive with Christ, forgave your sins, and freed you from the demands of the Law which he abolished on the Cross. There he disarmed and defeated all these hostile powers.

Therefore let nobody fault you on food or holy days or inveigle you into asceticism or angel-worship. To give way to this sort of thing would be to lose hold of Christ your head, who alone gives unity and growth to his body. When you died and rose with Christ, you lost all connection with these powers. Why then pay heed to those useless prohibitions connected with their worship (ch. 2)?

As men risen in union with Christ, aspire to the realm above where he now reigns. Have done with earthly passions – anger, indecency, greed, malice and the rest. Strip off your old bad habits and put on the new garments of God's people – compassion, kindness, humility, gentleness, forbearance, with love to bind them all into one. In God's new humanity old distinctions of race and caste are done away. Let Christ's peace rule your hearts; sing songs of praise to God; and do all in the name of the Lord Jesus.

A word, now, about your family life. In Christian households wives should defer to their husbands, and husbands love their wives. As children must obey their parents, their fathers should in turn treat them gently. Slaves should obey their masters, not as men-pleasers but as servants of the Lord, and masters should use their slaves considerately, knowing that they too have a Master in heaven (ch. 3).

Include us, please, in your prayers, so that God may open to us a door for the Word. With non-Christians deal wisely, and mix grace with wit in talking to them.

Brother Tychicus, whom I am sending with your own Onesimus, will give you all my news. Greetings from my fellow-prisoner Aristarchus, Mark (who may be coming to you) and Jesus Justus – my only Jewish Christian colleagues, but what a tonic[2] they have been to me! Greetings also from your own Epaphras, who works and prays tirelessly for the churches in the Lycus valley, from dear doctor Luke, and from Demas. When you have read this letter, have it read also to the Christians in Laodicea, and read the one from Laodicea.[3] And, by the way, tell Archippus to put his back into his ministry.

This greeting is in my own hand – Paul. Remember that I am in prison. God's grace go with you (ch. 4).

2. *The relevance of the letter*

What has this ancient letter to say to us today? This, to begin with: To all who would 'improve' Christianity, as the Colossian

---

[2] Greek *parēgoria*: a medical term. Perhaps Paul got it from doctor Luke.
[3] Ephesians?

heretics proposed, by tricking it out with the rags and tatters of (say) spiritualism, sabbatarianism, anthroposophy or any kind of modern 'higher thought', or *gnōsis*. Paul says in his letter: *In Christ we have all we need*. As 'the image of the invisible God' (1.15), he is sufficient as the revealer of God. As the one in whom God in all his fullness was pleased to dwell, and who 'has made peace by the blood of his cross' (1.19f.), he is sufficient as a redeemer. And he is sufficient, too, as the head of his body, the church (1.18); for on him the church depends, as to him it owes its allegiance. Therefore we need no extra mediators, no taboos, no false asceticism. To piece out the gospel with these spurious embellishments from alien cults is to corrupt, and not to enrich it.

And this, second: *The head of the church is a person of cosmic dimensions*. 'Your God is too small', J. B. Phillips has told us in his book of that title. What Paul says to the Colossian heretics – and to many modern Christians – is: 'Your Christ is too small. By his resurrection and exaltation he has been let loose in his Father's universe: all creation coheres in him; and towards him all history converges.' In other words, when we think of Christ, we must learn, as Teilhard and others tell us, to use bigger theological maps. For these soaring statements about him in the first chapter of Colossians do but say what any true christology must say, that the fact of Christ is somehow embedded in creation, which is all there with Christ in view, and that in some mysterious way the evolving universe carries the promise of Christ in it.

Here, as often, the poets are our best theologians. Paul, of course, lived long before the true immensity of the universe was known. But if he had ever read Alice Meynell's poem, 'Christ in the Universe', he would surely have said Amen to it.

We know, she begins, the facts of his earthly life:

> The signal to a maid, the human birth,
> The lesson, and the young Man crucified.

But

> No planet knows that this
> Our wayside planet, carrying land and wave...
> Bears as chief treasure one forsaken grave.

Nor, 'in our little day', may we guess at the risen Christ's wider work in God's great universe. But, she concludes:

But in the eternities
Doubtless we shall compare together, hear
A million alien gospels, in what guise
He trod the Pleiades, the Lyre, the Bear.

Oh be prepared, my soul,
To read the inconceivable, to scan
The infinite forms of God those stars unroll,
When, in our turn, we show to them a Man.

19

Saints in Salonica

In the British Museum you may inspect an inscription found in
Salonica and belonging to the first century AD. Once it stood on a
Roman arch, called the Vardar Gate, spanning the great highway
(the *Via Egnatia*) which ran through Thessalonica, and part of the
inscription's interest is that it styles the local magistrates 'politarchs' (a very unusual title), thus confirming the accuracy of Acts
17.6.

Ancient Salonica, or Thessalonica, was the capital of Macedonia
and its chief seaport. Acts 17.1-10 tells how Paul and his friends
first set foot there. Someone has said that, wherever the apostle
went, he caused either a riot or a revival. When he arrived there,
with Silas and Timothy, about AD 49, he caused both. Unbelieving
Jews organised the riot against him when his mission produced a
rich harvest of converts, some Jewish, more Gentiles, plus many
influential women in the town. Christ's messengers were therefore
compelled to move on to Beroea, where the same thing happened.
At this point Paul went south to Athens, whence he sent Timothy
north to find out what was happening in Thessalonica (I Thess.
3.1f.). He himself went on from Athens to Corinth (Acts 18.1),
where he stayed eighteen months. While he was there, he was
rejoined by his two friends, and Timothy brought a most reassuring report (I Thess. 3.6). The young church was in good heart and
standing up bravely to bitter persecution, but one or two matters
had arisen in the congregation which required Paul's guidance.
Sexual morality was not all it might be; some converts were idling;
and others were worried about what might happen to their friends

who had died before Christ returned. So Paul wrote his first letter to the saints of Salonica.[1]

We may date it with some precision. The famous Delphi inscription shows that Gallio (mentioned in Acts 18.11, and the brother of Seneca the philosopher) became proconsul of Achaia, whose capital was Corinth, in the spring or early summer of 51. By then Paul had been eighteen months in Corinth. He must therefore have arrived in Thessalonica in 49 or very early in 50. Since no long time can have separated his visit to the town from the writing of the letter, we may safely date it in AD 50.

I Thessalonians

Paul begins by giving thanks for the way in which the Thessalonians had welcomed the gospel and for their continuing witness to it amid suffering (ch. 1). Then, probably in answer to some Jewish insinuations, he begins an apologia: 'You remember,' he writes, 'our mission among you. We were completely honest with you, currying favour with no man; we treated you as gently as a nurse her children; we toiled and drudged for our own keep. And you, in your turn, received our messages as the word of God and not of men, though it brought you persecution from your fellow countrymen. Be assured that these men who oppose God's work will receive retribution' (ch. 2).

Then Paul explains why he had not returned. 'We tried to come back,' he says, 'but Satan thwarted us. So, while I stayed in Athens, Timothy came north to find out how you were faring in your troubles. And what good news of you he has now come back with! I can hardly express my relief and joy or wait to see you again. May God direct me to you soon' (ch. 3).

Then Paul takes up the matters in the report. 'Remember what we taught you,' he says, 'keep your bodies pure and get on with your work quietly. You ask about your loved ones who have died? Do not grieve like men who have no hope. If we believe that Jesus died and rose again, even so those who sleep in Jesus will God bring with him, and so we shall be for ever with the Lord. And when Christ comes in glory, your dear dead ones will be the first to meet him' (ch. 4).

---

[1] Acts 18.5 shows that Silas (=Silvanus) and Timothy shared Paul's work in Corinth. II Cor. 1.19 confirms this. So we may be sure that I and II Thessalonians ('Paul, Silvanus and Timothy', I Thess. 1.1.; II Thess. 1.1) were written from Corinth.

'Don't let the rumours about the end of the world unsettle you. Nobody can tell when the Lord will come. The important thing is that as children of light you should be vigilant. Salvation is sure: Christ died for us so that we, awake or asleep, might live in company with him.

Respect your leaders; admonish the careless; be joyful always; pray continually; and give thanks whatever happens. You ask about gifts of the Spirit and prophetic utterances? Test them all, keep what is genuine, and reject what does not ring true.

May God bless and keep you till Christ's coming. Greet all our brothers with the kiss of peace. See that this letter is read to them all. The grace of our Lord Jesus Christ be with you' (ch. 5).

II Thessalonians[2]

Paul's second letter to Thessalonica, which must have been written soon after the first one, was evidently designed to clear up some misunderstanding caused by Paul's words about Christ's coming in glory in I Thessalonians. If Paul had given the impression that the coming was imminent, so that some of his converts had downed tools, then they must know that certain events must first take place, and meantime there must be no idling.

Paul begins by giving thanks for his converts' steadfastness in persecution. They will be rewarded when Christ comes, as their persecutors will be punished (ch. 1).

Then he reaches the first reason for his writing – the prevalence of misconceptions about Christ's advent. 'Let no one deceive you,' he warns, 'the Day of the Lord has not come – as some are saying – nor will come until the Man of Sin[3] is revealed. Meantime he is restrained; but when he makes his last evil challenge, he will be slain by the Lord Jesus. But you, my readers, God has destined

[2] The authenticity of II Thessalonians has been doubted because it bears close resemblance at various points to I Thessalonians and because its eschatology is said to be different from that of I Thessalonians (cf. II Thess. 2.1-12 with I Thess. 5.1-11). Neither objection is convincing. See Wikenhauser, *New Testament Introduction*, Burns and Oates 1967, pp. 368ff.

[3] II Thess. 2.3: the 'Man of Sin' is Antichrist, a kind of Devil's Messiah who, in the evil days before the End, was expected to war on God and his saints. 'The Restrainer' (2.6f.) is probably the law and order of the Roman Empire. The notion that he is in fact Paul himself (advanced by the Danish scholar Munck) would make Paul a monomaniac – a kind of 'eschatological one-man band'. See W. Neil, *The Truth about the Early Church*, Hodder and Stoughton 1970, pp. 48f.

for salvation. So stand firm and hold fast the traditions I taught you' (ch. 2).

Finally, having asked their prayers for himself, he reaches his second reason for writing – the reports that some people had stopped working apparently on the excuse that Christ might return at any time. 'Avoid all such people,' he says, 'this is not what I taught, or showed by my example. What I said was: "The man who will not work shall not eat." So settle down and get quietly on with your work. Anyone who disobeys should be ostracized in a friendly way. May the God of peace be with you.'

Then, to authenticate the letter, he signs the greetings in his own hand (ch. 3).

These two letters have been called 'the Cinderellas' in Paul's correspondence. They tend to be ignored because they are undistinguished by any great theological passage and because they contain a mixture of plain commonsense advice and some uncongenial apocalyptic. Yet they shed a vivid light on conditions in one of the earliest Christian congregations; and when we pierce down to their abiding Christian message, they contain some salutary counsel for us still. What do they say? Three things of importance: first, that if we are looking for a carefree, untroubled life, we have not yet understood our Christian calling; second, that for Christians death, however it may come, has lost its sting, for those who are in union with Christ remain in him for ever: and, last, that in times of crisis our duty is to hold fast our rule of life, and get on with our work.

Once in New England, in one of those times of excitement about the end of the world, a sudden darkness descended at noonday while the assembly was sitting. Men cried in fear, 'It is the coming of Christ, it is the end of the world.' 'Bring in candles,' said the old president, 'and go on with your work. If the Lord is coming, how better can he find us than quietly doing our duty;'

This is the spirit of Paul's letters to the saints at Salonica.

20

Speaking the truth in love

Among the papyrus letters dug up, not so long ago, from the sands of old Egypt is one from a man named Aurelius Sarapammon to his agent. It runs:

I commission you by this writ to journey to the famous city of Alexandria, and search for my slave by name (the name is lost) about 35 years of age, known to you. When you have found him, you shall place him in custody, with authority to shut him up and whip him, and to lay complaint before the proper authorities against any persons who have harboured him, with a demand for satisfaction.

So runs this letter about a runaway slave. Now it happens that there is preserved in the New Testament another letter about a runaway slave written about AD 60. It is Paul's letter to Philemon; and a very human little document it appears when the story that lies behind it is unfolded.

1. *The story*

The scene of the little drama is laid first in Colossae, a town 100 miles east of Ephesus in Asia Minor, and the three chief actors in it are Paul, a citizen of Colossae named Philemon and his slave Onesimus.

When, through Paul's work in Ephesus, the gospel had found its way inland to Colossae, among the first converts were Philemon and his wife Apphia. They were good Christians, and the local congregation apparently met in their house. But unfortunately one of Philemon's slaves called Onesimus had helped himself to some of his master's money, and absconded. Whither he went on the first stage of his wanderings we do not know; but eventually he turned up in Rome, drifting there no doubt as similar persons today might drift to London if they had 'money to burn'. There providence took a strange but blessed hand in his affairs. About this time Paul had come to Rome to stand his trial as a Christian; and one day the door of his prison opened to admit—Onesimus. How he found Paul we cannot say; but we may imagine him blurting out his tale of shame to Paul with tears. The sequel was that Onesimus became a Christian and proved himself a great help and comfort to the apostle. But Paul, though he grew very fond of him, knew that it was his duty to send Onesimus back to his rightful master when the opportunity offered. It came soon. One day there arrived a messenger from Colossae reporting the outbreak of heresy in the church there and requesting Paul's guidance. So Paul sat down and wrote a letter to the Christians in Colossae – our Epistle to the Colossians – but before he put his pen away, he wrote a little note to Philemon about Onesimus. It is our letter, and in it Paul tells Philemon he is sending Onesimus back to him, asks him to reinstate him in his favour, and hints that he would like Philemon to release Onesimus for further Christian service with himself.

2. *The letter itself*

'Paul, a prisoner of Christ Jesus and our colleague Timothy' it begins, 'to Philemon our dear friend and fellow worker, and Apphia our sister, and Archippus our comrade-in-arms, and the congregation at your house.

'Grace and peace to you from God our Father and the Lord Jesus Christ.'

Then, with rare tact, Paul prepares the way for his chief point in writing:

'I always thank God when I mention you in my prayers, for, as I hear of your love and loyalty to the Lord Jesus and all God's people, I pray that the sharing of your faith may promote the knowledge of all the good that is ours in Christ. I have had great joy and encouragement over your love, because your action, my brother, has put new heart into God's people.'

Evidently some recent act of kindness by Philemon had reached Paul's ears. He is glad to mention it because he is about to say something which will put a severe strain on their friendship. Then, very delicately, he comes to the point:

'Hence, though I would feel quite free to order you to do your duty, I prefer to appeal to you for love's sake. Well then, as Paul the old man, who nowadays is a prisoner for Christ's sake, I appeal to you for my child whose father I have become in prison.'

If these last words must, momentarily, have puzzled Philemon, with his next sentence Paul lets the secret out: 'It is Onesimus I mean.' (Here we may note that the name Onesimus in Greek means 'Useful', and observe what happy play Paul now makes with his name.)

' "Useful" was anything but profitable to you in the past; but today he has become, true to his name, very profitable both to you and to me. I would fain have kept him, for in sending him back I feel I am parting with my own heart. But I did not want to do anything without your consent.'

'Perhaps (Paul goes on) this was why you and he were parted for a while, that you might get him back for good, no longer as a mere slave but as something more – a dear brother, dear indeed to me but how much more to you, both as a man and as a Christian.'

Then comes the final appeal: 'You count me a partner? Then welcome him as you would welcome me. Ah, but maybe you are still remembering the money he stole? Well, put it down to my account. Here is my IOU for the amount: I PAUL WILL REPAY, SIGNED WITH MY OWN HAND, PAUL. Come brother, let me get some use from you in the Lord. I write, confident that you will obey and do even more than I ask.'

With a request to get a room ready for him, since he hopes to be freed, Paul sends greetings from his friends (Mark and Luke among them) and ends with a blessing.

3. *The interest and value of the letter*

Three comments are worth making.

First: the fact that this tiny, semi-private letter has been preserved is surely evidence that Paul's plea did not fail. But we can go further. There is a strong hint[1] in vv. 19ff. that Paul wanted

---

[1] Paul says (v. 19), 'I want some benefit from you'. The Greek *onaimēn* is the verbal form of Onesimus. It is a Pauline pun. He is saying 'Let me make a profit of you', and his meaning is much clearer if Onesimus himself is the 'profit' he is after. So with 'more than I say' in v. 21. If Paul has not explicitly said he wants Onesimus returned to him, he has thrown out a broad hint. See John Knox, *The Interpreter's Bible*, XI, Abingdon Press 1955, p. 571.

Onesimus not merely reinstated in his master's favour but returned to him for active service. Did Philemon take the hint? Forty years later, Ignatius bishop of Antioch, writing to the Ephesian Christians, refers to their bishop, one Onesimus, whom he calls 'a man of inexpressible love'. It is likely that he is referring to the subject of Paul's letter. Paul's confidence had been justified. Onesimus had made good.

Second: somebody has called this letter 'the Magna Carta of the slave'. Of course it is not a tract on the emancipation of slaves, and some people are shocked because the New Testament never downright condemns slavery as an institution. They should remember that in the circumstances there was little – short of bloody revolution – which the early Christians could do. They had no real voice in public affairs, no vote. What they could do was to let the gospel, through their own words and acts, create such relations between master and slave that in time slavery would be seen in its own hideous light, and in large part abolished in the world. This letter is a good example of this principle beginning its beneficent work. That it took so long for Christians to set their faces steadfastly against slavery is a reflection not on the principle but on the failure of Christians to implement the power placed in their hands.

Third: this letter is not only what Renan called it, 'a masterpiece in the art of letter-writing'; it is also a perfect illustration of Paul's own phrase about 'speaking the truth in love' (Eph. 4.15). Dear, old, eccentric 'Rabbi' Duncan of New College, Edinburgh, summed it up as well as any: 'the most gentlemanly letter ever written.'

21

The Pastoral Epistles

The Pastoral Epistles, I and II Timothy and Titus, were so named by Paul Anton of Halle in 1726. The name was apt and stuck, for the letters consist mostly of advice to younger ministers on the defence of the faith, the care of their flocks and their own devotional life. Their chief aim, apart from denouncing false teaching, is to set up a high standard of Christian character and conduct and to urge loyalty to apostolic teaching. What is inculcated is 'sound doctrine and good works'.

But was 'the Pastor' Paul? Paul's name certainly stands at the head of each letter; but since the rise of modern biblical criticism in the early part of last century, many have doubted his authorship. Nowadays, indeed, scholars divide themselves into three camps:

Those who accept full Pauline authorship.
Those who think genuine Pauline fragments have been worked up by a disciple of Paul's.
Those who completely deny their authenticity.

1. *Historical.* It is urged that the letters cannot be fitted into the historical framework of Paul's life given in Acts. Let the difficulty be granted; yet this objection is not decisive, if only because no man can be sure that Paul's travels ended with the last chapter of Acts. We know from the Prison Letters that Paul hoped to be released from his Roman prison. He had every reason to hope so, for he had done nothing treasonable in the eyes of the Roman government. And there was a tradition in the early church that Paul was in fact acquitted and released, resumed his travelling, was re-arrested, condemned and martyred in Rome. If this is true, we

have found a place in Paul's life for the Pastoral Epistles.

2. *Ecclesiastical*. It is urged that the church in the Pastorals is organized to a degree unknown in Paul's time. This is undoubtedly a first impression: church polity does seem more advanced: we read of three types of minister – bishops, elders and deacons; and a roll for widows has been set up, with definite rules and regulations. But, again, the objection fails to convince completely. In the Pastorals 'bishops' and 'elders' (see Titus 1.5-7) are clearly the same men, 'elder' being their title, 'bishop' describing their function as 'overseers'. And we remember that Paul could call the Ephesian elders 'bishops' (Acts 20.17,28) and that Phil. 1.1 speaks of 'bishops and deacons'.

3. *Doctrinal*. Here it is urged that the heresies attacked are later than Paul's day and that the letters contain an un-Pauline stress on 'sound doctrine'. But the heresy denounced in the Pastorals (I Tim. 1.3-7; 4.1-5; 6.3ff.,20f.; Titus 1.10ff.; 3.9f.) is a 'Gnosticizing' Judaism. Is this so different from the Colossian heresy? Once again we must be cautious. Yet, on the purely theological side, we do seem to find un-Pauline features. For the Pastor 'faith' often seems synonymous with orthodoxy, and 'righteousness' is predominantly ethical. These features are hardly characteristic of Paul; and what the Pastor says about the Law (I Tim. 1.8-11) is not Pauline.

4. *Stylistic*. Here it is urged that the Pastor's vocabulary and style differ greatly from Paul's. This is perhaps the weightiest objection. For not only does the Pastor use 306 words (out of a total 897) not found in the admittedly genuine letters of Paul, but his sentences, in their primness and precision, contrast sharply with Paul's rugged and explosive periods. Finally, the Pastor's use of connecting words (e.g. *oun*) and particles (like *men* and *de*) differs much from Paul's.

How shall we conclude? The first and second objections are certainly not decisive, but there does seem to be substance in the third and fourth; and if you add them all together, the case against is undoubtedly impressive. Yet who can doubt that, in say, I Tim. 5.23; II Tim. 1.3ff.; 4.6-22; Titus 3,12-15, we are listening not to a disciple of Paul's but to the apostle himself? Passages like these make the 'hypothesis of fragments' attractive and probable. We may well believe that some genuine notes of Paul to Timothy and Titus fell into the hands of one of his followers, himself a church

leader, and that, using them in all good faith, he composed the
Pastorals. True, he issued them in Paul's name; but it was not
uncommon (in Jewish and Christian circles) thus to borrow the
authority of a great name for what you had to say. Besides, did not
the Pastor's letters contain fragments of the renowned apostle's
writing, and did they not give effect to much of his teaching?

The date of the letters as we now have them is probably
AD 90-100.

I Timothy

(Timothy, who had a Jewish mother and a Gentile father, became
Paul's assistant during his second visit to South Galatia [Acts
16.1ff.]. Thereafter he shared many of Paul's journeys as well as
his Roman imprisonment. This letter assumes he has been left in
charge of the church in Ephesus.)

Paul to Timothy:

As I urged, stay on in Ephesus and oppose these heretics who
deal in myths and genealogies. Certain would-be teachers of the
Law have renounced sound doctrine and the glorious gospel of
God's grace for sinners which is my trust. (You remember how I,
once a notorious sinner, found God's mercy.) So I give you this
charge (ch. 1).

See that prayers are said for all men. God wishes every man to
be saved. (There is only one God, as there is only one mediator
between God and men, Jesus Christ, who died to redeem us all,
and whose herald I am.) I desire the men to offer the prayers. The
women, who must dress modestly, I do not allow to teach. God
created women to bear children, and they will please him by
doing so (ch. 2).

As for bishops, let them be blameless men, married once only,
free from avarice, and fit to manage their own households. Recent
converts, who may be conceited, should not be chosen. Deacons,
too, should be men of high principle, temperate, married only
once, and good family men and managers.

I hope to come soon; but should I be delayed, this letter will
teach you how to conduct yourself in God's household, the church.
(What a wonderful revelation is ours in Christ – manifested, vindi-
cated, proclaimed, exalted!) (ch. 3)

Some (we are divinely told) may be led away by teachers of a
false asceticism, though we know that everything God made is

to be enjoyed. Stick to sound doctrine, keep yourself spiritually fit, and let no one despise your youth. Rather, be an example to your people, and cultivate your gift of teaching and preaching (ch. 4).

Treat all considerately: young and old, male and female. Widows really alone in the world assist, but if a widow has near relatives, it is their duty to care for her. About the Widows' Roll: for enrolment, a widow should be sixty, once married, and well reported for her Christian service. Don't enrol the younger widows – they are likely to be unreliable and given to idle gossip. Let them marry again and bring up families.

Elders who rule well should be well rewarded, as scripture says. Never entertain a charge against an elder, unless two or three witnesses support it. Reprimand publicly all errant ones; have no favourites; and never be in a hurry to ordain. Incidentally, stop drinking nothing but water; take a little wine for your digestion (ch. 5).

About slaves: They must respect their masters; and should these be Christians, this is no reason why they should respect them less; quite the contrary.

Insist on all these things. How far from sound doctrine is the conceited Gnostic who loves controversy and thinks religion should be a source of gain! Religion with contentment is great gain, but money-lust is the root of all evil.

So, man of God, run the great race of faith and keep your commission unsullied till Christ's appearing. Tell the wealthy to be rich in good deeds – these bring real life. And, for yourself, guard your commission, and turn a deaf ear to this nonsense calling itself 'knowledge'.

Grace be with you (ch. 6).

II Timothy

Paul to Timothy:

I thank God for you and for your Christian nurture, but I urge you to rekindle your ordination gift, and to testify bravely to the gospel of God's grace in Christ, whose apostle I am. Though I suffer now, my faith in his final sufficiency stands firm. Follow the sound teaching I gave you. All in Asia deserted me, but I recall how loyal Onesiphorus was, both in Rome and Ephesus. (May God be merciful to him at the Great Day!) (ch. 1)

Transmit the truth I gave you to faithful teachers, and be a loyal soldier of Jesus Christ, the Son of David and the risen Lord, as my gospel proclaims. Though I am fettered now, God's Word is not. Remember the (baptismal) hymn:

> If we with him have died
> With him to life we rise,
> If we but firm endure,
> A throne with him our prize.

Tell your people to avoid the godless chatter of the false teachers. In a great establishment like the church such men must needs exist, but keep clear of their senseless controversies (ch. 2).

These evils will get worse as the world nears its end; indeed, some men are already using vile caricatures of the gospel to ensnare others and serve their own lusts. You know through what sufferings as an apostle, in Antioch and Galatia, the Lord sustained me. So, in evil times, stay yourself on your Christian heritage and on Holy Writ, which can equip you as a man of God (ch. 3).

Before God and Christ I charge you to preach the Word of God earnestly and, in the bad times coming when false teaching spreads, to do the work of an evangelist. My time on earth is almost over, as my reward is sure. Come soon: except for Luke, I am alone. Bring Mark, that useful man, and the cloak and parchments I left at Troas. Beware of Alexander the coppersmith, a dangerous man, as I can testify. At my first defence, when all human helpers failed me, the Lord rescued me, as he always will.

Greet my friends in Ephesus (ch. 4).

Titus

Paul to Titus:

I left you in Crete to amend some defects and to appoint elders in every town. Choose men of integrity, once married and with children who are believers. Good bishops are needed, for many religious charlatans are at work (resembling the Cretans your prophet described – 'liars, vicious brutes, lazy gluttons'). They profess to 'know' God, but deny him by their actions, and they must be curbed (ch. 1).

Teach sound doctrine. Advise the older men to be temperate, sensible and sound in faith; the older women, to be reverent, abstemious, and apt to train the younger ones in the domestic virtues. Encourage the younger men to self-control, setting them an example by your own life and speech, and urge the slaves to be obedient and honest. So they will add lustre to the doctrine of God our Saviour, and we will all live as men redeemed by Christ's sacrifice and waiting for his appearance. Do this authoritatively (ch. 2).

Remind your people to obey the civil authorities, avoiding quarrels and showing courtesy to all. Remember that we, too, once hardened sinners, have been saved by God's mercy and justified by his grace. Steer clear of foolish speculations and controversies over the Law. Warn a heretic once, and once again, and then shun him.

Artemas or Tychicus will succeed you in Crete. Do your best to meet me at Nicopolis where I mean to winter. Help Zenas the lawyer and Apollos on their travels.

Greetings from all here, and grace be with you all (ch. 3).

These letters are part of the scriptural conversation between the Holy Spirit and the church in which the Spirit (using some fragments of Paul adapted and elaborated by one of his disciples) recalls and applies the gospel of Christ. Especially does the Spirit speak to the clergy, for the Pastorals form a kind of Bible within the Bible which specially belongs to them. Of course evangelism remains their primary task; but when the converts have been made, there remains the task of grounding them in sound doctrine and wholesome morals. Here the Pastorals are full of wise guidance, as they have also many valuable things to say about the minister's own spiritual life.

James Denney once said that Paul was inspired, but the Pastor only orthodox. This is fair comment; but the Pastor's times called for sound doctrine rather than inspiration, and his orthodoxy remains salutary to this day. It is easy to make jokes about 'sound doctrine' and to poke fun at the ultra-orthodox. But in a world like ours where so many un-Christian philosophies compete for men's allegiance and so many attempts are made to undermine the faith, who can deny the need for sound doctrine? If, as we must believe, it is no light thing to 'make shipwreck of the faith' (I Tim. 1.19), the Pastor's message is relevant.

Finally, all of us may profit from his commonsense. He always keeps close to realities, calls bad things by blunt names, and gives his rules in plain black and white. It may sound banal to tell

Christian men to be sober and Christian women to be chaste; but who will deny that these things still need to be said? In fine, in a world where we cannot all be expert theologians or profound mystics, the need remains for a plain, unmystical, straightforward Christianity of the kind the Pastor gives us. Let us be grateful for it.

PART FOUR

The Writings of the Other Apostolic Men

22

The Epistle of Priesthood

During the last decades of the first century there began to circulate in the young church a little masterpiece of religious thought. It had no title, but soon acquired one: 'To the Hebrews'. For the most part it was a finely-phrased discourse arguing that Christ was the perfect high priest, but it ended like a letter, with brief news and greetings. Unfortunately, the author did not put his own name to it, or that of his readers, or tell us plainly what moved him to write. Yet in his thirteen chapters he lets fall some clues. Let us see what we can make of them.

1. *Author, reader, occasion, date*

Who was *Auctor* (Latin for 'author'), as the writer is often called? The Authorized Version says he was Paul. But ancient opinion was divided for and against Pauline authorship; and it is quite clear to us nowadays that the style and thought are not Paul's. His Greek is purer and more rhythmical than the apostle's, and, though he and Paul share basic Christian beliefs, *Auctor* speaks of Christ, the Law and faith in ways which are not characteristic of Paul.

But if *Auctor* was not Paul, who was he? Conjectures have ranged from Barnabas to Priscilla, wife of Aquila (though, as a German scholar has said, there is really no evidence that Aquila was cursed with a learned wife!). But in the opinion of many modern scholars there is one much better claimant for the honour of authorship.[1] The reference in 13.23 to 'our brother Timothy' shows he belongs to Paul's circle. Can we go further? In Acts 18.24 Luke describes Paul's colleague Apollos thus: 'A Jew, an Alexandrian by birth, an eloquent man, powerful in his use of the scriptures.' Apollos was therefore (1) a Jew who had become a

[1] Luther was the first to make the suggestion.

Christian; (2) an eloquent preacher; (3) a native of Alexandria; and (4) an expert in the Old Testament. Now this fourfold description admirably fits the man who wrote Hebrews. He was a Jewish Christian. His rhetorical style, plus his habit of stopping to exhort his readers, betray the preacher. He interprets Christianity in terms of the Platonic philosophy which we know was current in Alexandria. And he makes massive use of the Old Testament, often allegorizing it as Alexandrian Jews like Philo did. If, then, we are to put a name on the title-page of Hebrews, 'the best bet' is Apollos. And if not Apollos, then, spiritually-speaking, his twin brother.

To whom did he write, and what moved him to it? Some modern scholars have held that his readers were mainly Gentiles, and that they were in peril of lapsing into irreligion. But this view signally fails to explain why a letter written to Gentiles relapsing into paganism should take the form of a long running contrast between Judaism and Christianity. Far sounder is the traditional view that the readers were Jewish Christians in danger of reverting to Judaism; and a modern variant of it, produced by William Manson,[2] makes very good sense indeed. Manson argues that the readers were a community of Jewish Christians in Rome who, threatened with persecution, were shrinking back under cover of Judaism.

The case for locating the readers in Rome is strong. The letter is first quoted there, about AD 95, by Clement. *Auctor* and Clement used the same Greek word (*hēgoumenoi*) to describe the church's 'leaders'. Timothy was well known in Rome (Col. 1.1; Philemon 1). And the phrase 'those who hail from Italy' in the greetings (13.24) probably points in the same direction.

Equally persuasive is Manson's argument that the readers were Jewish Christians who, threatened by persecution would fain have crept back under shelter of Judaism, a religion permitted by Rome as Christianity was not. Living too much in the Jewish part of their faith, they were remaining backwardly blind to the far horizons of their Christian calling. By contrast, *Auctor* was a man of the same bold, wide, forward-looking vision as Stephen the first martyr, as he appears in Acts 7. Like Stephen, he had glimpsed the universal significance of the Son of Man (compare Acts 7.56

---

[2] *The Epistle to the Hebrews*, Hodder and Stoughton 1951.

with Dan 7.13f.) and knew that the new Israel, the church, was destined to world-mission.[3]

This view explains many things in Hebrews: the writer's warning against 'drifting' from their Christian course (2.1-4); his call to his readers to 'hold fast the religion they profess' (4.14); his insistence in the main part of his letter (7.1-10.18) that the new means of grace brought by Christ offers the reality which Judaism could only foreshadow; his caution against 'shrinking back' (10.38f.); his summons in ch. 11 to the pilgrim life of faith; and his challenge to 'go forth to Jesus outside the camp, bearing the stigma that he bore' (13.13 NEB).

When was the letter written? Probably before AD 70 when the Jewish Temple was destroyed. Had the Temple fallen before he wrote, he must surely have pointed to its fall as proof that God had no further use for this focus of the ancient sanctities. The letter mentions two persecutions: one past, one pending. The first (10.32f.) could well describe the trouble in the Roman synagogues when the gospel found entrance there and the Roman emperor Claudius expelled the Jews from Rome (AD 49). The second (12.3ff.) suggests the first moves against the Christians which issued in the Neronian blood-bath of 64. A date about 63 seems likely.

2. *The contents of Hebrews*

Pausing in argument to exhort is a time-honoured preacher's practice. Our writer does it three times in his first six chapters, so that it is not always easy to disentangle the thread of his argument. But once we recognize his habit (and we shall note it as we go along) we can follow the march of his argument more easily. His discourse falls into two parts: (1) The main argument (1.1-10.18), and (2) the closing exhortation (10.19-13.25).

The main argument

First, in a prologue, *Auctor* declares that, in contrast to the Old Testament revelation, which was fragmentary and piecemeal, God has now, in this 'final age', made a complete self-revelation in his

---

[3] C. F. D. Moule, *The Birth of the New Testament*, A. and C. Black 1962, pp. 74-76, comes to much the same conclusion as Manson. 'Hebrews,' he says, 'is the end-product of the kind of debate in progress at the trial of Stephen.'

Son. Then he proceeds to prove Christ greater than the angels through whom, tradition said, the Law had been given (chs. 1-2). (But in 2.1-4 he pauses to warn his readers against 'drifting' from their Christian course.) Next, he shows Christ superior to Moses, as a son is to a servant in God's household (3.1-6). (Again he digresses in 3.7-4.13 to warn his readers against missing God's promised 'rest'.) Eventually he reaches his main theme – the high-priesthood of Christ – and finds the two qualifications of a high priest – sympathy with those he represents and divine appointment – fulfilled in Christ (4.14-5.10). (Once again, in 5.11-6.12, he stops to warn them against relapsing.) Then, at 6.13, he resumes his main thesis which continues to 10.18.

In ch. 7 Christ is shown to belong to a higher order of priesthood, represented not by Aaron but by that primeval priest Melchizedek mentioned in Gen. 14.18-20 and Ps. 110.4; and the Levitical priesthood is superseded by that of Christ the ideal high priest.

In ch. 8 he shows that Christ is not only the ideal high priest, but that he ministers in an ideal sanctuary, heaven, and his ministry has meant the establishment of the new covenant between God and man prophesied by Jeremiah (Jer. 31.31ff.).

In ch. 9 he shows that Christ, the ideal high priest, offers the perfect sacrifice for sins; and his argument climaxes in the proof of the futility of Jewish sacrifices and the finality of Christ's (10.1-18).

The closing exhortation

First he urges his readers to avail themselves of 'the new and living way' opened by Christ into God's presence, and warns them of the penalties attendant on backsliding. Then he praises their former fortitude in persecution, and reminds them that they stand in the succession of the great heroes of faith (10.19-11.40). Their present suffering, he says, is evidence of God's fatherly discipline, and he powerfully contrasts the terrors of the old covenant and the glories of the new (ch. 12). The last chapter (13) begins with various counsels and an appeal to imitate their leaders; warns them against strange teachings; and ends with a noble doxology and greetings.

3. *The message of Hebrews*

A picture at Catterick Camp, painted during the First World War, shows a signaller lying dead in No-man's-land. He had been sent out to repair a cable broken by shell-fire. There he lies, cold in death, but with his task accomplished; for in his stiffening hands he holds the cable's broken ends together. Beneath the picture stands one pregnant word – 'THROUGH'.

That picture is a parable of what *Auctor* is saying in Hebrews. Basically, the Christian religion means man entering into friendship with God, on the initiative of God – that is, a friendship made possible by what God has done in Christ. Before Christ, men were 'at odds with God' because their sin had snapped the contact between God and man. Christ, by his self-sacrifice, has brought the ends together has repaired the broken friendship between God and men. Or, as Plato might have put it if he had been a Christian, through Christ's sacrifice man is enabled to pass, as Judaism could not enable him, from the earthly world of shadows 'through' to the heavenly world of reality.

For, in *Auctor's* view, religion means primarily *access* to God mediated by worship; and it is sin which hinders access and impairs that communion with God for which man was made. If man is ever to attain it, he must somehow 'get through' to God. But how? The ritual of the Jewish Law – the whole system of priest and sanctuary and sacrifice – professed to take him there. Alas, it could not. Cleanse the *flesh* it might, but the *conscience* stained with sin it could not:

> Not all the blood of beasts
>   On Jewish altars slain
> Could give the guilty conscience peace,
>   Or take away the stain.

Christianity is the final religion because, through Christ's sacrifice, it secures that access to God which all the religious apparatus of Judaism could only shadow forth. With Christ, we pass 'out of the shadows into the truth'.

This is the theme of Hebrews: and *Auctor*, using Plato's two-storeyed view[4] of the world – the Shadow and the Real – draws, in chs. 8-10, a contrast between the material, make-believe access offered by Judaism and the spiritual and true access now made actual by God in Christ. Christ is the ideal high priest who, by

---

[4] The ground floor is this world of the shadowy and transitory; the upper floor is the world of the real and eternal.

offering the ideal sacrifice (that of his own perfect obedience to God, see 10.5-10), has pioneered a way into the Holy of Holies which is heaven. Thus Christians are able, by virtue of 'That one true, pure, immortal sacrifice', to pass by faith, here and now, into the heavenly world and have communion with 'the Father of spirits'.[5]

What has this first-century masterpiece to say to Christians today? Are not *Auctor*'s argument and exegesis outmoded and irrelevant? Doubtless we shall judge that, when he discusses Melchizedek in ch. 7, he reads much too much into the silence of Scripture, and his description of the 'lay-out' of the tabernacle may seem to have little more than antiquarian interest (9.1-5). Yet Hebrews strikes three notes which Christians still need to hear.

First, the *priestly* note. Even those who would scorn to be called 'high churchmen' and regard sacerdotalism with suspicion must feel the fascination of the world of Hebrews in which all is dominated by the figure of Jesus the great high priest 'seated at the right hand of Majesty on high' (1.3; 8.1), clothed in our nature, compassionate to our frailties. Presbyterians have never been lovers of 'priestcraft'; yet it was one of them, Michael Bruce,[6] the Loch Leven poet, who gave perhaps the finest expression to this note:

> Where high the heavenly temple stands,
> The house of God not made with hands,
> A great High Priest our nature wears,
> The Guardian of mankind appears.
>
> He who for men their surety stood,
> And poured on earth his precious blood,
> Pursues in heaven his mighty plan,
> The Saviour and the Friend of man.
>
> Though now ascended up on high,
> He bends on earth a brother's eye;
> Partaker of the human name,
> He knows the frailty of our frame.

[5] So 'we are all high priests', as Jeremias once said to me.
[6] Michael Bruce (1746-67) was pronounced by Southey 'a youth of real genius'. His verses are based on Heb. 4.14-16.

Our fellow-sufferer yet retains
A fellow-feeling of our pains;
And still remembers in the skies
His tears, his agonies, his cries.

In every pang that rends the heart
The Man of Sorrows has a part;
He sympathizes with our grief
And to the sufferer sends relief.

With boldness, therefore, at the throne
Let us make all our sorrows known;
And ask the aid of heavenly power
To help us in the evil hour.

If this is 'sacerdotalism', we cannot hear too much of it. And all talk of 'priestcraft' aside, do we not need the doctrine of Christ's heavenly intercession – found also in Rom. 8.34 and I John 2.1 – as a complement to faith in his atoning death? Only, as H. B. Swete says, we should never picture Christ as a suppliant pleading our cause before a reluctant God. Rather is he 'a throned Priest-King asking what He wills from a Father who always hears and grants his request'.[7]

Second: No less needing to be heard in these days when 'the world is too much with us', is the *pilgrim* note sounded in the wonderful eleventh chapter. There the heroes are no mere wandering adventurers but men bent on the search for the true fatherland of their souls, 'the city which has foundations, whose builder and maker is God' (11.10). The badge these men wear is faith, which is 'a venturing upon vision'. True, it is defined in the first verse as 'the assurance of things hoped for, the conviction of things not seen'. But it is an 'assurance' adventuring and enduring, as Abraham, Moses and the rest down to those 'refugees in deserts and on the hills' (11.18 NEB), the Maccabean martyrs, adventured and endured. In Jesus, 'the pioneer and perfecter of faith' (12.2), the end of their quest for the heavenly City is to be seen. He is faith's mightiest captain, who has blazed the trail and opened up 'a new and living way' whereby we too today may travel, to that heavenly Jerusalem, which is the last end of our soul's aspiring.

Third: only a rabid sectarian will find discordant that *ecumeni-*

[7] *The Ascended Christ*, Macmillan 1910, p. 95.

cal note which William Manson rediscovered for us. If we will, *Auctor* will teach us the unwisdom of clinging fearfully to the old securities when the clarion-call is for men to carry Christ's empire to the end of the earth. The church is not – or ought not to be – merely an ark of refuge to which the faithful flee from the snares of the world outside. The church becomes truly the church when, scorning to be only a rest-camp for the faithful, it goes militantly on the march; when refusing to be merely Christ's 'mystical' body, it becomes his *working* body in the world. If we may bring all this down to the congregational level, all our services should end with the idea not just that we are being sent *away* but that we are being sent *out*. One church admirably ends its service by dismissing the congregation thus: 'Our worship service is over, but our Christian service is just beginning. Go back with God into the world.'

A corollary of this last point may introduce what is perhaps the most important thing that *Auctor* has to say to us today.[8]

In Heb. 13.7f. we read: 'Remember your leaders, those who spoke to you the word of God; consider the outcome of their life and imitate their faith. Jesus Christ is the same yesterday, today, and for ever.'

Their first fathers in the faith had gone to their reward, leaving them noble examples to follow. But death had no more power over their Lord. *Yesterday*, he had lived and suffered and died for their sins. *Today*, and *for ever*, he lives in God's eternal kingdom, 'the Saviour and the Friend of man', able to help 'in time of need'. For, as *Auctor* says, 'the priesthood which Jesus holds is perpetual, because he remains for ever' (7.24 NEB).

But *Auctor*'s readers had to learn that, though theirs was an unchanging Christ, he was also onward-moving, always summoning his people to fresh ventures of faith. For their part, his readers were living in a changing world, to which they found it very hard to adjust. But outside, *in* that changing world, was their changeless Lord, calling them to 'go forth' to him.

Today we, too, live in a world where the old landmarks are fast disappearing and in a century of unparalleled change. In face of all its uncertainties and dangers we, too, are tempted to choose isolation, sitting tight in our old camps and enclosures, hugging the old ways. But to do this is both foolish and futile. We need

[8] I owe the substance of the closing paragraphs to F. F. Bruce's article on Hebrews in *Interpretation*, January 1969, pp. 16-19.

the ministry of the unchanging but ever onward-moving Christ. If we belong to 'a kingdom which cannot be shaken' (12.28), we must yet remember that the revelation we have in Christ is *dynamic*, is ever summoning to new dimensions of Christian thought and action. 'The Lord,' as Pastor John Robinson said in 1620, 'has yet more light and truth to break forth out of his holy Word.' Much land yet remains to be possessed in the name of Christ. We are called to go forward in the steps of this unchanging but always onward-moving Christ:

> On to the end of the road,
> On to the City of God.

23

The Epistle of Practice

'Give a dog a bad name,' says the proverb, 'and hang him.' Luther once gave the Epistle of James 'a bad name' and nearly succeeded in hanging it. 'A right strawy epistle,' he declared, 'with no tang of the gospel about it.' His outburst was intelligible. The letter seemed to contradict his watchword of *sola fide*, 'by faith alone'. But whatever else it is, it is not an epistle of straw. Theologically deficient it may be by Luther's standards, yet there is in the New Testament no man in stronger earnest about the practicalities of Christianity.

Who was James?

The answer of the letter itself is: 'James, a servant of God and of the Lord Jesus Christ' (1.). No claim is made here for apostolic authorship. Yet many have held that the letter is the work of the James *par excellence* in the New Testament – James 'the brother of the Lord' (Mark 6.3; Gal. 1.19; etc.). Disbelieving in Jesus during 'the days of his flesh', he had been won to belief by an appearance to him of the risen Christ (I Cor. 15.7). The book of Acts tells how he rose to a place of pre-eminence in the mother church, and we learn from Josephus that he was martyred in AD 62.

Three arguments can be advanced in support of this view. (1) The majestic simplicity of the self-designation (1.1). Had an unknown writer published this letter under the name of the Lord's brother, he would have added 'apostle' or 'brother of the Lord'. (2) The Jewish-Christian cast of the letter (e.g. 2.2; 5.4,11). (3) The ten echoes of Jesus' teaching to be found in the letter (1.5f.,22; 2.5,8,13; 3.12,18; 4.10,12; 5.12). On the other hand, the excellence of the Greek and the shyness of the church to admit the letter to the canon have made others wonder whether 'James the Just' (as he was called) could have been the author, and have led them to think that he was another James holding a position of authority in the church to which he belonged.

James wrote to 'the twelve tribes dispersed throughout the world' (1.1). Taken literally, this would refer to the Jews scattered throughout the world. More probably the phrase describes the church as the new Israel, the true people of God, dwelling afar from their heavenly homeland (cf. I Peter 1.1).

If the author was James the Lord's brother, the letter must have been written before AD 62. If he was another James, it may have been later. What seems certain from James 2.14-26 is that at the time of writing some people were caricaturing Paul's teaching about justification by faith, saying in effect that faith was everything and works did not matter.

The letter has been called 'an ethical scrap-book'. Certainly it has no clear shape or developing argument. James takes a topic of practical religion, and in a few terse sentences drives his point home before passing to a new one. But it is possible, by a little re-arrangement of his material, to find five little sermons in it:

1. Trials and temptations (1.2-8,12-18).
2. Riches and poverty (1.9-11; 2.1-13; 5.1-6).
3. Faith and works (1.19-27; 2.14-26).
4. The control of the tongue (3.1-12; 4.11f.; 5.12).
5. Patience and prayer (5.7-11,13-20).

Three short excerpts will show the quality of these sermons. Hear James first on his favourite theme of faith and works:

> My brothers, what use is it for a man to say he has faith when he has nothing to show for it? Can that faith save him? Suppose a brother or sister is in rags with not enough food for the day, and one of you says, 'Good luck to you, keep yourselves warm and have plenty to eat,' but does nothing to supply their bodily needs, what is the good of that? So with faith; if it does not lead to action, it is in itself a lifeless thing (2.14-17 NEB).

Next, hear him on the dangers of an unbridled tongue:

What a huge stack of timber can be set ablaze by the tiniest spark! And the tongue is in effect a fire. It represents among our members the world with all its wickedness ... We use it to sing the praises of our Lord and Father, and we use it to invoke curses upon our fellow-men who are made in God's likeness. Out of the same mouth comes praises and curses. My brothers, this should not be so. Does a fountain gush with both fresh and brackish water from the same opening? Can a fig tree, my brothers, yield olives, or a vine figs? No more does salt water yield fresh (3.5-12 NEB).

Finally, listen to him on the need for plain speech and prayer:

> My brothers, do not use oaths whether 'by heaven' or 'by earth' or by anything else. When you say yes or no, let it be plain 'Yes' or 'No', for fear that you expose yourselves to judgment (cf. Matt. 5.34-37).
>
> Is anyone among you in trouble? He should turn to prayer. Is anyone in good heart? He should sing praises. Is one of you ill? He should send for the elders of the congregation to pray over him and anoint him with oil in the name of the Lord ... A good man's prayer is powerful and effective (5.12-16 NEB).

Pithy, prophetic, practical – these three adjectives sum up James. He writes a pointed and often picturesque style. Thus he can say, 'Can you not see, you quibbler, that faith divorced from deeds is barren?' (2.20 NEB); or liken the heedless hearer to 'one who looks in a mirror at the face nature gave him' but, after one glance, goes off and forgets what he looked like (1.23f.). His prophetic soul burns with indignation when he contemplates those who make pleasure or money their God and oppress and defraud the needy (4.3-10; 5.1-6). But what James is driving at from start to finish is a Christian profession which will issue in practice. 'Be doers of the word and not hearers only' (1.22) is his demand, as the burden of his complaint is the same as his Lord's. 'They say and do not' (Matt. 23.3). And he sums it all up in a simile: 'As the body is dead when there is no breath left in it, so faith divorced from deeds is lifeless as a corpse' (2.26 NEB).

Is James then at odds with Paul on the issues of faith and works? No, what James denounces is a caricature of Paul's doctrine. By 'faith' and 'works' Paul and James mean different things. The 'faith' on which James comes down like a hammer is barren orthodoxy, mere lip-service to a creed – like that of the man who said to Stanley Jones, 'I believe in God, but not sufficiently to influence my conduct, except now and then'. By contrast, faith for Paul means utter and obedient trust in a living person. Moreover, by 'works' Paul means 'works of law' – what might be called 'earned credits in the ledgers of heaven'. By 'works' James means the lovely deeds of practical religion, e.g. helping widows and orphans in their distress (1.27).

Paul and James have different ways of putting things, and they lay the emphasis in different places; but there is no basic contradiction between them. For James would have agreed with Paul when he wrote, 'The only thing that counts is faith active in love' (Gal. 5.6 NEB); and Paul would have agreed with James that 'faith without works is dead' (2.26); and both would have agreed that the first thing to do with faith is to live by it. For, as P. T. Forsyth put it, 'Christians live by faith and work by love'.

24

The Epistle of Hope

R. L. Stevenson somewhere recalls a conversation which he had with a Fife labourer hard at work 'mucking a byre' (*Anglice*, but inadequately, 'cleaning a cowshed'). Their talk ran on many things, but especially on the aims and ends of life; and as they talked, the labourer let fall one remark which revealed the man: 'Him that has aye something ayont need never be weary.' That man had caught the accents of I Peter. It is the epistle of hope, not a mere witsful hoping for the best, but Christian hope – that lively and confident anticipation of heaven which rests on the God who raised Jesus from the dead and 'gave him glory so that our faith and hope might be in Him'.

It was to keep the lamp of that hope burning in dark days that Peter wrote his letter. But what dark days were these, who were the Christians who needed this summons to hope, and does Peter indeed stand behind this letter?

1. *The author and his readers*

'Peter, an apostle of Jesus Christ' – the letter begins. Three verses from the end we read: 'I write you this brief appeal *through* Silvanus, our trusty brother, as I hold him' (5.12). The letter purports to be the work of the apostle Peter, with Silvanus (the Silas of Acts 15-17) acting as his amanuensis.

Tradition is all in favour of this claim. In the early church the authenticity of the letter was never called in question. Moreover, the contents of the letter seem to confirm the tradition. The writer claims to have been 'a witness of Christ's sufferings', and also 'a partaker in the splendour that is to be revealed' (which reads like a reference to the Transfiguration – 5.1). I Peter 2.23 seems to show first-hand knowledge of the trial of Jesus, as the letter's doctrine of the atonement resembles that in Mark (which, according to tradition, reflects Peter's preaching). To this we may add that some ten or twelve sayings of Jesus are quoted, or echoed, in the letter.

Finally, on various points of detail – Jesus as the Suffering Servant of the Lord, the Cross as a 'tree', the 'stoneship' of Christ (based on Ps. 118.22) – we find a correspondence between the letter and the speeches of Peter in Acts.

But since we live in an age which questions every traditional view, it is not surprising that Peter's connection with the letter has been challenged and denied. We must therefore see what substance there is in these modern doubts and denials.

The first charge is linguistic. It is asked, could a Galilean fisherman who spoke Aramaic with a north-country accent have written the good Greek of this letter? To this we might reply that we have no right to assume that Peter could not have spoken Greek. 'Galilee of the Gentiles,' where Peter came from, was bilingual – the natives spoke both Aramaic and Greek. And Peter had a brother who boasted a Greek name, Andrew. But there is no need for this defence, for the good Greek of the letter can easily be credited to Silvanus. In other words, the voice may well be Peter's, though the literary hand is that of Silvanus. All we know about Silvanus suggests that it may well be so. Silvanus was a Jew but a Roman citizen; he was an early Christian 'prophet' and a devoted worker in the mission to the Gentiles. Such was his standing in the Jerusalem church that he was one of two commissioned to convey and explain the Apostolic Decree (see Acts 15.22f.) to Gentile Christians. Moreover, he had worked with Paul, and had been associated with him in the writing of the two epistles to the Thessalonians. (Not a few phrases in I Peter have parallels in these letters.) Thus the first objection will not stand.

The second charge is historical. It is said that the references to persecution in I Peter imply a time when it was an indictable offence to be a Christian, and therefore point to the time of the famous correspondence between the Emperor Trajan and Pliny, *c.* AD 112, when Peter was long dead.

But this objection is equally inconclusive. The references to slander and reviling in I Peter show that the readers' sufferings were due to the new life they were leading as Christians, and were real and heavy. But *state* persecution is not implied. (1) In I Peter

5.9 the *whole* church throughout the world is said to share in the suffering. Now all the persecutions before the third century were more or less local. The sufferings described in I Peter cannot therefore represent official state action against the Christians. (2) I Peter 2.13f. shows it is still possible to counsel loyalty to the civil authorities like the Emperor and governors (compare the very different position in Revelation). (3) The sufferings of I Peter all belong to the personal sphere and represent hatred and ill-feeling against a non-conforming minority. We are dealing not with state persecution but with something very like a pogrom – something which can be hardly less nerve-racking than official persecution.

The third charge is theological. It is said that I Peter contains too many echoes of Paul's letters to be the work of Peter. In proof of this we are pointed to the use of the phrase 'in Christ', to what the letter has to say about the atoning death of Christ, and to the section on Christian social ethics (2.13ff.). But once again the charge breaks down. In the social ethics section Peter, like Paul, is drawing on a common apostolic stock of ethical instruction[1] – something at the disposal of all early Christian missionaries. Moreover, when we remember how much of what used to be vaguely called 'Paulinism' is now shown to be common apostolic Christianity, we can lay no weight on the letter's teaching about the Cross or its use of the phrase 'in Christ'. Finally, we must never forget that Silvanus, who helped in the writing of this letter, had been a close friend and colleague of Paul's.

So we may follow tradition and attribute the letter to Peter, only adding that Silvanus was probably much more than a mere scribe or secretary. He may well have been the draftsman of the whole letter.

Who were the recipients of the letter? Answer: 'the elect of the Dispersion in Pontus, Galatia, Cappadocia, Asia and Bithynia' (1.1). Since the word 'Dispersion' commonly meant the Jews living in Gentile lands outside Palestine, we might, on first thoughts, take the readers to be Jews living in the four Roman provinces (administratively, Pontus and Bithynia formed a single province) of the address. But the letter shows that the readers were largely Gentiles (1.14,18 and especially 4.3); and there can be little doubt that the people addressed are Gentile Christians

---

[1] The technical term for this is *parēnesis* – moral instruction with a dash of exhortation.

(recently converted) in Asia Minor who form part of the true people of God scattered abroad in an alien world. The letter, whose purpose was to encourage them to firm faith in the face of persecution, was probably meant as a circular letter to be read in the various districts named.

2. *Place of origin*

Where was the letter written? The clue is to be found in I Peter 5.13: 'She who is in Babylon ... sends you greetings.' Peter had a wife, but it is quite improbable that he is referring to her here. 'She,' by general consent, refers to the church from which Peter writes (cf. Moffatt's translation: 'Your sister church in Babylon'). But 'Babylon'? Can this be the once famous city on the Euphrates with the hanging gardens? The answer must be No. There is not a scrap of tradition to connect Peter with that Babylon; but there is plenty of tradition to connect him with Rome. Accordingly, it is generally agreed that 'Babylon' in I Peter is what it is in the book of Revelation (see Rev. 17.5; 18.2), a pseudonym for Rome.

3. *Date of the letter*

We have already dismissed the view that the letter belongs to the time of Pliny's correspondence with the Emperor Trajan; and we have seen that there is no cogent reason for denying that Peter, who perished in Rome in the Neronian persecution, stands behind the letter. A date, therefore, of about AD 63 would fit the facts implied in the letter. Let us remember that it is still possible to advise loyalty to the Roman Emperor, and that the language of the letter suggests an impending rather than an actual persecution. We may therefore surmise that the letter was written just before the great outrage of AD 64, when the persecution brewing in Rome looked like spreading to the provinces, and that for this reason the writer used 'Babylon' as a pseudonym for Rome as a precautionary disguise.

4. *The letter itself*

After the opening address and a noble doxology for the risen Christ, Peter describes the fulfilment of the prophecies in the gospel of their salvation and calls on his readers to respond to it by holy living (1.1-2.3).

As the people (or temple) of God, of which Christ is the living head, they are summoned to a service which is both priestly (the offering of spiritual sacrifices) and prophetic (to tell out the triumphs of the God who has called them out of darkness into light – 2.4-10).

Peter then instructs them in various patterns of Christian social behaviour (2.11-3.12), before facing them with the prospect of persecution : if and when it comes, he says, they should endure it in the temper of Christ and live as converted men should, by the will of God (3.13-4.6). In this critical time let them use their various gifts for God's glory and the good of their fellows (4.7-11).

The ordeal of persecution should not surprise them; rather they should count it joy to suffer for Christ's sake, though never as malefactors or mischief-makers (4.12-19).

As a 'fellow-elder' and a 'witness of Christ's sufferings', Peter urges the elders to shepherd their flocks faithfully, in hope of the Head Shepherd's reward (5.1-5). Let them be humble, vigilant and steadfast in trial, relying always on the gracious God who has called them to glory (5.6-11).

Then, with a mention of his amanuensis, Silvanus, and 'his son Mark', Peter sends greetings (5.12-14).

In I Peter there are two main themes. One is steadfastness in persecution. The other is that of good behaviour (*anastrophē* is the Greek word, and of 13 examples in the New Testament, 6 occur in I Peter). But the dominant theme is the summons to Christian hope in dark days. 'Blessed are they,' said Jesus, 'who are persecuted for righteousness' sake' (Matt. 5.10). There is no better commentary on the Beatitude than this letter. Here is no 'grey and close-lipped Stoicism' which can only grin and bear it. Here is a document which has caught the true temper of that master who, for the joy that was set before him, endured the cross – which, though the skies lour and the enemy press hard and heavy, glows with that hope of 'an inheritance which is imperishable, undefiled and unfading, kept in heaven for you' (1.4).

NOTES

In the body of the letter there seems to be a break between 4.11 and 4.12. Not only do we have a doxology and an Amen at 4.11, but in vv. 12ff. persecution seems to have begun, whereas earlier it was only a possibility.

I Peter was addressed to all the churches of Asia Minor, but it looks as if some were being persecuted, others were not. It has therefore been suggested that Peter sent two forms of his letter – one a general warning of the danger, the other advice to those in the thick of it. No doubt the messengers were told to read in each congregation the form suited to their own situation.

1 Peter a baptismal sermon?

In 1911 a German scholar named Perdelwitz not only proposed to split I Peter into two parts, but argued that the first and main part of the letter was a sermon to the newly-baptized. In the doxology and new address ('beloved') he found evidence of a clear break between 4.11 and 4.12, and he insisted that, whereas the persecutions of 4.12ff. are present facts, those in the earlier chapters are simply possibilities. His theory was, therefore, that I Peter contains two letters. The main letter which ends at 4.11, is the baptismal sermon; the remainder is a letter to a persecuted community.

In our time other scholars, smitten with what has been called 'pan-liturgism', i.e. the tendency to find the influence of early Christian worship everywhere, have supported this theory.

But there is no real justification for it. (1) It posits a complete break between 4.11 and 4.12. But we have already given a more convincing explanation of this difficulty. (2) It writes off as fictions, quite unwarrantably, the opening address and the personalia at the end. And (3) it forces baptismal meanings on quite general passages. To explain the language of I Peter 1-3, all we need to assume is that the readers had been recently converted and were being recalled to their baptismal vows. And it is a firm count against the baptismal-sermon theory that in the letter new birth is linked not with baptism but with the Resurrection (1.3) and the Word of God in the preached gospel (1.23).

The conclusion, therefore, is that I Peter is not a baptismal sermon but an ordinary letter written to newly-converted Christians, in order to encourage them amid imminent dangers and to testify to the power of faith to triumph over all hardships.

25

The Correspondence of the Elder

1 John

If, among the General Epistles (as they are called) Hebrews is the epistle of priesthood, James the epistle of practice, and I Peter the epistle of hope, I John is the epistle of life. For St John, 'life' or 'eternal life' – and they mean the same thing – is another name for salvation: the salvation of which God in Christ is the author. (Note: To 'have eternal life' is the equivalent of 'being in the kingdom of God' and of being 'in Christ'.) With 'life' John begins (1.1), and with 'life' he ends (5.20). If we ask what he means by 'life' the answer is: the life which is life indeed, life lived in fellowship with God through Christ its mediator, life freed from the slavery of sin, life whose finest fruit is love, life that can never die.

1. *The author, his aim, and his readers*

Though the Epistle is anonymous, its author was obviously some venerable father-in-God, whose ripe Christian experience enabled him to write this pastoral letter to his 'little children'. Who was he? If style and thought prove anything, the Epistle is by the same hand as the Fourth Gospel. Not only do we find in the letter the same distinctive idioms and phrases, but there is hardly a thought in the letter which has not its parallel in the Gospel; and the same great contrasts of light and darkness, good and evil, love and hate, life and death, pervade the Epistle no less profoundly than they do the Gospel. I John is therefore probably the work of John the Elder, the disciple of the apostle John.[1] (In II and III John, which

[1] For a good brief defence of the common authorship of the Fourth Gospel and the Johannine Epistles, see Neil Alexander, *The Epistles of John*, SCM Press 1962, pp. 23-26.

are almost certainly by the same hand, he calls himself 'the Elder'.)
The place of writing will then be the same: Ephesus or its neigh-
bourhood; the readers will be the local churches in the 'diocese' of
Ephesus; and the letter will belong to the last decades of the first
century.

Which came first, Epistle or Gospel? Since many passages in
the Epistle need the help of the Gospel to explain them, it probably came second. The Gospel was written in order that men
might have life by faith in the Son of God (John 20.31); the Epistle,
to explain how John's readers might know that they had that life
(I John 5.13).

St John wrote primarily to build up his readers in the Christian
faith by stressing its fundamentals. But he had another aim. Para-
doxically, this epistle which has so much to say about Christian
love (*agapē*) is also strongly polemical. If its first aim is to edify,
its second aim is to attack – to attack 'the spirit of error' (4.6) and
its propagators who were 'misleading' the faithful (2.26). The 'error'
was Docetism, which was a special brand of Gnosticism. Docetism
(derived from the Greek verb *dokein*, 'seem') was an early Christian heresy which said that Christ only *seemed* to be a man, that is,
denied the reality of the Incarnation. Among the Docetists was a
man called Cerinthus who lived in and around Ephesus towards
the end of the first century. According to him, Jesus and Christ
were two separate beings, 'Christ' being a heavenly power who
descended on the man Jesus at his Baptism and left him before the
Crucifixion. It is this 'Cerinthian' heresy which John attacks in
I John 5.6: 'This is he who came with water and blood: Jesus
Christ. He came, not by water alone, but by water and blood.'
(Here 'water' represents the Baptism, 'blood', the Crucifixion.)

The followers of Cerinthus, who had 'seceded' from the church
(2.19; 4.1), were therefore going about saying in effect, 'The Incarnation is not real. With our superior knowledge, we are *past*
sin, and morals do not matter.'

If we read I John carefully, we shall catch echoes of John's
controversy with the 'Cerinthians'. Whenever a sentence begins,
'If we claim to be sinless' (1.8), 'If anyone says ...' (2.4), or John
pillories a man who, professing to love God, hates his brother
(2.11 etc.), or strongly affirms that Jesus is the Son of God come
in the flesh (4.2), we may be sure he has the heretics in mind.
And yet the Epistle is far from being all polemics; for time and

time again John lifts the whole matter out of the dust of mere polemics into the lucid atmosphere of eternal truth.

2. *The plan of the Epistle*

At first glance the Epistle appears to be plan-less – a collection of meditations 'spiralling' round a few main themes. But a verse like I John 2.3, 'Here is the test by which we can make sure that we know him', gives us the clue to the true nature of the letter. It is really an apparatus of 'tests' for the possession of eternal life (as Robert Law's book on I John, *The Tests of Life*, rightly suggests.) These 'tests' are based on three great conceptions of God: God is light, God is life, God is love. So we may divide the letter into three sections, introduced – the second not very clearly at 2.25 – by these conceptions. Under each head the question examined is: Are we walking in light? Are we children of God? Are we dwelling in love? And the three 'tests' proposed under each section are: right living, genuine loving and true believing.

With this clue to its structure we may analyse the letter thus:

Prologue: The Word of Life in Jesus (1.1-4).

God is light: Do we walk in the light? Then we must: Dwell in the light, and live as Christ lived (right living: 1.5-2.6). Love our brother, and not the world[2] (genuine loving: 2.7-17). Believe that Jesus is the Christ, the Son of God (true believing: 2.18-24).

God is life: Are we children of God? Then we must: Do right as his children (right living: 2.25-3.10). Love our brothers, not in talk only but in act (genuine loving: 3.11-18). Confess that Jesus Christ has come in the flesh (true believing: 3.19-4.6).

God is love: Do we dwell in love? Then we must (here the tests melt into love):

Obey his commandments.

Believe that Jesus is the Christ who came by both water and blood (4.7-5.12).[3]

Epilogue: The assurance of eternal life and the Christian cer-

[2] As often in John, 'the world' here means 'human society as it organizes itself apart from God'.

[3] The words in the Authorized Version of I John 5.7, 'For there are three that bear record in heaven, the Father, the Word and the Holy Ghost: and these three are one', are a later scribal gloss. They do not occur in our earliest MSS.

tainties. (We know that our worthy prayers are heard, that the Son of God keeps God's child safe, that we belong to God's family, and that the Son of God enables us to know the true God.) Beware of all bogus gods (5.13-20)!

3. *The value of the epistle*

Even polemics, under the providence of God, can yield their happy fruits. For the twin glories of this Epistle are, first, its emphasis on the Incarnation and, second, its emphasis on Christian love. You might entitle it (as the NEB does) 'Recall to Fundamentals': for what it says is that (*a*) true Christian faith is faith in the Incarnation, and (*b*) true Christian life is the life of brotherly love.

The core of the Christian doctrine of the Incarnation is that 'God was in Christ' – that in Jesus, the man of Nazareth, the transcendent God stooped low for us men and our salvation. Cerinthus and his followers, by reducing the Incarnation to a mere semblance, drove John to reaffirm its reality with all the spiritual passion at his command. To all their speculations he replies uncompromisingly, 'Jesus Christ has come in the flesh.' 'No one who denies the Son has the Father. He who confesses the Father has the Son also,' and, 'He who has the Son has life.' Of course St John was right. If God was not really in Christ, the gospel is 'a tale told by an idiot, full of sound and fury, signifying nothing'. The Incarnation is the root and crown of all Christian truth.

The other glory of the Epistle is its magnificent insistence on the primacy of love in the Christian life. Time and time again he insists that 'only love is true churchmanship' and that 'the unloving knows nothing of God' (4.8). This teaching comes to its climax in I John 4.7-21, which is as truly John's Song of Songs in praise of Christian love as I Cor. 13 is Paul's.

All this is really only the practical corollary of John's doctrine of God in Christ. It is because love is the law of God's being – all his activity is loving activity, whether he creates, or rules, or judges[4] – supremely shown in the sending of Christ his Son, that we must love our brothers, and by so loving, show we are really God's children. 'Beloved, if God so loved us, we also ought to love one another' (4.11).

Yet, as Carlyle says, 'there is nothing inexorable but love'; and though John never tires of saying, 'Little children, love one an-

[4] C. H. Dodd, *The Johannine Epistles*, Hodder and Stoughton 1946, p. 110.

other,' he blazes out indignantly at that pseudo-Christianity which, feigning love for God, looks with loveless eyes upon its Christian brethren. 'If any one says "I love God" and hates his brother, he is a liar; for he who does not love his brother whom he has seen, cannot love God whom he has not seen' (4.20).

Of St John, then, we may fitly say (in Browning's words):

> Like Dante, he loved well, because he hated –
> Hated wickedness, and all that hinders loving.

II John

Imagine a venerable 'bishop' who, hearing of the spread of false doctrine in his diocese, writes a pastoral letter about the danger, and then, hearing of a particular congregation being badly affected, decides to send it a brief note containing the gist of his previous letter. This is the relation between I and II John. II John is a miniature of I John, with hardly a phrase not found in the bigger letter; and its author, 'the Elder', must be the same, John the Elder of Ephesus. That 'the lady chosen by God' (NEB) named in the first verse is a church, not a woman, admits of little doubt. So 'the children of your sister, chosen by God' (v. 13) who send their greetings, are the members of the Elder's church.

Evidently some members of the congregation addressed, on a visit to the Elder, had given him a report which both pleased and vexed him. He was pleased that some of the congregation had remained loyal to the truth, but he felt the need to reiterate the duty of Christian love (vv. 4-6). What vexed him was the news of the spread of an 'advanced' doctrine which denied the reality of the Incarnation. (Clearly, as in I John, these *avant garde* Christians were Docetists.) In his reply, which paves the way for a personal visit, the Elder declares that any 'advanced doctrine' which severs itself from the historic Christian faith is delusive – lose the true doctrine of Jesus as the Son, and you lose the Father too – and he bids his readers boycott the heretics. 'Shut your doors on them,' is the burden of his advice, 'and cut them in the street'. Drastic counsel indeed, which seems at variance with the Christian law of love! To this the Elder might have retorted that in face of the perilous situation no toleration was possible. In a situation like this the problem (and it is ours as well as the Elder's) is to find a way of living with those whose concept of Christ seems sadly defective, a way which neither infringes the Christian law of love nor compromises our loyalty to Christian truth.

III John

III John, probably written from Ephesus about the same time as I and II John, might be called 'the Johannine Philemon', because it is a private note concerned with personal relations. Yet, as in Philemon, there is a local church in the background – perhaps the very one to which II John was sent.

It was a 'row' in the congregation which evoked the letter, and the chief persons concerned in it were:

The Elder, who wrote the letter;
Gaius, its recipient;
Diotrephes, whose action provoked it; and
Demetrius who carried the letter.

Diotrephes, who held the chief office in the church (and 'loved his pre-eminence', comments the Elder grimly) evidently resented any 'direction' from the Elder in Ephesus. Not only had he refused to welcome some missioners from the Elder, but he had even expelled local church members who gave them hospitality. So, in this letter, the Elder writes to his friend Gaius (perhaps the minority leader), thanking him for his past kindness to the missioners and asking his support for them on their second visit (vv. 2-8). He hopes himself to come soon and 'have it out' with Diotrephes. Then, after commending Demetrius who is to carry his letter (and may have been the leader of the missioners), he sends greetings.

Was Diotrephes presbyter or bishop? Canon Streeter[5] held that you cannot be 'a Jack in office' unless the office is there already, and went on to argue that Diotrephes was in fact the first 'monarchical bishop' in Asia. Did this kind of 'bishop' exist as early as the last decades of the first century? Is it not as likely that Diotrephes was a presbyter – a presbyter who 'had a grand memory for forgetting' that he was only such *inter pares*?

Whatever be the truth about Diotrephes, what is the use of having a name which means literally 'Cherished by Zeus', if your conduct is condemned by Christ? 'Whoever wants to be first', he said, 'must become the willing servant of all' (Mark 10.44 NEB).

[5] B. H. Streeter, *The Primitive Church*, Macmillan 1929, p. 85.

26

Contending for the Faith

Who was Jude? If he was 'the brother of James' (v. 1) he was the Jude of Mark 6.3 and 'Founder's kin' (the grandsons of this Jude were leaders in the churches of Palestine and lived on into Trajan's reign, 98-117). Certainly his knowledge of the Old Testament and the book of Enoch (vv. 14f.) suggests a Jew. If he was another Jude, Streeter's guess that he was Jude, the third bishop of Jerusalem, is as good as any. Where his readers lived is matter of conjecture – possibly in Syrian Antioch. Take the writer to be the brother of James, and a date for the letter later than 70-80 is unlikely. If he was another Jude, it may belong to the end of the first century.

But we do know why he wrote. He was 'contending for the faith once for all delivered to the saints' (v. 3). The loyalty of the faithful was being menaced by heretics. These men were apparently Christian antinomians or libertines (v. 4) who by their unbelief, irreverence, insubordination, carousing and immorality were disgracing the fair name they bore. It is no part of a Christian's duty to call people by soft names when they merit hard ones. In this spirit Jude denounces the heretics. First, however, he holds out before his readers, as an awful warning', the fate which overtook the disobedient Israelites in the Wilderness, the rebellious angels, and the cities of the plain. Then he turns on the trouble-makers. 'They are blemishes on your love feasts,' he says, 'as they boldly carouse together, looking after themselves.' And his anger blazes into magniloquence: 'Waterless clouds ... fruitless trees ... wild waves, casting up the foam of their own shame, wandering stars for whom the nether gloom of darkness has been reserved' (vv. 12f.).

But when he has emptied the vials of his vituperation on the heretics, his denunciations give place to a series of noble imperatives:

> But you, beloved, build yourselves up on your most holy faith; pray in the Holy Spirit; keep yourselves in the love of God; wait for the mercy of our Lord Jesus Christ unto eternal life. And convince some, who doubt; save some, by snatching them out of the fire; on some have mercy with fear, hating even the garment spotted by the flesh (vv. 19-23).

It is New Testament teaching that Christians are 'kept by the power of God' (I Peter 1.5), a truth which Jude recognizes in his noble doxology addressed to him 'who can keep you from falling and bring you safe to his glorious presence, innocent and happy' (24).[1] But since God has given men free will, it is always possible for some to sin themselves out of shelter of the divine love. Jude reminds us that God's loving vigilance must be matched by man's vigilant effort – what we call 'Christian perseverance'. The man who expressed the truth in the memorable phrase 'Keep yourselves in the love of God' surely deserves a place, however humble, in the New Testament canon.

[1] Jerusalem Bible translation.

27

The Promise of his Coming

We have separated II Peter from I Peter and put it after Jude for three reasons: (1) It is almost certainly not Peter's work, (2) it borrows freely from Jude, and (3) it is the latest book in the New Testament.

Why do scholars believe Peter did not write the letter? First, because early Church Fathers like Origen and Eusebius had grave suspicions about it. Second, in tone and substance it bears no kind of resemblance to I Peter. Third, its rather baroque Greek was surely never written by a Galilean fisherman. Fourth, it borrows wholesale from Jude (II Peter 2.1-3.3 showing at least a dozen debts to Jude 4-18). Fifth, it refers to Paul's letters as 'scripture' (3.16). These five considerations compel every honest scholar to refuse the letter to Peter and to ascribe it to some church leader who, about the middle of the second century, borrowed the authority of Peter's great name to enforce a warning to his readers.

Our author was worried by the activity of false teachers in his community. That they were libertines is clear enough; but it was their scoffing attitude to the hope of Christ's second advent which mainly moved him to write. They were saying to the faithful: 'Where is his promised coming? Generation after generation has gone by, and still he has not come. Let us abandon this foolish expectation.' To these men our author has his answer, as we shall see.

The letter itself consists of a 'Be zealous', a 'Beware' and a 'Be prepared'. First, calling himself 'an eyewitness of his (Christ's) majesty' (a clear reference to the Transfiguration), and reminding them of the sure word of prophecy, he bids them be zealous to 'make their calling and election sure' (ch. 1). Next, borrowing

most of Jude's 'sanctions', he tells his readers to beware of the
heretics. 'They promise you freedom' he warns, 'but they themselves are slaves of corruption' (ch. 2). Then, rounding on the
scoffers, he declares the coming of the Day of the Lord to be certain, and bids them follow the advice of 'our beloved brother
Paul' and be prepared for it by growing in the saving knowledge
of Christ (ch. 3).

A modern German scholar, Ernst Käsemann, thinks II Peter
should be excluded from the canon because in it 'orthodoxy, based
on a fictitious Peter, has replaced faith'.[1] Would we have been the
poorer if the men who helped to form the canon had left it out?
Perhaps not. Yet we should have lost a lovely sentence like 'until
the day dawns and the morning star rises in your hearts' (1.19),
a wry comment on Paul's letters ('they contain some obscure passages which the ignorant and unstable misinterpret to their own
ruin', 3.15f.), and, above all, a wise word about Christ's second
coming.   ,

We may, or we may not, believe that the world is destined to
go up in flames 'with a loud noise' (though some of our scientists,
with the proliferation of nuclear weapons, would not discount the
possibility); but, like pseudonymous Peter, we must believe that
one day God is going to 'wind up' the scroll of history and make
a final end of evil. So we may still find a salutary message in what
he says to the scoffers, quoting Ps. 90.4: 'With the Lord one day
is as a thousand years, and a thousand years as one day. The Lord
is not slow about his promise as some count slowness, but is forbearing toward you, not wishing that any should perish, but that
all should reach repentance' (3.8f.). Till the Day of the Lord comes,
it is our duty to continue steadfastly in the faith and grow in grace
while 'according to his promise we wait for new heavens and a new
earth in which righteousness dwells' (3.13).

This is surely well said, and was worth saying.

[1] R. M. Grant, op. cit., pp. 230f.

28

The Judgment and Victory of God

James Denney once likened the book of Revelation to a tunnel
with light at the beginning and light at the end, and in the middle,
as he put it, 'a long stretch of darkness through which lurid objects
thunder past, bewildering and stunning the reader'. This is the
ordinary reader's first reaction to it. He can make some sense of
the letters to the seven churches in the first three chapters; he can
thrill to the vision of the New Jerusalem in the last two. But that
'long stretch of darkness' in between – what on earth, he asks, is
it all about? Nor will he be wiser if you tell him that it is about a
throne and a scroll, seals, trumpets and bowls, four horsemen, a
beast no. 666, and a scarlet woman, with a millennial reign for
God's saints, and a lake of fire for the devil. The true answer to his
question is that it is about the judgment and victory of God. But
this will not be immediately obvious to him. So he may be comforted to learn that, if the book puzzles him, it has puzzled many
down the centuries. The early church hesitated long before letting
it into the canon, and at the Reformation Luther thought its inclusion a mistake. Yet, for reasons to follow, we may be glad that
it got in, and none can deny that it serves to round off the New
Testament with a Hallelujah Chorus – 'And they shall reign for
ever and ever' (22.5).

1. *Apocalypses and the Apocalypse*

Scholars commonly call this book 'the Apocalypse'. 'Revelation' is
the Latin equivalent. The word means 'unveiling', and Revelation
is the finest Christian specimen of apocalyptic literature, i.e. writings which 'unveil' the last things and reveal the final victory and
judgment of God. (Many of us, incidentally, have an apocalyptic

streak in our make-up – like the little lass who, on being told that 'Granny had gone to be with God', exclaimed, 'Gosh! How posh!' Somehow she divined that, though it had been 'sad about Gran', it was going to be all right now that she had gone to be with 'the Good Man above'.)[1]

Our book was by no means the first apocalypse. Between 200 BC and AD 100 the Jews, groaning under the yoke of foreign oppressors, produced many, the first and greatest being the OT book of Daniel. (Others include II Esdras in the Apocrypha and the Book of Enoch.)

Apocalypses represent man's search for an interpretation of history which will embrace catastrophe and transcend immediate tragedy. They are 'tracts for bad times', books written to nerve the faithful in their ordeal by lifting the veil and letting them see the final issue of God's purpose. Inevitably they take the form of visions – visions of what lies beyond the doom-dark horizons of history.

But why should the images of an apocalypse be so fantastic, its numbers so queer, its scenery so 'out of this world'? There are two answers. For one thing, these books attempt to utter the unutterable, to describe what the eye of sense has not seen, to peer into the undisclosed future; and it is only in the language of myth and symbol we can do this. Second; apocalypses appear in a time when freedom of speech is in eclipse. They are a kind of underground resistance literature. Therefore your apocalyptist dare not deal in plain speech: he must wrap up his message in a kind of cypher to which he hopes his readers will have the key. Thus our author must refer to Rome as 'Babylon' and its persecuting emperor as the 'beast'.

We may now turn to the Apocalypse. What crisis produced it? Who were its recipients? And who its author?

Irenaeus says the book was written near the end of the reign of the Roman Emperor Domitian (AD 81-96), probably therefore about AD 95. Study of its contents confirms this. In AD 64 Nero had begun to persecute the Christians, and about thirty years later the smouldering fires of persecution blazed out again. This time the excuse for harrying the Christians was 'emperor worship'. (This was, in intention, an attempt to bind the far-flung Roman Empire

---

[1] Another bit of evidence is our liking for Blake's 'Jerusalem' with its 'dark satanic mills', its 'unfolding clouds', its 'chariots of fire'.

together by giving it what it lacked, a common religion.) Earlier emperors had not taken this cult of themselves too seriously. Domitian did, demanding that state officials address him as 'Our Lord and God', and the cult was rigorously enforced in Asia where the seven churches were. Statues of the Emperor were erected, priests appointed, and the subject peoples commanded to accord divine honours to Domitian. (Cf. Rev. 14.9-11 with its reference to 'worshippers of the beast and its image'.)

Christ or Caesar? A very serious issue this was for the good Christian. One only deserved the name of 'Lord'; and yet to defy the imperial edict was to court banishment and even death. Our writer had defied it, and found himself exiled to the lonely Aegean isle of Patmos where the Romans kept political prisoners. Here he saw the visions recorded in his book. He calls it a 'prophecy' (1.3); and if a prophet means one who has been admitted to the inner counsels of God, he has a right to call himself one (cf. Amos 3.7: 'The Lord God does nothing without revealing his secrets to his servants the prophets').

Who was he? He was a Jewish Christian named John (1.4,9; 22.8). But if style is any test, he was not the man who wrote John's Gospel and Epistles. The evangelist writes with the profound simplicity of a Bunyan; the prophet of Patmos (who writes a very Hebraic Greek, with a grammar all his own) has the forked-lightning style of a Carlyle describing the French Revolution. (The parallel goes even further, for Carlyle saw the Revolution as a vision of judgment in which the wrath of God was visiting the sins of a corrupt and sinful generation.) The authoritative tone of his writing shows him to have been a church leader in Asia. To distinguish him from the Fourth Evangelist, and to describe his special gift, he is commonly called 'John the Seer'. His purpose was to fortify his fellow-Christians in the day of their ordeal.

2. *The contents of Revelation*

His book takes the form of a letter – a pastoral letter – and was meant to be read to the seven churches of Asia. But it is best regarded as a *drama* of divine judgment and victory in which the action moves forward to a tremendous *dénouement*. For his materials John has drawn on his own visions (1.10, etc.), the Old Testament (especially the book of Daniel), Jewish apocalyptic, the apostolic *kērygma*, and even international myths (like that of the Woman, the Child and the Dragon). But all are skilfully woven into a unity, and the drama flames to its climax in the destruction of Babylon (Rome) and the vindication of God's people (the church).

We can divide the book's contents into seven sections:

1. Prologue (ch. 1).
2. Letters to the seven churches (chs. 2-3).
3. The open door in heaven (chs. 4-5).
4. Visions of judgment (chs. 6-16).
5. The fall of Babylon (chs. 17-19).
6. The consummation (ch. 20-22.5).
7. Epilogue (22.6-21).

Before we fill in this outline, let us note two features of the book.

First: one of John's dramatic devices is *the principle of parenthesis*. Just as a musician may introduce a light movement between two sombre ones, so John, when his visions of judgment become almost intolerable, has a way of relieving the tension by switching the scene from the agonies of earth to the beatitude of heaven. There is one such interlude in ch. 7 when, right in the middle of the seven seals of judgment, John gives us a glimpse of the redeemed martyrs in glory, arrayed in white robes. Another one comes in ch. 14 with the picture of the church triumphant and the Son of Man in power.

Second: a feature of apocalypses is *double happenings* – events in heaven which have their counterparts on earth. Thus in ch. 12 the archangel Michael's victory over Satan in heaven is the counterpart of Christ's earthly triumph over evil on the Cross.

Now let us attempt a running synopsis of the book:

In the prologue John salutes the seven churches and tells how 'Christ in majesty' granted him visions of what must soon take place (ch. 1).

In the following letters to the seven churches (Ephesus, Smyrna, Pergamum, Thyatira, Sardis, Philadelphia and Laodicea), John, as Christ's mouthpiece, speaks in encouragement and in reproof to the various congregations whose spiritual states he knows well. The brightest light falls on loyal Philadelphia, the darkest shadow on lukewarm Laodicea (chs. 2-3).

With chs. 4 and 5 the revelation proper begins. Through an open door in heaven John sees the ineffable God on his throne worshipped by the heavenly hosts. In the Almighty's hand is a scroll fastened with seven seals (the book of God's plan for the world). Only one is found worthy to open it, a lamb bearing the marks of slaughter on him. (At once we think of one who was led 'as a lamb to the slaughter', Isa. 53.7. John is depicting Jesus as the suffering and victorious Servant of the Lord.) With the opening of the sealed book the visions of judgment begin. There are three series of seven – seven seals, seven trumpets, seven bowls. Heavenly counterparts of what is happening on earth, they probably represent not successive periods of history but variations on the theme of divine judgment.

First come the judgments inaugurated by the breaking of the seven *seals* (chs. 6 and 8.1). Four horsemen ride forth to spread pestilence and death in the earth. With the breaking of the fifth seal the martyrs are heard calling on God to vindicate them. They are given white robes and told to 'rest a little longer'. The sixth seal brings a world-wide earthquake, and with the seventh – after the parenthetical glimpse of the redeemed in glory – comes 'a brief silence in heaven'; but it is only the lull before the re-gathering storm.

After the seals come the *trumpets* (chs. 8-9 plus 11.15). The first six herald hail on the earth, fire in the sea, the poisoning of the rivers, the eclipse of the heavenly bodies, a plague of stinging locusts and angelic cavalry dealing death to men. Then, after two obscure parentheses (the Angel and the Book, the Temple and the Two Witnesses, 10.1-11.14), the seventh trumpet sounds (11.15) and a great shout is heard in heaven: 'The sovereignty has passed to our Lord and his Christ, and he shall reign for ever and ever.'

With ch. 12, in what might be called a parenthetical 'flash-back', there appears a woman (the church) giving birth to a child (Christ) who is menaced by a dragon (the Devil). When the child is caught up to heaven (the Ascension), the dragon pursues him thither, only to be conquered and cast out by Michael and his angels. Then, on earth, the dragon attacks the woman's offspring, helped by two beasts. The first (the Roman Empire) wars on God's people, while the second (the Caesar-cult) acts as his bestial accomplice.

With ch. 14 comes another parenthesis supplying the eternal background to what is taking place. In it John sees the church triumphant and the Son of Man in power. Then angel after angel announces the coming harvest of judgment.

In chs. 15 and 16, to the sound of the victorious martyrs singing in glory, seven angels go forth bearing the *bowls* of God's wrath. The first four bring ruin to the land, the sea, the rivers and the sun; the fifth plunges the beast's realm in darkness; and when the sixth is outpoured on the Euphrates, foul spirits muster the kings of the earth for the last great battle[2] between God and the forces of evil. The seventh brings an earthquake which devastates the cities.

With chs. 17 and 18 we approach the climax. In a vision John sees Babylon (Rome) as a great harlot astride a beast and drunk with the blood of God's people. Then he hears 'great Babylon's doom pronounced by heaven's command', while the kings of the earth, the merchants and the sea-captains lament her fall.

The resultant Hallelujahs in heaven have hardly died away when Christ, the Word of God, rides forth on a white horse to vanquish the beast and his worshippers (ch. 19).

The victorious Christ now reigns on earth with his martyrs for a thousand years. Then the devil, who has been bound in prison, is let loose to make his final attack on God's people; and after his defeat and consignment to the lake of fire, comes the last judgment: 'I saw a great white throne and him who sat on it ... and I saw the dead, great and small, standing before the throne, and the books were opened' (ch. 20).

Finally, with the darkness of Doomsday past, we emerge from 'the tunnel' into the light. Like a new Moses, John stands on his Pisgah peak and surveys the promised land. With the old heaven and earth gone, he is granted a glimpse of 'the holy city, the new Jerusalem' where 'the Lord God will be their light, and they shall reign for ever and ever' (ch. 21-22.5).

In the epilogue John is assured that the fulfilment is near, and with a curse on all who tamper with his book, he writes a benediction (22.6-21).

3. *The interpretation of the book and its value*

No book of the Bible has suffered more at the hands of its interpreters or been a happier hunting-ground for cranks. One grievous error has been to turn it into a kind of Old Moore's Almanac replete with veiled allusions to persons lying, so to speak, in the

[2] Armageddon. Its meaning – and proper spelling – are still in doubt. See the Bible dictionaries.

womb of the future. Thus the beast of 13.18, whose number is 666, has been identified, according to the interpreter's time and taste, with Mohammed, the Pope, Luther, Napoleon and Hitler. John was probably thinking of the wicked Emperor Nero.[3] The only cure for such fantasies is to read Revelation in the light of the times for which John wrote.

Another mistake has been to interpret John's symbols with a crude occidental literalism – to regard, for example, the last two chapters as a divinely-inspired ordnance map of heaven. Thus, when John describes the new Jerusalem as a cube-shaped city of pure gold, with twelve gates each bearing a pearl, and having a wall 1500 ft high with the names of the twelve apostles written into it, his interest is not in statistics but in symbols. His aim is to suggest the indescribable magnitude and perfection of the Eternal City. Here it is not the celestial map-makers but the poets – like St Bernard in his 'Jerusalem the Golden' – who have best caught his meaning. Like the poet William Blake who wrote that apocalyptic hymn 'Jerusalem' and, as he was dying, 'burst out singing of the things he saw in heaven', John of Patmos had not only a vivid sense of the reality of the unseen but also a command of what psychologists call 'archetypal images', e.g. the old dragon, the book of life, war in heaven, the morning star, which he employs without explanation, leaving the rest to our imaginations.

Again, the man who would understand Revelation must familiarize himself with John's mystical theology of numbers. Thus 3 is the number of heaven, 4 of earth, 7 the perfect number. (A 'broken' 7 – 'a time and times and half a time' – i.e. $3\frac{1}{2}$ years, stands for the period of the supremacy of evil.) 12 is the 'church number. The triple 'Holy, holy, holy, Lord God Almighty' exemplifies the heavenly 3 (4.8). As there are four winds, so there are four corners of earth (7.1). Again we note that the book of God's redemptive plan for the world has seven seals (5.1), as his judgments fall in sevens on the ungodly. No less interesting is the number of those sealed for salvation in 7.4: 144,000. This is twelve times twelve multiplied by one thousand; and by it John means us to think of the vast completeness of those

---

[3] The Greeks and the Hebrews used the letters of their alphabets as numerals. The Greek NERON KAISAR, transliterated into Hebrew script, produces 666 – a number which persistently falls short of the perfect number seven.

who, with their leaders,
Have conquered in the fight.

Thus (to repeat) John's book must be read in the light of the times
when it was written, his allusions looked for in the persons, events
and even rumours[4] of the last decade of the first century AD.

Here it is worth raising an old question to which an able modern
scholar, G. B. Caird, has given a new answer.[5] In Rev. 1.3 we read:
'The crisis (*kairos*) is near.' What crisis is this? All agree that it
is the persecution of the church by Rome. But in the visions which
follow, this crisis is set against the background of the crisis to end
all crises, the end of the world. Did John expect the world to end
soon? Most would answer Yes. But since John expected his prophecies *in their entirety* to be soon fulfilled, the likelier answer is
that the crisis of 1.3 is not the world's end but the persecution of
the church. This crisis John sets against the backdrop of the
supreme crisis in order to show prospective martyrs the real nature
of their suffering and its place in God's eternal purpose.

To take an illustration. In the Interpreter's House, Bunyan's
Pilgrim is perplexed to see a fire burning against a wall, which
flames still higher when a man throws water on it. The Pilgrim's
puzzlement only ends when the interpreter takes him to 'the back-
side of the wall' where he sees a man with a jug of *oil* in his hand.
So history has a backroom into which the man of faith can look
and see the inner meaning of the events in which he lives. Such a
man was John of Patmos. His aim in writing was to show Christians who might be haled before the Roman magistrates 'the back-
side of the wall'. In other words, the martyrs were to know that
their suffering was a part of the purpose of God, attested by his
Christ (1.2), 'a purpose as old as the world and as ultimate as the
crack of doom'.

Seen thus, Revelation takes on a new relevance and can speak
its Word of God for the times in which you and I are fated to live.
It has in fact a threefold value.

To begin with, it is *a message for a crisis*. It is trite but true to

---

[4] A widely current one, echoed in Rev. 13.3 and 17.8, was that Nero,
who had killed himself in AD 68, would return from the underworld, to
renew his beastliness.

[5] *The Revelation of St John*, A. and C. Black 1966, p. 12. See also his four
articles on 'Deciphering the Book of Revelation' in the *Expository Times*,
Oct. 1962-Jan. 1963.

say that ours is an age of crisis, both for the world and for the church. In this century evil has been unleashed in the earth on a scale unprecedented in history; man's ingenuity has hung over the human race the dread fear of nuclear holocaust; and in many lands Christians have had to suffer obloquy, persecution, and even martyrdom. Inevitably, the hearts of many have failed them for fear of what is coming on the earth. So this strange book, now nineteen centuries old, can again become a trumpet-call to stead-fast faith in a time of chaos and calamity. To us it can say as long ago Isaiah the prophet said to his people in a day of national crisis, 'He who really puts his trust in God shall never be rattled' (Isa. 28.16).[6]

Second: Revelation is *a noble affirmation of true Christian optimism*. A great modern prophet, Reinhold Niebuhr, once wrote a book called *Beyond Tragedy*. It is John the Seer's 'beyond-tragedy' optimism which sounds through all the songs of redemption which are such a feature of this book. (Some have thought they were based on hymns actually sung in the Christian worship of his time.) John's is no facile, fair-weather optimism which has never known 'the cloudy and dark day'. Rather is it the optimism which has looked into the very abyss of evil unaffrighted – un-affrighted because it knows that the world belongs to God and not to the devil. This world, John believes, with all its values as God's handiwork, and with all its evils as the fruit of man's crimes and follies, is still the stage and venue of God's redemptive purpose. To its mystery the key is Christ, the glorified Lamb of God who, bearing the marks of that sacrifice which has redeemed the race, now reigns with God on his throne. Because of Christ's victory over evil on the Cross, John knows that 'the evil world will not win at last because it failed to win the only time it ever could. It is a vanquished world in which men play their devilries.' The words are P. T. Forsyth's,[7] written during the hell of the First World War, but they express the 'beyond-tragedy' optimism of John of Patmos.

Finally: Revelation is *an abiding witness to the reality of heaven*. Beyond any other New Testament writer John has power

---

[6] For the translation see A. C. Kennedy's essay on Robertson Smith in R. Selby Wright (ed.), *Fathers of the Kirk*, Oxford University Press 1960, p. 250.

[7] P. T. Forsyth, *The Justification of God*, Independent Press 1948, p. 223.

to infect others with his own certitude of the unseen and eternal world. As he assured his first readers, so he can still assure us, that at the end of the Christian road there is a city – the City of God; that, whatever else heaven means, it means an end to the sorrows of earth; and that the last reward of the loyal and pure in heart will be to see God and his Christ face to face in the presence of 'ten thousand times ten thousand and thousands of thousands'.

But let the Seer himself have the last word:

> I, John, saw the holy city, new Jerusalem coming down from God out of heaven prepared as a bride adorned for her husband. And I heard a great voice out of heaven saying, Behold the tabernacle of God is with men, and he will dwell with them, and they shall be his people, and God himself shall be with them, and be their God. And God shall wipe away all tears from their eyes; and there shall be no more death, neither sorrow nor crying, neither shall there be any more pain; for the former things have passed away (21.2-4 AV).

Note on the millennium (Rev. 20.1-10)

This passage is unique in the New Testament, though it has never failed down the centuries to produce 'Millenarians' who have taken it quite literally. It declares that before Christ's second coming in glory he will reign with his martyred saints on earth for a thousand years. Some have said that John derived this doctrine from pre-Christian apocalyptic. But G. B. Caird (op. cit., p. 250ff.) points out that evidence for this is lacking, and argues that the idea of such a reign was an indispensable element in John's thought. After his Resurrection Christ has two lives: (*a*) his reign at God's right hand; and (*b*) his saving activity in the world. So the seer believes that the martyrs, though now in glory, are to be 'let loose in the world' to set forward the progress of the gospel. 'John expected the reign of Christ and the martyrs to be different in degree but not in kind from the reign which Christ has exercised ever since his resurrection.' Christians must believe there will come a time on earth when it will be true to say that 'the sovereignty of the world has passed to our Lord and his Christ' (11.15 NEB). Otherwise Christ has won only a Pyrrhic victory, leaving the powers of evil in possession.

This is a courageous attempt to find Christian truth in a perplexing passage. Of Millenarian doctrine in general *The Oxford Dictionary of the Christian Church*, p. 901, says: 'Though Millenarianism has never been formally rejected by orthodox Christianity, it may be doubted whether there is adequate justification for it in scripture or in Christian tradition.'

The Unity of the New Testament

The New Testament, from a literary point of view, is a study in variety. More plainly, it is a literary hotch-potch. Here are all sorts of literary forms: first, four books called Gospels, in some ways resembling biographies, in other ways not; then a volume of history by one who, though a Gentile, reads history with Hebrew eyes; then a very mixed epistolary 'bag' which includes a massive theological treatise (Romans) and a charming private letter (Philemon), a rhetorical homily (Hebrews) and an ethical scrap-book (James); and the whole is rounded off with a Christian apocalypse (Revelation).

The diversity does not end there; it extends to subject-matter. When we study the contents of the various books, our first impression may well be that their writers are all discussing different themes. To take one example: the dominant theme of the Synoptic Gospels is the kingdom (or reign) of God; of Paul's letters, communion 'in Christ'; and of John's writings, 'life' or 'eternal life' (the terms being interchangeable). True, the person of Jesus Christ is closely bound up with all three themes. But how? Have we not here three messages, or 'gospels', not one?

A little knowledge of the New Testament (as Bacon might have said) may incline a man to this view; but deeper study will bring his mind round to a conviction of its basic unity. For when, guided by modern scholars, we study the three themes just mentioned, we begin to see that when Jesus proclaimed, both by word and by work, 'The reign of God has begun', viz. in his own person and ministry; and Paul wrote, 'In Christ God was reconciling the world to himself'; and John affirmed, 'The Word (or saving purpose) of

God became flesh', i.e. expressed itself in a human being, they were using different concepts to express their common conviction that in the coming of Christ and the kingdom God had spoken and acted decisively for the salvation, or rescue, of his people.[1]

In short, beneath the plain diversity of the New Testament lies a fundamental unity of message: a unity that must have been felt by the men who gathered the twenty-seven books into a canon. To take a musical analogy: if in the New Testament there are many musicians – and there are at least a dozen – playing different instruments, one dominant theme sounds through all their music. What is it?

It is 'the story of salvation' – the story of how 'in the fullness of time' (i.e. the divinely-appointed time) God decisively intervened in human history in Jesus Christ, completed his saving purpose for his people by sending his Son, the Messiah, for their deliverance. This statement needs some explanatory comments.

To begin with, the message of the New Testament is precisely what we have called it – a *story*, the story of God's decisive intervention in human affairs in Jesus Christ. It is a story in form so simple that a child can grasp it, though its profound implications for man and the world and history must be worked out by theologians from Paul and John in the first century to Barth and Bonhoeffer in this. It is a story that needs for its expression the use of active verbs, such as 'God spoke' or 'sent' or 'gave'. It is a story which finds its classical expression in John 3.16: 'God so loved the world that he gave his only Son that whoever believes in him should not perish but have eternal life.'

Next: this story is the *consummation* of God's purpose for his people. 'The New Testament,' said Augustine truly, 'lies hidden in the Old Testament; the Old Testament is made plain in the New.' We cannot understand the New Testament rightly unless we see it as the fulfilment of a story which begins in the Old. The Bible is not only a collection of records tracing the development of religious ideas among Israelites, Jews and Christians, but also and chiefly the story of God's saving purpose for his people, begun with their rescue from Egypt, continued in his later dealings with them recorded in history and prophecy, and consummated in the sending of his Son the Messiah. In the words of Myers' poem 'St Paul':

[1] See note at end on the equivalence of some cardinal NT phrases.

God, who to glean the vineyard of his choosing,
  Sent them evangelists till day was done,
Bore with the churls, their wrath and their refusing,
  Gave at the last the glory of his Son.

The parable of the Wicked Vinedressers (Mark 12.1-9) shows that the chief actor in the story saw it so – found in the Old Testament not the prophets' thought of God but God's action in Israel by prophet, priest or king – and knew his own ministry to be the culminating act in God's invasion of his race. His apostles saw it in the same way, for the first plank in their *kērygma*, or 'proclamation', was the fulfilment of the scriptures.

It is the same God who speaks to us in both Old and New Testaments – the God of Abraham, Isaac and Jacob is the Father of Christ – as it is one purpose of God which is being fulfilled in both Testaments. This truth finds its classical expression in the prologue to Hebrews: 'God having of old time spoken to our fathers by the prophets in many and various ways has in these last days spoken to us by a Son' (Heb. 1.1f.). This is why we cannot consent to 'scrap' the Old Testament. To throw away the Old Testament would be to throw away the key to the New. The Old Testament promises and prefigures the salvation fulfilled in Christ and the Church.

Third: this story of salvation, though one and indivisible, can be resolved into three elements: a Saviour, a saved (and saving) people, and the work of salvation itself; or, if you will, One Lord, One Church, One Salvation. These form three strands in a single cord – a trinity in unity – and that unity is the story of salvation. This triune story runs through the whole New Testament, and we must now spell it out in a little detail.

1. *One Lord*

In the beginning (as we have seen) was the *kērygma*, or preached message of salvation through Christ; and it sounds through the whole New Testament, from Gospel to Apocalypse. Mark, the earliest Gospel, is simply an expanded form of the *kērygma*; and so, with differences, are Matthew, Luke and John. All are '*kērygma*-built'. This same message is the burden of the apostles' sermons in Acts. It is the ground-work of Paul's gospel (see I Cor. 15.3ff.). You may catch its characteristic notes, in Hebrews, I Peter, I

John and even in the visions and hymns of Revelation.[2] Thus, to change the metaphor, through the variegated fabric of the New Testament, now clear and conspicuous, now veiled and hidden, runs the golden thread of the *kērygma*, the good news of God's saving act in Christ. This is the thesis which was convincingly argued by C. H. Dodd in his book *The Apostolic Preaching* published in 1936; but twenty-three years before Dodd, P. T. Forsyth[3] had taken the main point: 'There was no universal theological formula,' he wrote of the New Testament situation, 'there was not an orthodoxy, but certainly there was a common apostolic gospel, a *kērygma.*'

Now take a step farther. This *kērygma* centred in Christ. ('We preach Christ,' said Paul.) And just as one *kērygma* sounds through the New Testament, so implied in it is one common religious attitude to Christ, *one essential christology*, one basic estimate of his person. What is it? While holding fast his real humanity, the New Testament writers all set him on that side of reality we call divine. Or, to put it more simply, all say, '*Kyrios Jesus* – Jesus is Lord.'

The prayer of the mother church *Marana tha* – 'Our Lord, come' (preserved in I Cor. 16.22) is proof that the primitive church did so. Though Paul uses many titles and categories to express Christ's meaning for faith, he agrees with his fellow-apostles on the essentials: Jesus, he says, was true man, 'born of woman', *and* 'Jesus is Lord', a being to be named in the same breath with God. The writer to the Hebrews does not differ. No New Testament author dwells more movingly on the human Jesus 'who in the days of his earthly life offered up prayers and petitions, with loud cries and tears, to God' (5.7); yet none is surer that he is 'the impress of God's essence' and 'the appointed heir of all things' (1.2f.). No less certain is Peter that, though Jesus had once been a man facing his accusers with a noble non-resistance (2.22f.), he is now Lord and Christ (2.13; 3.15), a being to be named with God and the Holy Spirit (1.2). The seer of Revelation is concerned to depict 'Christ

[2] For detailed proof see F. F. Bruce, *Interpretation*, Jan. 1969, pp. 3-19 (Hebrews); A. M. Hunter, *The Interpreter's Bible*, XII, Abingdon Press 1957. pp. 51-53 (I Peter); C. H. Dodd, *The Johannine Epistles*, Hodder and Stoughton 1946, pp. xxvii-xxxvii (John) and R. N. Flew, *Jesus and his Church*, Epworth Press 1938, p. 237 (Revelation).
[3] P. S. Forsyth, *The Principle of Authority*, Independent Press 1952, p. 127.

in glory', occupying the throne with God the Father. Yet this 'Christ in majesty' is the same Jesus, born of David's line (5.5) who had gone to Golgotha for men's salvation and still bears the marks of his sacrifice (5.6,11, etc.).

It is not otherwise with the four evangelists. For Mark, Jesus is at once a real man and the divine Son of God. For Matthew, Jesus the Messianic Son of David, the preacher of the Sermon on the Mount, is 'Emmanuel – God with us' (1.23; 28.20). No reader of Luke can doubt that for him Jesus had once been a real man among men; yet just as surely he regards him as 'the Lord', a being divine in his origin and destiny (1.35; 24.44f.). Finally, if John (both in his Gospel and Letters) is at pains to stress the real humanity of Jesus, yet for him he is the

> Word of the Father
> Now in flesh appearing.

a being who speaks in the accents of divinity ('I am what I am', 8.24,28,58; 13.19), One who confronts men in the truth and power and love of the Eternal.

To sum up. Despite great differences in thought, phrase and title among the New Testament writers, *one essential christology underpins the whole New Testament*, perhaps best summed up in the earliest Christian confession of faith, 'Jesus is Lord.'

'There is a unity in all these early Christian books,' wrote James Denney, 'which is powerful enough to absorb and subdue their differences, and that unity is to be found in a common religious relation to Christ, a common debt to him, a common sense that everything in the relations of God and man must be and is determined by him.'[4]

What is this but to say that for all the New Testament writers there is but *one Lord*, one only name given under heaven whereby men may be saved? For them Jesus was not merely 'the man for others' as he is for some today (though of course he was incontestably that); he was 'Jesus Christ our Lord', the only Son of God.

2. *One church*

If the first strand in the cord of 'the story of salvation' is 'one Lord', the second is 'one church'.

A saviour and a message of salvation necessarily imply a saved

[4] James Denney, *The Death of Christ*, Tyndale Press 1951, p. 101.

people. However differently evangelists and apostles express themselves, *one essential doctrine of the church as the new people of God pervades the New Testament.*

The roots of this doctrine go back to the Old Testament and the conception of Israel (or, as in the prophets, 'the faithful remnant') as the *qĕhal Yahweh* (LXX: *ekklēsia Kyriou*) the people of God, God's holy community. What we have in the New Testament is the church's claim to be the *new* people of God, created through Christ, and called to do what old Israel had failed to do – to be 'a light to lighten the Gentiles'.

We begin with Jesus and his disciple-band. Study what Jesus says about the advent of the kingdom (or rule) of God; his conception of himself as Messiah, or bringer of the kingdom; his words about himself as the shepherd and his disciples as God's 'little flock'; and it is clear that the end Jesus had in view was the gathering of a new Israel, a new people of God, a new church.

First: the coming of the reign, or rule, of God, which was the burden of Jesus' preaching, implies a people living under that rule. So in parable after parable – the Mustard Seed, the Drag Net, the Wheat and the Tares, the Great Supper – Jesus shows that his purpose is to form a new community. If he calls men to follow him, he is gathering the nucleus of this people of God.

Second: this is confirmed by Jesus' conception of his Messiahship. He interpreted it in terms of Daniel's Son of Man and Isaiah's Servant of the Lord. Both are 'societary' figures. Each implies a community. When Jesus called himself 'the Son of Man' (and it was his favourite title), he saw himself as the head of a special people, 'the saints of the Most High'.

Third: when Jesus described himself as doing a shepherd's work and his disciple-band as a 'flock', OT passages like Ezek. 34 and Micah 5.4 show that he was using pastoral language to describe his Messianic task of gathering God's people.

This is the theory, or theology, of the matter. If now we observe what Jesus actually does, we see him clothing his purpose with reality, translating it into fact. We may put the issue in one sentence. *When Jesus called twelve disciples (a number pregnant with symbolism), when he gave them a new 'law' for living (as in his great Sermon), when he sent the disciples forth on their mission to proclaim the advent of God's rule and to gather believers, and when on his last night with them, he instituted a new 'covenant' –*

all these facts show him fulfilling his God-given task of creating a new Israel, the true people of God, to replace the old Israel which had proved disobedient to God's will for it.

But Jesus also knew – had he not learned it in communion with his Father and in his study of the scripture? – that 'the planted seed of the kindom must be watered by the bloody sweat of his passion', that only by his own obedience unto death and his victory over death, could the 'little flock' become the great one God intended. Only so could he gather together (as he says in John's Gospel) 'the scattered children of God', 'not of this fold', so that his Father's purpose would be fully realized, and there would be 'one flock, one shepherd' (John 10.16).

So Jesus goes to the Cross that, by the sacrifice of his life and by his triumph over death, he may establish the new 'covenant' and make the new people of God a reality. Had he not said, 'I will destroy this temple made with hands and in three days build another made without hands' (John 2.19)? This is not only a prophecy of his personal triumph over death; it is the prophecy of a new church. Beyond death he looks to the time when there will be a new shrine 'made without hands' for the worship of the little flock now become a great one. On the day of Pentecost that *ekklēsia* comes truly into being;[5] and the new Israel, now empowered by the Spirit, begins its great career in the world.

So we turn to the apostles and the church. Inevitably in the years just after that Pentecost the young church did not at once fully realize its nature and destiny. Yet even in what Luke says about its beginnings, we can discern its glimmering sense of *four things*. It is the true people of God. It owes its allegiance to Christ. It is empowered by the Spirit. And it is called to mission. This last point Stephen sees more clearly than the rest, and pays for his vision with his life.

Now pass down three decades to the 'fifties' of the first century AD. The third decade is that in which Paul wrote his letters, and in them we see the first great Christian theologian spelling out the nature and role of the church with a vision which outpasses even Stephen's, As the *ekklēsia* of God, it is 'a third race' alongside Jews and Gentiles (I Cor. 10.32). Its common allegiance finds expression in 'Jesus is Lord' (I Cor. 12.3; Rom. 10.9; Phil. 2.11). It knows itself to be the 'fellowship of the Spirit', the fellowship created and

[5] Pentecost is not the *birth* of the church, but its *coming of age*.

energized by God's Spirit (II Cor. 13.14; Phil. 2.1). And its out-reach, as Paul sees, is meant by God to be truly 'ecumenical'.

Similarly, in the early 'sixties' Peter (with the help of Silvanus) depicts the church as the true people of God (I Peter 2.4-9), rever-encing Christ as Lord (3.15), hallowed by the Spirit (1.2), and called to 'tell out the triumphs of him who has called them out of dark-ness into his marvellous light' (2.9).

When *Auctor* (the writer of Hebrews) writes to the Christians in Rome, he is equally persuaded that the church is the true people of God (Heb. 2.12; 4.9), that its allegiance is to Christ his Son (3.1; 4.14), that the power at work in it is the Holy Spirit (2.6; 6.4f.). But it is the *mission* of the church which he thinks his readers have forgotten. Instead of 'shrinking back' under cover of the old securi-ties, they are called to go out, adventuring, out into the wide pagan world, under the leadership of the unchanging Christ.

If we now turn to John and Ephesus (say, about 80-90) we see that John has the same conviction about the nature and destiny of the church. The church is the true Israel, as the parable of the vine and its branches shows (John 15.1ff.). (The vine was a favour-ite symbol for Israel as God's people.) If 'Jesus is the Son of God' rather than 'Jesus is Lord' seems to express his *Credo* (I John 4.15; 5.5), he has no doubt where its allegiance lies. In this *ekklēsia* the Holy Spirit bestowed by the risen Jesus (John 20.22), indwells Christ's followers, acting as remembrancer, witness-bearer, and advocate (see the five 'Paraclete' sayings in John 14-16). And its mission is to be universal; for Jesus is uplifted on the cross in order to 'draw all men to himself' (John 12.32); he has 'other sheep not of this fold' (i.e. Jewry, John 10.16), and his death is not for the nation alone but for the ingathering of 'the scattered child-ren of God' (John 11.52).

Finally, even through the visions of John of Patmos we may discover his view of the church's nature and role. His words about the rule of the saints (Rev. 1.6; 5.9f.), based as they are on Dan. 7, are his way of declaring the church to be the true people of God. The church's allegiance is to be seen in his metaphor of the church as the Bride of Christ (22.17), and heard in the hymns of adora-tion addressed to the regnant Lamb. Nor is the work of the Holy Spirit forgotten. By that Spirit's inspiration John sees his visions (1.10; 21.10); and the presence of the Spirit in the church is attested by the invitation, 'The Spirit and the Bride say, Come' (22.17). How wide is the church's outreach? To it belong men of 'every tribe and tongue and people and nation', as the Song to the Lamb is sung by 'ten thousand times ten thousand and thousands of thousands' (5.9,11f.).

3. *One salvation*

One Lord, one church – we come now to the last strand in the triune cord, one salvation.

The problem here is the sin of man and God's solution to it. If we compare the teaching of Jesus with Paul's, we find that, though their language greatly differs – Jesus' teaching being tenderly human, Paul's often scholastic – the Lord and his apostle agree that in God's sight all men are sinners who cannot save themselves.[6] So also, in their various ways, Peter, John, *Auctor*, and the seer of Patmos agree that the cause of man's spiritual malaise is the sin which disrupts his fellowship with God.

It is axiomatic for Peter that 'all we like sheep have gone astray' (cf. I Peter 2.25) and that it was for 'unrighteous' men that Christ died (3.18). For John, Christ is 'the Lamb of God who takes away the sin of the world' (John 1.29), and he says bluntly, 'If we say that we have no sin, we deceive ourselves' (I John 1.18). Like Jesus (see Mark 7.14-23), *Auctor* knows that what defiles a man comes from within, and that it is for a conscience stained with sin that a remedy must be found (Heb. 9.9,14). 'To him who loves us and has loosed us from our sins by his blood be the glory,' cries John of Patmos (Rev. 1.5), acknowledging that 'loosing' from his sins is man's deepest need.

But if human sin poses the problem to be solved if man is to attain true blessedness, the New Testament writers concur that the solution is to be found in Christ and his Cross. True, they have their own distinctive angles on what we call 'the atonement'; yet all agree that in Christ crucified and risen is to be found God's remedy for sin. Deeper than all their differences we can trace *a unity of approach* to the Cross and him who 'hath given us rest by his sorrow and life by his death'.

Right from the beginning – witness I Cor. 15.3 (where Paul quotes 'tradition' he had received) – it was a part of the Christian *Credo* that 'Christ died for our sins according to the scriptures'.

[6] See my *Unity of the New Testament*, SCM Press 1943, pp. 90-104, for detailed proof.

That is to say, his death was vicarious, related to human sin, and fulfilled the scriptures (which must surely be a reference to Isa. 53). Further, the apostolic writers hold that the atonement originated in God's gracious will, that it was made necessary by man's wrong-doing, and that, as its means was a Cross-death, so its aim was restored fellowship with God.

When they come to describe what Christ did on the Cross, they say that his act was not only vicarious but *representative* (Jesus being who he was, the Son of Man, the Servant of the Lord, our great high priest etc.) and that it was a *sacrifice* (all refer to 'the blood of Christ', i.e. his life sacrificially released by death for the benefit of others). And they agree that the spiritual end of the atonement was the reconciliation of sinful man to God – whether, with Paul, they call it 'peace with God', or with Peter and *Auctor*, 'access' to God, or with John, 'eternal life', i.e. life lived in fellowship with God.[7]

To say that there is one single uniform doctrine of the atonement in all the New Testament writers would be untrue. What is true is that 'through the New Testament runs one mighty thought: Christ died for our sins: he bore what we should have borne: he did for us what we could never have done for ourselves: he did for God that which was God's good pleasure.'[8]

One word more. Though the atonement is presented in the New Testament as 'a finished work' – something done once for all – it is not something done outside of man. Man has to make its benefits his own. It is not complete till man makes his response to that 'love so amazing, so divine' manifested in the Cross. This he does in three ways: first, by faith, when he commits himself to Christ for God and eternity; second, in the Holy Communion, when, still by faith, he appropriates the virtue of Christ's passion symbolized by the broken bread and the outpoured wine; and, third, by sacrificial living, when, remembering what Christ has done for him, he gives himself in sacrificial love to others.

This, then, is the triune story of salvation of which the New Testament is the abiding record. This is 'the Word from the Beyond for our human predicament', which gives the New Testament a unique place in the religious literature of the world. And this story

[7] For detailed proof of these statements see Vincent Taylor, *The Atonement in New Testament Teaching*, Epworth Press 1940.

[8] J. K. Mozley, *The Doctrine of the Atonement*, Duckworth 1915, p. 93.

of salvation, old but ever new as the Holy Spirit makes it so, is the basis of all sound Christian doctrine, the inspiration of all true Christian living, and the foundation on which rests any true belief in the life everlasting.

Note on the equivalence of some cardinal NT phrases

The Synoptics speak of 'the gospel of the kingdom of God'; St Paul, of 'the gospel of Christ' (Rom. 15.19 etc.); St John of 'the word of life' (I John 1.1). So far as words go, they appear to be discussing different things. But it is not really so.

Consider the Synoptics. Here the kingdom (or saving rule) of God and the person of Christ are inseparably bound up with each other. Jesus embodies God's rule. 'If *I* by the finger of God cast out demons. then the kingdom of God has come upon you' (Luke 11.20). Further, to be a disciple of Jesus is to 'be in the kingdom'; for where he is, the kingdom is. It was their perception of this which led Origen to coin the phrase *autobasileia* and Marcion to say, 'In the gospel the kingdom of God is Christ himself.'

Next take Paul. His equivalent for 'the kingdom of God has come upon you', viz., in the person of Jesus, is 'the righteousness of God (i.e. God's saving activity, God putting things right) has been manifested', namely, in Christ (Rom. 3.21ff.). Moreover, for Paul to preach the gospel is to preach Christ. (Compare Rom. 1.16, 'The gospel is the power of God for salvation', with I Cor. 1.23f., 'We preach ... Christ the power of God'.) *The gospel is Christ.*

Now consider John. 'Life', or 'eternal life' (they are interchangeable expressions), is the dominant idea of his writings. Where the Synoptists speak of 'the kingdom of God', John speaks of 'eternal life'. But for John this supreme blessing is so bound up with Christ that he can say in the gospel, 'I am the life' (John 11.25; 14.6), and John himself declares in his First Epistle, 'This life is in his Son ... he who has the Son has life' (I John 5.11f.). *The life is Christ.*

Thus we shall not stray far from the truth if in reading the New Testament we make the following equations:

1. The gospel of the kingdom=the gospel of Christ=the word of life.
2. To 'be in the kingdom'=to 'be in Christ'=to 'have life'.

Books for Further Reading

Translations

The Revised Standard Version
The New English Bible
The Jerusalem Bible

Introductions

W. C. van Unnik, *The New Testament*, Collins 1964
R. M. Grant, *A Historical Introduction to the New Testament*, Collins 1963
A. Wikenhauser, *New Testament Introduction*, Burns and Oates 1967
C. F. D. Moule, *The Birth of the New Testament*, A. and C. Black 1966

Language

B. M. Metzger's article on the subject in *The Interpreter's Bible*, Vol. VII, Abingdon Press 1951, pp. 43-59

Text and Canon

B. M. Metzger, *The Text of the New Testament*, Oxford University Press 1969
J. N. Sanders' article on the canon in M. Black and H. H. Rowley (eds.), *Peake's Commentary on the Bible*, Nelson 1962, pp. 679ff.

Background

G. Ernest Wright and Floyd V. Filson (eds.), *The Westminster Historical Atlas to the Bible*, SCM Press 1946

H. H. Rowley (ed.), *A Companion to the Bible*, T. and T. Clark 1963

A. C. Deane, *The World Christ Knew*, British Publishers' Guild 1947

G. Adam Smith, *Historical Geography of the Holy Land*, Fontana Books 1966.

E. Bevan's article in C. Gore, H. L. Goudge and A. Guillaume (eds.), *A New Commentary on Holy Scripture*, SPCK 1929

T. R. Glover, *The Conflict of Religions*, Methuen 1909

Jack Finegan, *Light from the Ancient Past*, Princeton University Press 1959

C. K. Barrett, *The New Testament Background. Selected Documents*, SPCK 1957

K. Stendahl (ed.), *The Scrolls and the New Testament*, SCM Press 1958

The Theology of the New Testament

Alan Richardson (ed.), *A Theological Word Book of the Bible*, SCM Press 1950

J. Jeremias, *The Central Message of the New Testament*, SCM Press 1965

A. M. Hunter, *Introducing New Testament Theology*, SCM Press 1957

Alan Richardson, *An Introduction to the Theology of the New Testament*, SCM Press 1958

C. H. Dodd, *The Apostolic Preaching and its Developments*, Hodder and Stoughton 1963

R. N. Flew, *Jesus and His Church*, Epworth Press 1938

Vincent Taylor, *The Person of Christ*, Macmillan 1958

The Four Gospels

(a) The Synoptic Problem

C. S. C. Williams' article in M. Black and H. H. Rowley (eds.), *Peake's Commentary on the Bible*, Nelson 1962, pp 748ff.

(b) Form criticism

Vincent Taylor, *The Formation of the Gospel Tradition*, Macmillan 1935

A. T. Hanson (ed.), *Vindications*, SCM Press 1966

(c) The parables of Jesus

J. Jeremias, *Rediscovering the Parables*, SCM Press 1966

(d) The miracles of Jesus

D. S. Cairns, *The Faith that Rebels*, SCM Press 1954

Alan Richardson, *The Miracle Stories of the Gospels*, SCM Press 1941

C. S. Lewis, *Miracles*, Fontana Books 1960

(e) The life and teaching of Jesus

T. W. Manson, *The Sayings of Jesus*, SCM Press 1949

A. M. Hunter, *The Work and Words of Jesus*, SCM Press 1950

H. E. W. Turner, *Jesus Master and Lord*, Mowbrays 1954

T. W. Manson, *The Servant-Messiah*, Cambridge University Press 1953

G. Bornkamm, *Jesus of Nazareth*, Hodder and Stoughton 1960

H. Zahrnt, *The Historical Jesus*, Collins 1962

C. H. Dodd, *The Founder of Christianity*, Collins 1971

Acts and Paul

G. B. Caird, *The Apostolic Age*, Duckworth 1955

C. K. Barrett, *Luke the Historian in Recent Study*, Epworth Press 1961

W. Neil, *The Truth about the Early Church*, Hodder and Stoughton 1970

I. H. Marshall, *Luke, Historian and Theologian*, Paternoster Press 1971

A. W. F. Blunt, *The Acts of the Apostles*, Oxford University Press 1934

F. F. Bruce, *The Acts of the Apostles*, Tyndale Press 1952

W. M. Ramsay, *St Paul the Traveller and Roman Citizen*, Hodder and Stoughton 1895

A. M. Hunter, *The Gospel according to St Paul*, SCM Press 1966

The Writings of the Other Apostolic Men

William Manson, *The Epistle to the Hebrews*, Hodder and Stoughton 1951

C. E. B. Cranfield, *I and II Peter and Jude*, SCM Press 1960

Robert Law, *The Tests of Life*, T. and T. Clark 1909 (on I John)

G. B. Caird, *Revelation*, A. and C. Black 1966

Commentaries

These comprise:

(a) One-volume commentaries on the whole Bible, like *Peake's Commentary on the Bible* and *A New Commentary on Holy Scripture* (see above), and W. Neil, *Bible Commentary*, Hodder and Stoughton 1962.

(b) Series of commentaries on the various New Testament books, like the Torch Commentaries, the Moffatt New Testament Commentary, the Clarendon Bible, the New Century Bible, The Interpreter's Bible, Black's New Testament Commentaries and the Anchor Bible. These are all based on English translations.

(c) Large commentaries on the Greek text, like Vincent Taylor, *The Gospel according to St Mark*, Macmillan 1952; E. G. Selwyn, *The First Epistle of Peter*, Macmillan 1947; C. K. Barrett, *The Gospel according to St John*, SPCK 1956.

Index of Subjects

Index of Authors